GENERATIONS

@Pastor.How @Pastor.Lia

A weekend service at
Imaginarium, Heart of God Church

GenerationS Volume 1: How to Grow Your Church Younger and Stronger
The Story of the Kids Who Built a World-Class Church

Published by Generations Pte. Ltd.

Copyright © 2021 by Tan Seow How and Cecilia Chan

Library of Congress Control Number: 2021941991
ISBN (hardcover): 9781662918797
ISBN (paperback): 9781662915482
ISBN (electronic): 9781662915499

Special market sales: Organisations, theological seminaries, churches, pastors and small group leaders can receive special discounts when purchasing this book in bulk. For information, please email team@generationsmvmt.com

Volume 1

GENERATIONS

How to Grow Your Church
YOUNGER and STRONGER

The Story of the Kids Who Built a World-Class Church

@Pastor.How @Pastor.Lia

GenerationS

This book is dedicated to our spiritual grandchildren,
great grandchildren and beyond whom we might not have
the privilege of meeting or teaching.

You may not be in this world yet but you are already in
the mind of our eternal God and in the hearts of
Pastor How and Pastor Lia.

All royalties and proceeds from this book will advance
the cause of GenerationS in HOGC and globally.

I hope that this Book
will sow a vision in you.
And also seed the
dream in you.
Always give God the
BEST years of your life!

Prov 13:22

How
2021

This is
my Life's Work and
Legacy. It will not
end... many shall rise
after me...
I prophesy into the future
and call forth leaders
who will build
GenerationS!
Isaiah 55:12

lia
2021

GenerationS

WHAT LEADERS SAY ABOUT *GENERATIONS*

Having visited Heart of God Church over 25 times in the last 15 years, we have seen up close how this spiritual home has grown to become the very best example anywhere in the world of a church that fully believes in the young generation and fully trusts them with advanced ministry at an age when most pastors would not even know these young people existed in their church at all.

The beauty of this did not emerge from cheap copy/paste principles but from the genuine passion and loving parents' hearts of our dear and close friends, Pastors Tan Seow How and Cecilia Chan. We are honestly more excited about their book than any other in the previous decade.

JOAKIM & MARIA LUNDQVIST
Senior Pastors, Word of Life Church Sweden

There are moments in life that you never forget! The first time I walked into Heart of God Church in Singapore was life-changing. Yes, Imaginarium is epic, and yes, the technology at work making the weekend services happen is outrageously world-class. However, none of this would have happened if it were not for the courageous, imaginative, faith-filled and out-of-the-box leadership of my friends, Tan Seow How and Cecilia Chan. Whether it is the 15 and 16-year-olds running the tech, or the young adults leading the masses, the ministry of Heart of God Church is simply mind-blowing.

GenerationS is not a once read but will be a regular read for leaders wishing to grow younger and stronger churches!

GLYN & SOPHIA BARRETT
Senior Pastors, !Audacious Church
National Leader, Assemblies of God in Great Britain

Heart of God Church left me impressed by their strength and innovation. Here I saw thousands of Gen Z not just engaged and on fire, but empowered to lead and serve. These digital natives not only consume online content, they are unleashed to create it. Every leader should come and experience this world-class church.

Having spent time with Pastor How and Pastor Lia, I know that *GenerationS* is the handbook that every senior pastor and their team needs to reach generations and future-proof their church.

BOBBY GRUENEWALD
Pastor & Innovation Leader, Life.Church
Founder, YouVersion

Pastor How and Pastor Lia left an indelible mark on us. It's rare to meet people with rare leadership gifts, bold vision, and relentless courage, who at the same time remain so down-to-earth, grounded in character, and committed to serving the generations to come.

ERWIN RAPHAEL MCMANUS
Founder and Lead Pastor, Mosaic
Creative Director, McManus Gallery

In this mindset-shifting story of discipleship, leadership development, and church growth, Pastors Tan Seow How and Cecilia Chan present a Spirit-led process in which kids become leaders. As a person involved in the higher level training of their pioneer "kids," I had the privilege of observing these pastors' strategic work to transform young people into skillful ministers and world-class leaders.

This volume presents a church that values academic, social, and spiritual development of young people and considers them today's leaders. In this sense, as Saint Paul was to the Gentiles, Pastors How and Lia are to the GenerationS. The lessons learned and the concepts developed at the Heart of God Church deserve duplication in nations around the world.

THOMSON K. MATHEW, D. Min., Ed. D.
Professor Emeritus and Former Dean
College of Theology and Ministry, Oral Roberts University (USA)

少豪牧師和曾牧師，他們看見「教會傳承」的需要，他們不是為了自己教會的接班人而重視傳承，而是為了整個世代的需要，他們所投入的心力，讓人非常感動。這個世界變化得很快，年輕人要面對的挑戰，不單來自於「科技」、「文化」，甚而是「品德價值」、「家庭觀念」的挑戰。教會如何幫助他們在這樣的風暴中可以站立得住，是教會面對的挑戰。我們需要更多像「少豪牧師」和「曾牧師」一樣的牧者，在這個世代中為主站立!! 教會界的「少豪牧師、曾牧師們」快快站起來!! 加油!!

ZHANG MAOSONG 張茂松
Founding Pastor 創會牧師
新店行道會

Pastor How and Pastor Lia have dedicated their lives to young people... Proof of their work is evident in the passion witnessed at Heart of God Church and in the unparalleled quality I've experienced in the business they lead.

PAUL JACOBS
President and CEO, Premium Audio Company,
parent company of Klipsch Group, Inc.

After 30 years of doing mass events for youth with 3 million attendees, the most common question I have received from pastors is, "How can I do this in my city or my church on a regular basis?" I knew of no example to point them to, until now. Heart of God Church, led by Pastors How and Lia, is the most profound example on the planet of an Exponential Church building a pipeline of passionate followers of Christ emerging into adulthood as firebrands of faith with deep roots of maturity!

RON LUCE
Doctorate Strategic Foresight
Global Church Strategist, *www.exponentialpastor.com*

There are few people in the world that I know, who are positioned and have shown the ability to understand this generation as Pastor How and Pastor Lia do. *GenerationS* beautifully and boldly spotlights the mindsets that need to shift for the Church to grow and thrive both now and in the future.

ROB HOSKINS
President of OneHope
Senior Advisor to the World Evangelical Alliance (WEA)
Co-author, *Change Your World: How Anyone, Anywhere Can Make a Difference*

Pastor How and Pastor Lia's passion to raise generations of youth leaders... has awakened many evangelical leaders throughout Asia and beyond.

BAMBANG BUDIJANTO, Ph.D.
General Secretary, Asia Evangelical Alliance (AEA)
CEO, Leadership as Discipleship - UNLEASHED

每一次到新加坡「神之心教會」，都令我深深地震撼。這裡的年輕人充滿對神的熱情，對信仰的堅信。相信 Pastor How 和 Pastor Lia 筆下所流露出的，就是他們生命為年輕人付出所結的果子。我很期待這一本書，成為領導者和牧者的靈感，給予我們新的視角來思考如何帶領下一個世代。改變需要耐心毅力，成長需要澆灌呵護，這條道路並不孤單，這本書就是你的朋友！

Sandy Yu 游智婷
CEO / Producer 事工負責人 / 專輯製作人
Stream of Praise Music Ministries 讚美之泉

We have known Pastor How and Pastor Lia since 2008. They proved their insight and wisdom to build a world-class church by reaching and parenting young generations into strong leaders. This book will shift your mindset and show you their ropes and hooks to conquer the mountain of sustainable church growth.

PETER & ILONA PAAUWE
Senior Pastors, DoorBrekers Church (Netherlands)

Pastor How and Pastor Lia in this book demonstrate... rare insights born out of revelation and practice... This book is a must for any minister who intends to stay relevant seeing the growth rate of the younger generation.

POJU OYEMADE
Senior Pastor, The Covenant Nation (Nigeria)

It is impossible to mention youth revival and generations, and not place Pastor How and Pastor Lia in the same sentence. We travel all over Brazil and the nations, but the experience we had when visiting Heart of God Church forever changed our lives and ministry.

FELIPE & MILA PARENTE
Senior and Co-Senior Pastors, Bola de Neve Church (Brazil)

You are holding a book in your hand that I wish every Christian would read. Pastor How and Pastor Lia are sharing a message that has to do with the future of the church. Nothing is more important than reaching out to the next generation. I HAVE BEEN WAITING FOR THIS BOOK.

CARL-GUSTAF SEVERIN
Missionary, Evangelist
Author, *Russia Stole Our Hearts*

Heart of God Church has succeeded in showing the world what boys and girls can do for God when somebody believes in them, gives them the proper training, and puts them into action.

MATTS-OLA & RANDI ISHOEL
Senior Pastors, Word of Life Church Moscow (Russia)

---

* Excerpts only. Full version on **GenerationSmvmt.com**

CONTENTS

PREFACE - HOW ✈

As we write this book, we just celebrated our church's 20th anniversary.

When Lia and I started the church in 1999, it was an experiment. So when I was asked to write a statement to summarize our last 20 years, this was what I came up with...

> Heart of God Church started as a divine experiment to build a prototype Youth Church. Now it has developed into a proof of concept that Youths can build a STRONG CHURCH.

We had a dream of a church built by youths, for youths, to reach youths but there was no church we could model after. No pastor we could follow as a reference point... so it was mostly by trial and error (more error actually). A lot of mistakes and grace later, we would like to think that we are a proof of concept that youth churches are synonymous with strong, growing churches.

A youth church is built by youths, for youths, to reach youths!

So as you read this book, hopefully we will help you avoid delays and detours so that you can get there faster than our 20 years.

This book evolved into two volumes quite by accident. As Lia and I wrote what's on our minds and hearts, it quickly became almost 100,000 words. We tried to cut it down, but everyone in the focus groups who read the draft urged us to leave it in. So the best solution is to release it in two volumes.

So you can consider these two volumes as the director's cut. A director's cut is not just longer, but it is not edited to Hollywood's commercial taste. Similarly, Volume 2 includes the heart and heartbreaks behind raising and leading youths. It would go against our integrity to just leave you with a rosy picture of working with youths. It is a false narrative that every youth will grow up to become a God-fearing, grateful, loving Christian leader. That's the fairy tale ending we all want, but reality is not happy and perfect like Wanda's town of Westview. So there are four chapters in Volume 2 dedicated to stories of disappointments and hurts. True accounts of sins, immorality, and crimes committed by youths who grew up in HOGC. It will be real and raw. And more importantly, we will share how God led us through the valleys of youth work. You could say that Volume 1 is knowing the power of His resurrection while Volume 2 is sharing in the fellowship of His sufferings (Philippians 3:10).

Is HOGC the finished version? Certainly not... We think of what we are doing like building the plane as we fly it.

A group of aeronautical professors were flying to a seminar.

After they were seated comfortably on the plane, the pilot came out and said, "Your students wanted to surprise you. This plane is entirely built and maintained by your students. You should be so proud."

All the professors stood up and ran out of the plane in panic.

All except one.

The pilot asked that one professor who was seated calmly, "Wow, you really have confidence in your students."

He replied, "Oh yes... Knowing my students, I am confident that this plane will not even get off the ground."

Well, in Heart of God Church, we buckled up and went for the ride of our lives. We are flying on the plane built by our youths.

If you say you believe in the next generation, are you willing to bet your life on it?

It is like Elon Musk putting himself on the first SpaceX rocket to Mars.

In HOGC, we bet our entire ministry on our youths... we are all in.

We let them build and fly the plane... *and we sit in it.*

Scary, yes, but that's the pioneering faith and start-up adventurous spirit we thrive on...

Come fly with us.

And to all the HOGC members and leaders reading, Pastor Lia and I wrote with you in mind. You could have joined our church years after we wrote this and become our 20,000th member. Or you could be toddlers now as I write and by the time you read this, you are 14 years old.

This book is not just another book to you.

This book is our story and history.

It is His story.

It is like a book of our DNA and culture.

It is like a letter written from your founding pastors about our vision and values.

It is a chronicle of how God brought a youth revival.

As the Psalmist said:

> Psalm 78:2-4 (NLT)
>
> ... I will teach you *hidden lessons from our past—**stories*** we have heard and known, ***stories*** our ancestors handed down to us. We will not hide *these truths* from our children; we will tell the ***next generation*** about the *glorious deeds* of the Lord, about his power and his mighty wonders.

If you are reading this in 2029 or 2050, verses 6 and 7 will be Pastor Lia's and my prayer:

> Psalm 78:6-7 (NLT)
>
> so the ***next generation*** might know them—even the children not yet born—and they in turn will teach their own children. So each generation should set its hope anew on God, not forgetting his glorious miracles and obeying his commands.

PREFACE - LIA ⚾

Heart of God Church was a divine experiment. I am relieved that it actually worked. And now I live to tell the world that it is possible to grow your church younger and stronger. That mantra is my oxygen.

It is such a privilege to have had a front row seat to witness kids who built a world-class church!

I write this book to bring spotlight to the youths. *GenerationS* is a message that carries two pioneering voices. In this book, you will find How's voice and my voice. It is often hard to tell where How ends and Lia begins, except for different vocal tones and styles. But that proves what I have always believed in — cohesion without erosion. You and your spouse can be a complementing team without eroding each other's gift and eclipsing each other's personality.

You can almost hear the beam in our voices that we are both very proud of the young people in our church. Like proud parents, we know the youths in Heart of God Church are world-class Jesus followers and first-class servant leaders.

So if you catch me bragging about the youths, then yes, guilty as charged. They deserve the highlight like the boy who gave up his lunch, or like the boy who guided a blind Samson or like a young Samuel.

So yes, excuse us for raving about them.

#SorryButNotSorry.

And if you find me raving about God, then yes... guilty again. This book is not about me or How, it is about God.

This book is a #HumbleBrag about the youths, the adults who believed and supported them and Jesus who built HOGC.

Pause. Before you think that loving young people is a story that is all delightful and felicitous, an honest word of caution. The Bible says:

Proverbs 14:4
Where no oxen are, the trough is clean;
But much increase comes by the strength of an ox.

An ox brings strength. An ox is like a youth. Where there are on-fire youths, there is strength in the church. But with oxen around, the trough is also messy. Sometimes, youths equal mess. There will always be disorganised work spaces, missed deadlines, hurt feelings and broken equipment.

Pause again. Youths can do more than break your equipment carelessly. They can shatter your hearts.

We love the heroic story of David and we wish the HOGC story is all that. But reality tells us that David's life is also bookended by Saul and Absalom.

Like a fatherly influence, Abraham journeyed with Lot but Lot made dubious choices. Separation ensued.

A young Samuel growing strong in the temple also stood in the ominous shadow of the growing sins of Eli's sons. Same temple but so different paths.

In the midst of the 12, Jesus had given bread to a Judas. Likewise, we did too.

So when we raise youths, there will be wheat and tares.

The prodigies and prodigals grow side by side. Only one out of four types of soil is good ground.

How and I had our fair share of them. We had some Sauls and lots of Lots.

What I love about the Bible is that it is so real and does not whitewash the sins and sinners. I hope our book will also be real too, not just a flex fest. How and I want the readers to be inspired but also know the costs. That's why in Volume 2, we wrote about the heartbreaks when youths grew up and not only walked away from God but attacked the House that they grew up in.

In ministry life, sometimes you will find yourselves in situations which are held together by just duct tape and prayers. Attacks from our spiritual children were one such circumstance, sickness was another. So I also wrote a chapter in Volume 2 called *But If Not*. It talks a bit about my cancer journey. God not only healed me, but out of that healing came a new dimension of Miracles & Breakthroughs Services in our church. In that cancer year, we also took all of my insurance payout and together with our savings plus monies from our personal family business, we gave $1 million to our church Building Fund. We have included *But If Not* as a bonus chapter at the end of this book. 😌

It has been a long journey but I can assure you, this book will show you that out of brokenness comes great blessings. What was an unexpected blessing was that, out of this message, we had the opportunity to sit in a room with Matt Redman (#theREALdeal) and collaborated on a song called *But If Not* (#surREAL)!

In all our experiences, betrayal from our own spiritual children needed the most duct tape applied on ourselves. So if you catch me crying, I am also guilty as charged.

However, when I am writing this book, I close my eyes and imagine.

All I can see are the faces of GenerationS of Heart of God Church youths who are *still* following Jesus passionately.

I see their flinty faces of commitment. I keep typing... for them.

This book is for them and GenerationS that will keep rising.

For as long as I have breath, I will breathe and build GenerationS!

HOW TO NAVIGATE THIS BOOK

Just before you come fly with us...

1. Two voices in this book – two authors

Two Senior Pastors co-pioneered and built HOGC so it takes both voices to tell the full story. Even though Lia and I walked together on the same journey, our thoughts, feelings, and reactions are sometimes different, so it will be interesting for you.

I'd like to think How and I are as different as night and day (I am a late sleeper much to his chagrin and he is an early riser much to mine), we know that after 20 years of pioneering a church together and seeing each other almost every day (fun fact: we have never had separate offices), our voices may be distinct but our hearts beat in unison. So in order to help you distinguish who is talking in the book, we have incorporated some identifiers.

You may have already noticed *two different fonts.* Throughout the book you will also see *two different icons.*

Since I (Pastor How) am a bonafide WWII history buff (the only kind of buff I can get away with 😜), whenever you see an RAF Spitfire, that represents my voice.

My (Pastor Lia) voice will be marked by a baseball/softball – my only vice (other than coffee). Confession: I forced my husband to spend our 20th wedding anniversary holiday watching other men... eight straight days of Giants baseball games. 😄

2. More voices – contributing writers

At the end of some chapters, you will be able to read from our friends across the globe. These contributors bring different perspectives. Our friends have built great churches and ministered in some of the world's pre-eminent conferences. Their experience, exposure and expertise will add invaluable insights.

Thank you Dr Robi Sonderegger, Bishop Dale Bronner, John and Lisa Bevere and Matt Redman. I thank God for such good friends who willingly and enthusiastically gave your time and effort to write about what Heart of God Church means to you. You have encouraged, influenced and inspired us more than you know. We need to hang out more!

How

There are HOGC contributing writers as well who will bring in-house insights. From their POV, they share about growing up as a youth leader in HOGC or give the inside look into HOGC. Most of their contributions are at the end of the book because we saved the most interesting for the last. Don't miss it.

And we will top it off with words from our own daughter. (We are now bribing her to write good things about us.) I think the truest test of a youth church is that our own children are in revival too. If it works in church, it's gotta work at home. If it works for the youths in church, then it's gotta work for our own children too. *As Christians – don't just pass down our money but our mission. Don't just pass down our valuables but our values.*

> **Don't just pass down money but mission.**
> **Don't just pass down valuables but values.**

3. Money should never be an obstacle

Lia and I did not write this book to make a profit. Youths are our crusade so *GenerationS* is like our manifesto. We see this book as a resource. Money should never be an obstacle for the move of God. No one should miss out on this resource because of financial constraints.

If you are a pastor or leader who wants your whole team to read this book...

If you are a Bible school dean or lecturer who wants to equip your students to raise GenerationS...

If you would like us to partner with you for your conference...

We are happy to help you and your team get your hands on the book. Just go to **GenerationSmvmt.com** for more details.

4. All royalties and proceeds go to the GenerationS Fund

All royalties and proceeds from the sale of this book will go to the GenerationS Fund*, which will be used to advance the cause of GenerationS in HOGC and globally. We are thankful to God that He has already provided for Lia and me through our personal family business.

We are giving away the book royalties and proceeds in hopes of inspiring others to support the GenerationS Fund. Your giving will be used to resource and equip pastors and leaders in HOGC and all over the world.

Just head to **GenerationSmvmt.com**.

---

* The GenerationS Fund is a fund under Heart of God Church Singapore, established to advance the cause of GenerationS in HOGC and globally.

5. GenerationS Digital Companion

Words alone cannot tell the full story of GenerationS. So we came up with a digital companion to supplement your reading journey. Just scan the QR code at the end of each chapter to browse bonus videos, interactive materials, pictures, and the most touching testimonies!

Go ahead. Check it out. Get a feel and the vibe of Heart of God Church before you continue reading... To get you started, here's the first QR code.

Come, fly with us!

GenerationS
Digital Companion

GenerationS

GenerationS is not just reaching My Generation or even the Next Generation. But it is reaching many GenerationS.

Lia 🎾

Everything that has the words *generation* or *youth* usually pulls my eyeballs in. On social media, I see many pastors talking about *My Generation* or the *Next Generation*. I love it! Even up until the 2010s, few pastors would even talk about youth. Now, it is getting headlines!

With this book *GenerationS*, How and I hope our 20-plus years of experience building GenerationS can open up a further horizon and give ministries a longer range of impact. Imagine how strong their churches will be, going from *My Generation* and *Next Generation* to *many GenerationS*? After all, God declared Himself to be the God of Abraham, Isaac and Jacob – well, there are at least three GenerationS mentioned here.

Mark Twain once said, "If the hammer is the only tool you have, you will treat all of life's problems like they are nails." How and I are first and foremost, builders. Like all passionate builders, we like many options in our toolbox. So it is against this backdrop of retooling and widening the options for church-building that I am throwing another mindset into the mix. Think – *GenerationS*!

WHAT IS THE DIFFERENCE?

What is the difference between GenerationS and other widely adopted philosophies of reaching youths? I believe many had pioneered youth groups in the late 1990s and early 2000s all over the world. They were brilliant. They were so successful with young people. But if you look around now, these youth groups are no longer youth movements.

One generation. They only went with the flow of one youth generation. In the typical scenario of their church history, they arduously reached other youths in *their* generation or at most, the *next* generation. But 20 years later, they have become parents and are reaching other parents. Understandably, they are reaching those of their own kind. But sadly, they no longer have a vibrant youth ministry in their church – which was their original strength! They have not reproduced more than one or two generations of young leaders.

The difference with GenerationS is that we do not just focus on reaching *My Generation* or even the *Next Generation*, but we keep on going back down for another generation, another generation, another generation and making sure there are always 13–16-year-olds in the House.

> **GenerationS is not just reaching *My Generation*
> or even the *Next Generation*.
> But it is reaching *many GenerationS*.**

In HOGC, how we define GenerationS is not a 40-year gap or even 20 years in between generations. Every generation is only about three to five years apart! Every few years in HOGC, we start a new youth group as the preceding generation grows up. Every generation gets to Grow Up and Grow Old together. With each generation, there are hundreds of leaders and volunteers, serving together and growing up together. Now, we are already in our 6th Generation. This is how we ensure longevity, renewal and an endless pipeline of ignited youths!

That is why this book is called *GenerationS.* It is not named *Next Gen* or *My Gen*! All good if your church is using a *Next Generation* or *My Generation* approach for your youth ministry. But today, I am proposing that you *add on* another way, another mindset. Honestly, building GenerationS in Heart of God Church does not make us greater – it just makes us more tired!

All pastors know it is hard work growing a church bigger. But it is even harder labour growing the church *younger*! It is a moving target. No, let me correct that. It is like running down an upward escalator! You will pant, you will plant another group but you will never have time to pat yourself on the back.

But God has been good to us. Right now, we have 6 GenerationS of young HOGC leaders serving God all at the same time. Homegrown pastors, leaders, staff and young parents have come out of the 1st Generation while the 6th Generation are our youth who became leaders when they were as young as 14 years old. And the beautiful thing? The average age of our church is still 22 years old after 20 years! At this point, I see the 6th Generation still carrying the torch to produce GenerationS beyond theirs! They have joined us on the escalator run! In fact, as of the writing of this book, we are in the midst of launching our 7th Generation. This is what our rally cry has been for the last two decades: *GenerationS are Not Replacements. GenerationS are Reinforcements.*

GenerationS are Not Replacements.
GenerationS are Reinforcements.

When you build GenerationS, the endless pipeline of leaders continues and the pool of leaders serving God keeps on expanding. The older generations are *not replaced* but *reinforced* as the younger generations join the ranks. Layers and layers of leaders serving *at the same time*!

My Life Verse: Isaiah 58:12
"... You shall raise up the foundations
of many *GenerationS*..."

Let me take you on a visual journey through the 6 GenerationS so you have a reference point of what it looks like in our church. Most of these youths are not from Christian families but they were saved in our church and got planted. They are the first and only Christians in their home. They were not brought to church by Christian parents. In fact, it is the other way round. The youths were the ones who brought their unsaved parents to church and inspired them to become Christians!

We started our first generation of youths with nine teenagers. These are some from the *1st Generation* of youth leaders we had.

1ST GENERATION

Pastor Lynette*   Pastor Charleston*   Pastor Garrett*

Jian Ming   Daniel   Valerie*

Dominic   Yvonne, Elaine, Joanne

---

* Read their contributions in the later part of this book.

This is the origin. They came when they were as young as 8 years old and now they are all in their 30s... Oooold! Meaning, if they are dinosaurs, How and I are fossils!

As you can see in their before photos, they were so cute! And now, they are all still good-looking – plus they have become parents with cute babies to replace their former cute selves. Many in this 1st Generation are pastors and full-time staff.

But we did not stop there. We went back down to reach the next generation.

This is the *2nd Generation*. Again, they came when they were young and now they have all grown up! (Don't you love before and after photos?) They are all leaders right now. Some are staff and board members. Some are lawyers and doctors. And many of them are pastoral leaders. What is inspiring is that most of them hold a full-time job outside and yet serve at such a high capacity.

2ND GENERATION

Megan
Leads 570

Ee Loo
Leads 480 Youths

Darryl
Leads 330, Head of Video Production

Sabrina
Worship Leader,
SOW Instructor

Dr Leonard
Board Member

Shi Hao
Leads 180

But we did not stop there. We went back down for the *3rd Generation* and again for the *4th Generation.*

3RD GENERATION

Leads 250   Leads 130 Youths   Head of Media Operations

Head of Events
Contents Lead

Head of Photography
Leads 85

Head of Analytics
Sermon Screens Lead

4TH GENERATION

Media Operations Leader   Worship Team Leader   Head of Events

Head of Youth Events
Leads 55

Social Media Leader

Drummer
Leads 40

In all these generations, I am only showing you photos of a few but in every generation we actually have hundreds of them. So imagine this, in your church, hundreds and hundreds of each generation coming up to reinforce the previous generation! The previous generations are still at the frontlines serving, but then they have another generation coming up as *reinforcements.*

So at the end of the *4th Generation,* guess what? We did not stop. We went back down for a *5th Generation.*

5TH GENERATION

Youth Events Team Leader
Assoc. Producer (Online Church)

Media Team Leader*

Leads 30*

Leads 50

IT Ministry Lead Developer

Assistant Head of Testimony

And you get the idea, we did not stop there. After a few years, we went back down for the *6th Generation!* And they form another layer of leaders and people serving in church.

---

* No, you're not seeing double – these twins are on fire and serving God!

6TH GENERATION

| Leads 130 | Leads 50 | Media Operations Leader |
| Social Media Trainer* | Head of Youth Innovation | Assoc. Producer (Online Church) |

| Photography Team Leader | Worship Team Leader | Sound Ministry Team Leader |
| Leads 15 | Leads 30 | |

As of this writing, we are in the midst of launching the *7th Generation.* (Watch out for stories from the different GenerationS later in this book or in the Digital Companion.)

And let me tell you what the greatest blessing of raising young people and GenerationS is. My daughter is an on-fire leader in the *6th Generation*! When you build young people, remember, it goes around and it can come right back to bless you!

So this is what we mean. Layers and layers of leaders *at the same time.* Nobody is replacing anybody. GenerationS are *not replacements*. They are *reinforcements*!

GenerationS is *not just an experiential concept* that I am talking about just because our novel experiment has proven successful. It is a *biblical concept*!

> 2 Timothy 2:2
> And the things that you have heard from me among many witnesses, commit these to faithful men who will be able to teach others also.

---

* Read her contribution at the end of Chapter 11.

There are at least four generations of believers mentioned here! Serving God at the same time!

Paul ➛ Timothy ➛ Faithful Men ➛ Others

The Bible urges us to build GenerationS!

As you read this book, many of you will be inspired and you will catch a vision. Inspiration sustains you. Vision propels you. But it is *faith* that will ultimately and actively put your hands on the plough to build GenerationS. So I have planted many visual images in this chapter just to awaken faith in your heart! These visuals will nail themselves to your mind and embed their powerful resolution in your psyche. Images in this chapter shout — "It is powerful and *possible* to build GenerationS!"

DEEP BENCH

Here is an iconic photo in our church showing how the GenerationS work together.

Iconic Photo: A common sight in HOGC — three GenerationS serving together (L to R: supervisor, trainer, crew standing on a stool).

Three generations of youths are reflected here serving together in one service. The skills the oldest youth has learnt, he is committing these to another faithful younger man who is able to teach the youngest – a 12-year-old boy who had to stand on a stool to reach the lights board! No age nor height is going to separate him from his love to serve God! Three generations serving at the same time!

Here is another photo from more recent times.

HOGC Training Ground: Three GenerationS serving on the keyboard (L to R: supervisor, trainer, 12-year-old playing on a lowered keyboard).

There are so many images similar to this, taking place in every HOGC department. Photos like these flesh out the concept of *Deep Bench*. There has been a great interest in the phrase *Deep Bench* ever since I talked about it years ago. Many pastors and leaders have asked me to teach more on it. Therefore in this book (Chapter 8), I have deep dived into what *Deep Bench* is about.

GenerationS and Deep Bench are more than just phrases or quotable quotes. Therefore reproduce GenerationS and don't just replicate its quotes. The hippie musician Jimi Hendrix said it best, "I've been imitated so well I've heard people copy my mistakes."

HOGC is nowhere near Jimi's legendary iconic status *but he is right – don't just copy.* That is why we have painstakingly written this book so that the *spirit* and *heart* for GenerationS and Deep Bench will be caught. Use your understanding, see the longer range and be challenged to build. Pastor How and I hope that this book will help broaden your toolbox as you hammer out a longer future for GenerationS to come!

And after going at it for more than 20 years, I am so glad we ran down that ascending escalator! Having 6 GenerationS of leaders serving together churchwide has made our church strong indeed. We have grown our church younger and stronger.

GenerationS! Never before have we loved the letter 'S' with such precise passion!

In Heart of God Church, we are still going for that 8th, 9th, 10th Generation. Right now, we are still hustling in the same manner. Join us on this escalator run?

HOGC vibes? This 16-year-old captured it perfectly! Scan for more videos.

Lisa Bevere

New York Times best-selling author of *Without Rival*
Co-Founder of Messenger International

REPLACED OR REINFORCED

The first time I heard Pastor Lia teach on the concept of GenerationS was in Chiang Mai, Thailand at a conference that Messenger International hosted and Heart of God Church supported with their excellent time and talent. In addition to ministering, Pastors How and Lia brought a large team along to cover worship and volunteer at the event.

As I sat in the back of a crowded auditorium, Pastor Lia spoke to the Thai church leaders on the importance of valuing and empowering their youth. The very fact that so few youth were in attendance confirmed that this idea was completely foreign to the audience who'd gathered in her afternoon session. But everything was about to shift. It's one thing to hear about a generational dynamic and quite another one to see it played out.

As she spoke, Lia invited a small number of her group to join her on the stage. They were core leaders who'd been with Heart of God Church since its inception. They were musicians, admins, and pastors that How and Lia had mentored from their teens who were now in their thirties and had become integral leaders of their core team. After Lia explained each of their relationships and roles, she invited another group to join them on the stage.

This next group represented those who were just a few years younger than the first group. In addition to being mentored by Pastors How and Lia, the second group was mentored by the first. After each of their ages and roles were explained, they called up the group they had poured into who were just a few years younger than themselves.

This phenomenon continued until the stage was crowded with beaming youth filled with God's love and divine purpose. Some were no more than teens.

Each age group was flanked by honor and welcome. It was so evident that each generation celebrated the growth and potential of those who were younger. I didn't sense any comparison, pride, or competition. Then Pastor Lia shared this insight that put it all into perspective.

"The next generation are not our replacements, they're our reinforcements."

I was struck by the simplicity and power of her words. This changed everything! You'd train a reinforcement very differently than a replacement. You'd invest more in someone who was coming alongside you than you would in someone who was taking your place.

Our beautiful broken world has become a war zone. We risk losing far too much if the generations remain disconnected from one another. We need the strength, questions, and zeal that is woven into the youth just as they need the wisdom and insight of those who have walked the road before them.

I often hear Millennials and Gen Zs described as entitled. But let's pause a moment. Can any of us possibly earn the gracious gift of salvation? Is it possible that anyone could redeem themselves? Never! This is the very reason that Jesus paid the ultimate price for all of us. I want to challenge you to read this kingdom parable with the perspective of generational reinforcement.

> "God's kingdom is like an estate manager who went out early in the morning to hire workers for his vineyard. They agreed on a wage of a dollar a day, and went to work."

Our Lord invites each of us to work his vineyard. Initially we're excited by this privilege. As the harvest increases the estate manager realizes he needs more laborers.

"Later, about nine o'clock, the manager saw some other men hanging around the town square unemployed. He told them to go to work in his vineyard and he would pay them a fair wage. They went.

"He did the same thing at noon, and again at three o'clock. At five o'clock he went back and found still others standing around. He said, 'Why are you standing around all day doing nothing?'

"They said, 'Because no one hired us.'

"He told them to go to work in his vineyard."

Four times in the course of one day the manager returns to the town square to enlist those who are idle. Because the last group was hired at 5:00pm, you know it was a long day of hard labor for those who began early. In a time of harvest, you must grab the fruit when it is ready.

"When the day's work was over, the owner of the vineyard instructed his foreman, 'Call the workers in and pay them their wages. Start with the last hired and go on to the first.'

"Those hired at five o'clock came up and were each given a dollar. When those who were hired first saw that, they assumed they would get far more. But they got the same, each of them one dollar. Taking the dollar, they groused angrily to the manager, 'These last workers put in only one easy hour, and you just made them equal to us, who slaved all day under a scorching sun.'"

We all get their frustration, but listen and hear why they are wrong.

"He replied to the one speaking for the rest, 'Friend, I haven't been unfair. We agreed on the wage of a dollar, didn't we? So take it and go. I decided to give to the one who came last the same as you. Can't I do what I want with my own money? *Are you going to get stingy because I am generous?*'

"Here it is again, the Great Reversal: many of the first ending up last, and the last first."

And this is the question we must answer with our actions and attitude.

"Are you going to get stingy because I am generous?"

God forbid that we would dishonor our generous Lord! I pray that those who labor long and hard will rejoice with the Lord of the Harvest and celebrate His generous nature. Thinking generationally will keep us on the right course.

Lisa Bevere

Lia talks GenerationS, Lisa talks Godmothers! Watch as they swap insights.

The Kids Who Built a World-Class Church

Start Empowering Youths.
Stop Entertaining Them.

There is a 15-year-old leader in church. She is leading a connect group (CG) of 43 other youths. She is preaching, worship leading, and discipling. Her group invited 46 new friends over for Christmas services and 29 of them made decisions for Christ. 10 of those friends came back the following weeks and just like that, her group grew to 53. This surge was the result of weeks of preparation, prayer, and dedication.

She is buzzing with euphoria but she also knows the hard work has just begun. Now it's all hands on deck. She is connecting with the new friends through Instagram and TikTok. In one week, she gives 12 one-on-one Bible studies to these new Christians. She is also organizing the rest of her leaders to be responsible for integrating the new youths.

Even when the 2020 pandemic hit, she didn't hibernate but hustled. Although Easter was online, her group invited friends to Zoom in and they hit 182 in Easter attendance. All things worked for good. It was even easier to invite youths when services were online. That unforgettable Easter will always be reminisced about as Easy Easter.

Every CG and zone broke through. By the end of April, her group was averaging 100 in weekly attendance. In 5 months, this leader grew her CG from 43 to 100-ish. Today she is a leader of 130 youths.

Her personal vision is to grow herself to become a Zone Leader with the capacity and capability to lead 200. And she added in her own words, "Not just 200 but Strong 200." So she knows that in order to lead 200 and survive school (crazy Asian, exam-heavy, high-stress school), then she needs to raise up many leaders of 20s, 10s, and 5s. She needs a team of leaders. So at night, she is having conference calls with her leaders to disciple them. She is training, building, and delegating. She understands the revival is spelled W-O-R-K. (You can read more of her story at the end of Chapter 11.)

In HOGC, this leader is not unique. She is not the only 15-year-old leader. There are others like her who lead 70–80 youths. She is also not the first youth leader. There are hundreds who have been leading before her. Now they are older and in university or in the marketplace, still leading and serving.

She will not be the last too. There are 13 and 14-year-olds coming up after her. They are being trained to lead smaller groups now.

This is what a ***Strong GenerationS Church*** looks like.

There is a pipeline of leaders and church builders.

There is a culture of evangelism and discipleship.

There is a cycle of reaching out, recruiting, refining, and releasing – then hit repeat.

It is possible.

God did it here in Singapore. God brought revival to Millennials, Gen Z, and Gen Alpha in a first-world city. Lia and I have the privilege of watching this youth revival from the front row. However, I also know that God wants to bring a youth revival to every church and every city.

One ignited youth can make a difference. What happens when they come together? You get a combustion of faith, energy, vision, and good vibes.

Four HOGC students were saved and planted when they were 18 years old. The next year, they enrolled into university as freshmen. They decided that they were not going to be thermometers but thermostats. They were going to be different and make a difference.

The four of them were from different faculties – Law, Business, Engineering, and Economics – but they had the same vision to bring revival to their campus. They worked together as a team, praying, reaching out, organizing EV (HOGC lingo for evangelistic) activities, initiating meet-ups, etc.

We will just zoom in on one of them. Chelsea had an unhappy childhood, so naturally she struggled with insecurities, but the love of God filled her heart and she found a home in HOGC. The same way God changed her life, now she wanted her friends to experience God too.

One of the first friends she wanted to reach out to was Nicholas. She had never invited anyone to church before. She didn't know what to do. So she did the only thing she knew – *pray*! I think God loves to hear the nervous and simple prayers of new Christians, especially when the prayers are selflessly for others. Nicholas didn't know what hit him. He came to church, encountered Jesus, and was planted.

When Nicholas became a Christian, his friends were shocked. When he stopped getting drunk and clubbing, and started going to church, they thought his body had been taken over by aliens. His best friend, Brendan, couldn't believe it. So he followed Nicholas to church and got saved too.

God spoke to Nicholas to invite another friend, Melvyn, for Easter services. Melvyn didn't want to come because "religion is not really my thing." But he decided to just come once and never again. Well, he got saved and is planted in church too.

So now we have Nicholas and Melvyn in church. And Chelsea is just getting started. She is now like a spiritual hitman. Next in her crosshairs is a law student, Nicole. Chelsea reached out to her for a whole year but Nicole rejected her for a whole year. That whole year was not wasted because Chelsea was simultaneously praying for her too. Who can resist a whole year of targeted prayer? Persistence breaks resistance. Nicole not only got saved, she is now a pastoral leader of 140.

I think Chelsea over-prayed for Nicole and she OD-ed on prayer. Nicole became a super evangelist. Now she wants to reach out to her entire Law faculty. These were the best and brightest students, and their brilliance was only matched by their atheism.

But by now she is not alone. There's Chelsea plus the other three original revivalists.

Add on fuel like Nicholas and Melvyn.

Then turbocharge the team with high-octane Nicole.

Through these revivalists, more than 100 Law students have stepped into church!

What you read here is a single chain of revival from Chelsea. There are three other chains of revival from the original gang. These four freshmen brought hundreds to church and soon there were 40 university students saved and planted in church. Their little connect group became a zone. And in another 10 months, that zone doubled to 80!

More than just the number added, out of this university revival came a wave of leaders and volunteers. At the last count, there are:

- 6 full-time church staff
- 9 part-time church staff
- 55 pastoral leaders (who lead anywhere from 3 to 200)
- 120 serving in various ministries

They even started a lawyers' group. Besides reaching out to more lawyers, they are helping out in the church's legal work.

This is what a **Strong Youth Church** looks like.

Students reaching students.

It is not event-based or preacher-centered but ignited young people reaching other young people.

Self-motivated. Self-initiated. Ground-up.

It's a viral revival.

How did this happen?

How can it happen for churches in the world?

Well, it starts with a complete overhaul of our mindsets.

How often have you heard leaders say this: "Youth are the future."

Or pastors saying, "I am building the leaders of tomorrow."

No!

That's a false start right out of the gate. Of course, youth are leaders of tomorrow – no argument about that. But, youth are also leaders *today*!

This small but foundational mental adjustment is the game changer.

If youth are leaders now, then we want them to lead now.

If they are leaders today, then we let them plan, organize, implement, and execute today.

Since the beginning, Lia and I have had this conviction: Youth are leaders *today*, not just tomorrow!

That is why 14-year-olds are leading other 13-year-olds who are leading other 12-year-olds.

13-year-olds are planning and running youth camps for hundreds.

14-year-olds are sound engineers, operating a professional, concert-grade soundboard.

15-year-olds are media directors, coordinating 16 professional live feed cameras like a maestro.

Youth are leaders TODAY, not just tomorrow!
- Pastor How & Pastor Lia

When we start believing in our heart of hearts that youth are leaders now, it will translate into massive application implications. It means that we start empowering the youths and stop entertaining them.

Instead of getting them to join our ministry, they own the ministry. In fact, it is their ministry. In our church, we have a slogan: *You don't just belong to HOGC, but HOGC belongs to you.*

It is a fallacy to delay youths from leading "till they are older." It's like getting youths to watch soccer from 12 to 25 years old and expecting them to be star players when they are 25. That's not gonna happen.

Empower the youths, Don't Entertain them!
- Pastor Lia

They have to be playing competitively at their age groups. They have to be in real games – hustling, adrenaline pumping, scraping their knees, taking clutch shots, tasting victory, dealing with defeat, and learning to work as a team.

Even just training and practicing without actual games is not enough to develop youths into professional soccer players. This is because it takes more than technical skills. A successful athlete requires a holistic set of psychological, emotional traits such as discipline, self-motivation, and a winning mindset.

Same for developing church leaders. Youths have to be in the real game. We need to involve the youths in every aspect of church life and deep into the epicenter of ministry. They must be running on the field, not sitting in the stands. Give them the ball!

Just asking them to attend youth nights or come join a cool event is like asking youths to watch their friends have fun through the window.

Just putting youths in permanent training mode – Bible studies and Scripture memory only (don't get me wrong, Bible studies are important) is like telling youths to practice without a tournament.

Just letting youths say the occasional opening prayer or make the announcements is like getting them to be ball boys or girls in a tennis match while the grown-ups play. You can touch the balls but not the racket.

Just getting the youths to do a once-a-year youth takeover is like putting them in a game with five minutes left, once a season.

Can you see the colossal mistake of "waiting till they are older"?

While we are "waiting for them to be older," their hearts are being captivated by another vision. Year after year, we lose them emotionally and spiritually. By the time we deem them "old enough," we would have lost them physically too.

Can you see the blunder of not getting youths to lead *today*?

We have to move youths from the spectator stands to the sidelines to the front lines.

How?

It's not rocket science – just let them lead.

We will talk more about this in Chapter 6.

Now let me tell you about Charmaine.

Charmaine is an Operations Coordinator in the media department. She is overseeing eight ministries: Live Feed, Lights, Effects, Visuals Production, Motion Graphics, Projection, Sermon Screens, and the other Ops Coordinators. She is a pro, spewing technical terms like "VP can standby title bar and UFS video with QR code on banners. Don't loop. Lights make sure facelights on correct setting. P1 standby contin!"

I try to sound intelligent when she explains to me how things work. When I am overwhelmed by her professional jargon, I interrupt her with Bible verses to remind her that I am holier than her. 😊

Her team has a crew of over 100.

This sounds like a job for a 37-year-old industry professional whom the church hired to head the department with a half million-dollar budget.

But Charmaine is 20.

She has been doing this since she was 12.

She is not a full-time staff. In fact, she is still in university.

She doesn't look the part... She looks like she is 16 and the sweetest girl next door.

By the way, she also leads 3 connect groups totalling 70 youths – and scores a GPA of 3.9.

This is what happens when you believe in youths and get them to lead at 12. Charmaine is just one of many Operations Coordinators. In fact, she is already one of the older ones. There are two 14-year-olds coming up to reinforce the team.

This is what a youth leader looks like.

This is what a Strong Youth Church looks like.

What a weekend service run by HOGC youth volunteers looks like!

THE KIDS WHO BUILT A WORLD-CLASS CHURCH

Soon after our auditorium, Imaginarium, was built, a sought-after lights and sound consultant plus stage designer visited our service. He was in town because another megachurch in the city paid him to design their auditorium. I did not know him so our team hosted him and brought him to our Media Control Room where the 14–20-year-olds were running the entire service. I met him after service ended. After all the pleasantries, he delivered his pitch. He sold me on how we can make the lights better, stage nicer, camera work more professional, and how we can be ready for a global TV ministry. Then he ended his pitch with, "Now that you are successful and on the map, it's time to take it up to the next level. *It's time to get rid of the kids and let professionals* [like him] *take over."*

I didn't even get his email.

Don't get me wrong. We certainly need improvements all the time. We regularly hire consultants and professionals to help us out. But "get rid of the kids"?! It's the kids who put us on the map. It's the kids who built this church.

"Getting rid of the kids" is like putting the cart before the horse. For Lia and me, the purpose of all the screens, media, and tech is for the kids to be involved and to give them opportunities to serve. HOGC is not a show to entertain Christians or a production to impress global TV audiences. HOGC is the gymnasium for the youths. It is where thousands of Charmaines are developed.

The consultant saw better lights and nicer screens.

I see better youths and greater leaders.

A walk-through with Dr Robi in our Media Control Room: Meet the kids who run a world-class service.

Bishop Dale C. Bronner

Founder/Senior Pastor/Author
Word of Faith Family Worship Cathedral, Atlanta, Georgia, USA

I have had the privilege of teaching and preaching on every inhabited continent in the world, yet I've found Heart of God Church to be the most powerful demonstration of youth being discovered, developed, and deployed to produce a world-class ministry for Jesus Christ. HOGC beautifully illustrates the power of diligence, consistency, and starting with a remnant seed, in this case—children, to produce a glorious harvest for Jesus Christ in every realm of influence in the world.

My first time stepping into HOGC was an impacting moment for me. One of the first things that struck me was the sense of excitement and expectation in the eyes and attitudes of the church. It felt like a big family at Christmastime with great expectation of food, presents, and fun. There was an electric kind of energy that permeated the packed auditorium. It made me feel like a youth again! It was everywhere—in the music, the colors, the fun-looking fonts on all the graphics, the décor, their attire, their social media presence, the humor, the fun, the vibrant cell groups, and their awesome, passionate hunger for God. They have uniquely created an inviting place to belong, to believe, and to become. They have a contagious Christianity in a way that I would imagine that the first followers of Christ had during the time Jesus walked the earth.

For more than a decade, I have observed HOGC. I have watched how they have intentionally trained up children to live in the right way, serve with the right attitude, and passionately share their faith with people in their sphere of influence. I've watched them create a champion spirit of excellence in youth through discipling them in Christian principles, creating authentic friendships, valuing education, empowering them in entrepreneurial endeavors, and serving with joy and more. They do a great job in making the next steps clear as they grow in Christ.

Prior to witnessing the levels of discipline and excellence at HOGC, I never knew that youth could be trained and trusted to fulfill serious responsibilities in ministry. I didn't know that teenagers could be trusted to handle being on time and serving with excellence in technical skills by operating sophisticated computers, cameras, lighting, digital screens, networks, learning to play instruments, ushering, accounting, hospitality, etc. They intentionally set high expectations for the youth. They don't limit their realm of possibility. They inspire them to dream and imagine a better future and world.

HOGC has proven that people rise or fall to meet your level of expectations for them. Pastor How and Pastor Lia have modeled what responsible, committed Christianity looks like. They have modeled generosity, a commitment to lifelong learning, business acumen, and how to serve with excellence. They have refused to lower their standards for their youth, despite others who refuse to raise their standards for youth.

HOGC is a place that stirs the imagination and empowers dreams to be experienced. At HOGC they help you believe in Jesus, then believe in yourself, and then believe in your dreams. They help to nurture excellence and then use that excellence to serve the purposes of Jesus Christ on the earth.

HOGC values people, no matter how young or old. Then they add value to people. Then they live out those good values with one another in community. Then they share those good values with others outside of the church. This is what authentic Christianity is all about.

Bishop Dale C. Bronner

Bishop preaches from Genesis to Revelation in 5 minutes?! Every HOGC member remembers this! Don't miss many other powerful clips too.

The Heart of God Church Story - The Journey of a Dream

Heart of God Church started as a divine experiment to build a prototype Youth Church. Now it has developed into a proof of concept that Youths can build a STRONG CHURCH.

Words have meaning but a name has its own life. Many of you can recognise offhand that our church name has its roots in the Bible character King David.

> Acts 13:22 (NLT)
> ... David, a man about whom God said, 'I have found David... *a man after my own heart.* He will do everything I want him to do.'

We want to be a church who expresses God's heart and desires on the face of the earth. We started pioneering with that intent. And so against a backdrop of greying churches, HOGC stumbled onto a sweet spot – youth.

Hindsight after 20 years tells us that God really wanted a youth church that builds GenerationS to exist. Heart of God Church was an expression of God's desire on earth. I believe a church will always live out its name. Now we are so privileged to be able to tell the story. This is a Journey of a Dream that captures mountains, valleys, the in-betweens, mistakes, hurts, disappointments and joys of pioneering.

Heart of God Church began as a small group of five people including How and myself. The journey of our youth church started on the top floor of my late brother's house. Three of my brothers offered their houses for use in our pioneering days. They were saved in our church! Amusing as it may sound, they were also a little worried that I had resigned from my job as a journalist. Opening up their houses for our church use was their way of expressing support for their little sister's bewildering life choices. Asian brothers, what can I say, I love them!

One of my brothers' houses had three levels for use. Exactly how we needed it! Pastor How would lead the adult small group downstairs. I herded the kids upstairs, then shut the door and tried to keep them focused and bring Jesus to them. Those four steps were always in that sequence, by the way. Mayhem seems to be every kid's middle name especially when you try to cater from ages 4 to 10 in one group.

Over time, we moved out of the homes and rented a space in my father-in-law's office building located in a small industrial park (Henderson). My ministry partner and husband How ran an adult service. I ran a proper children's church service concurrently. It was in those children's church services that I noticed a group of teens who were either too cool to be engaged or too cold to be enlivened. Whether they were cool or cold, they were definitely not on fire for Jesus. At a glance, you knew they were too old for children's church and too young for adult service. And I was too burdened for them. Everything in my heart went out to those bored faces.

So I took nine of these teens out of the children's church and started a teens small group in my father-in-law's office which was unused during the weekends. Little did I know that the Strong Youth Church of thousands we now have would come out of this first small group!

First kids' camp in Pastor Lia's house.

Running youth connect group at Pastor How and Pastor Lia's home in Woodlands.

Pastor Lia running children's church upstairs while Pastor How led the adult small group downstairs at the home of Pastor Lia's brother.

Pastor Lia prophesying at a youth camp – out of this group came pastors and full-time staff.

Pastor Lia and Pastor How in Henderson (our first worship venue, 1999–2004).

Running children's church in Pastor How's father's office.

Pastor Lia prophesying over 11-year-old Pastor Lynette.

Taking out these nine to pioneer a youth group was a monumental step. Oh, they were a monument in themselves. I called them the 9 Stones because they would not worship, would not pray, refused to respond when you spoke to them and they didn't smile. Their grand silence made them aloof and alone all at the same time, a terrifying monument indeed. They were just a bunch of teenagers. Stony-faced ones. But Jesus said even the rocks will cry out and praise His name. Thank God. They grew spiritually! In fact, several of our homegrown pastors and full-time staff have emerged out of these 9 Stones.

The 9 Stones not only grew spiritually, the entire youth group exploded in growth. The ever self-deprecating How quipped that if we ever split, my young church would be bigger than his. But I told him that his side of the church with older demographics would be richer than mine.

So that was how we started. In a small industrial park, all kids. Many of our well-meaning pastor friends and relatives urged us to reconsider building a youth church. Everyone said youths had no money to contribute. It was not sustainable. It was just not possible to build a youth church.

To some extent, they were right. Money was not the only thing lacking. We had no musicians, no millionaires, no mature leaders. We had to kick and punch just to stay above the water.

Undeterred, we ploughed on. For the first few years of pioneering the church, we did not take a salary. Living on a dream and fresh air is what Asians call it. We had a vision that we could build a church operated by youths, for youths, to reach youths. To bus in the kids, I used my savings. The small group of adults in the church also gave generously to the church. We invested limited finances into the youths but poured limitless time to disciple and train them.

THE MIRACLE IS IN THE HOUSE

In the pioneering days, we read a book by Tommy Barnett, *There's A Miracle In Your House*. His challenge that the miracle is found within our House confirmed what we had been believing for! Encouraged and emboldened, we started carving out Miracles in the Mundane. We put musical instruments into the hands of ordinary kids who had zero music experience and told them, "You play the drums", "You go learn the bass." They miraculously did pick up skills.

Adults had always been the only ones playing on our worship team in our humble beginnings. But there was in-fighting and immorality. Some were good, some gave a lot of grief, some quit. So I let go of almost all of the adult worship team members. It was time to bring higher honour and greater commitment into the House of the Lord. It was time for a rebuild.

I spoke to a 14-year-old boy, Dominic. He had been learning the keyboard. I told him, "This coming Sunday, you will be playing the keyboard."

"Oh, in the small group," he surmised.

"No, in the main service on stage – alone with me. You will be the only musician. I am worship leading. Just you and me," I clarified.

Quiet. He was quiet. So I filled in the quietness by summoning up my most faith-filled pastoral voice and told him, "Dominic, why don't you spend the time worshipping God on your keyboard and you will find your breakthrough." He must have been thinking, *You are Pastor Lia, add one more letter 'r' to your name – and you are dangerously close to being over optimistic about this!* If he thought I was a Lia-r, I definitely didn't see it because he had a poker face.

Dominic and Pastor Lia rehearsing for the main service.

Being the faith-filled boy he was, he took up the challenge. He spent the whole week in worship. In fact one night, he felt the Holy Spirit tell him to switch off the room lights, play in the dark, close his eyes and worship without being bothered about whether his fingers would miss a key. That night, God's presence filled his room. He came the next morning to play in the main service. That morning, God's presence filled the room. (And I got to keep my name Pastor Lia!)

The miracle is in the House! There are Miracles in the Mundane as you build kid by kid, youth by youth, teenager by teenager!

Meet Charleston, a handsome and trendy 13-year-old. His desire to serve God was as big as his huge, baggy jeans. Being a man of vision,

he envisaged himself reaching his friends for Jesus. Charleston loves soccer as much as he loves Jesus. During a soccer game one day, it was raining. His friends challenged him and said, "If your God is real, pray and ask Him to stop the rain." He prayed and the rain really did stop. Out

13-year-old Pastor Charleston on the drums.

of that bold act of faith and one-on-one reaching out, he led many of them to Christ personally. In fact, he brought 40 of his friends to church! That was our very first student revival. Many leaders rose up subsequently and the church continued to grow!

If you are a pastor and you have no musicians, millionaires and no mature leaders, take heart. There are miracles in your House waiting to be watered and grown. Give your all and expect God to pour in His all!

The tide turned. More and more caught the vision and became our young leaders. Soon enough, our entire worship department was also run by youths, for youths, to reach other youths. We started the School of Worship where we trained even more young musicians to serve in His House.

A common sight since the beginning of HOGC – Pastor Lia training, leading and discipling youths (photo from 2000).

HOGC iconic story – Pastor How was the one who taught a little stony-faced boy named Daniel his first few simple chords on the guitar. Today Daniel is the Music Director who had enjoyed a study stint at the Musicians Institute in Los Angeles. We call him our HOGC John Mayer. He is an anointed, consummate practitioner of his craft. Daniel is not only an exceptional worship leader and guitarist, he is a committed preacher and pastoral leader. He leads 210 people currently! In HOGC, that is where he keeps the heart of his music focused – on people!

God has multiplied the five loaves and two fish we put into His hands. Today we have five full worship teams serving, all homegrown and house-proud. Layers and layers of young leaders have risen up!

Our first worship team guitarists, young Pastor Garrett on the acoustic and Daniel rocking his electric guitar.

12-year-old Pastor Lynette as a singer on the worship team.

Truly, the miracle is in the House! Don't look at your neighbour's green pastures. The turf is greener on the other side until you discover it is AstroTurf, of course. So stop comparing with other pastors and start discovering the miracles in your own House!

"YOU WILL RUN INTO MY PROVISION"

I have always taught our church that prayer is our Declaration of Dependence on God. That understanding was chiselled into my heart during deep times of prayer for our fledgling church. Scarcity and lack drove us to dependence on Him. Breathless audacity of pioneering drove us to our declaration of faith.

During one such personal time, God spoke so clearly to my heart. He said, "You will run into My Provision!" He did not say that He would provide. Neither did He say He would make sure goodness and blessing would follow me all the days of my life. He said 'run into My Provision'. That means – *before* the needs of our church would come up, God had already prepared a *provision* for that need! Provision will not *follow* us. It will not even come *beside* HOGC but it will be *ahead* of HOGC. That is why we will *run into* His provision!

What a sturdy word for hopeful pioneers! Like How always says – pioneering a church is hard enough but pioneering a church with youths is bordering on stupidity. He says youths come with empty pockets and even emptier stomachs!

In those days, we truly felt like a father and mother with 12 poor kids. Our church had about 800 students and 150 adults then. Take away some working adults who did not tithe or give. Then take away other adults who did not have income, we were left with few sacrificial remnants. So the reality was perhaps 70+ tithers supporting a church of close to 1,000. That sense of lack was all the more accentuated when we were outgrowing the space at our second venue (Dhoby Ghaut). Not having enough space was a good problem but good problems still needed solutions.

Service at Dhoby Ghaut (second worship venue, 2004–2007).

After searching, we had laid eyes on renting a venue that used to be a sports hall. Perfect. No pillars (I can see all the pastors nodding to this), near a train station (yes! Our youths had no cars!) and high ceiling (I see all lights and media crew smiling at this). Perfect. Except for the price (I am not smiling at this).

We contacted the relevant real estate agent and asked if he could negotiate the rental down for us. He took one look at us and the poor youths we had, stood up and ended the meeting. He said, and I will always remember to this day the dismissive look in his eyes, "If you can't afford, just go back to your old place." And he walked off. We were shocked. Firstly, it was not even the owner of the building we were asking, we were asking an agent who was brokering the deal! Secondly, did he have to be that curt, blunt and rude?

Talk about being humbled. We were humiliated! Who needs the devil when we can have real estate agents from hell?

To all pastors reading this: The journey of fighting for young people and their destinies in God has never been and will never be an easy one. You have to thicken your skin if you want to build a youth church! Above all, you have to fortify your heart with His Word.

The perfect worship venue we had laid eyes on went up in a puff. But God was not done yet. We will run into His provision, remember?

And God says He will resist the proud and lift up the humble – or the humiliated in our case.

Days after our failed attempt with the real estate agent, HOGC was holding an evangelistic event featuring a world-renowned classical guitarist. We went around and greeted the new friends during the concert. One of our leaders, Jin Chiew, who was a lawyer, had invited his friends. Amazingly, it turned out that one of them was from the very same company that owned that building we wanted to rent! So his friend offered to put us in contact with the relevant department and we negotiated *directly* with them. What happened next could only be God. We got our building at a good rental price! We secured it at a price even lower than what we offered the real estate agent. And the best part of it all was that we did not have to pay any commission or fees to the agent! Yes!

God will lift the humiliated! We will run into His provision! He had prepared ahead – a friend to open doors even *before* HOGC's need for rental negotiation came up! When God wants to provide for you, He will make sure you get to His provision no matter what route you take! Nothing, absolutely nothing can separate you from the provision of God!

For more than two decades it is stories like these that spurred us on to continue building a youth church, no matter the cost. The Heart of God Church story is really about the Journey of a Dream and how God was with us every step of that journey.

All four of my brothers were saved in HOGC in the pioneering days and three of them have since gone home to be with the Lord. From offering their humble homes for church use to SingPost (our third worship venue), they would have been proud to see how this Strong Youth Church has grown!

That SingPost miracle? It was awe-inspiring fuel for us to keep dreaming and walking. And in this venue, we grew from 1,000 to 3,000!

SingPost worship venue pre-renovation – you can still spot the badminton court outlines at this former sports hall! We didn't have enough chairs so we had to rent the (red) chairs behind.

Fully packed service at SingPost (third worship venue, 2007–2015). Here we grew from 1,000 to 3,000.

How ✈

We were in SingPost from 2007 to 2015. I would say that this is the place where we established ourselves, going from a start-up to an organized church. We implemented HOGC 2.0 to put in systems, processes, and structured training. In those days, the mantras were:

- SYSTEM = Save Yourself Stress Time Effort Money
- Administration = Love
- Details determine destiny

A few years later we ran out of space again. We were already running four services to the brim. On Big Days like Christmas and Easter, it was so packed, we had to take turns to breathe. It was obvious that we needed another venue. At the time, it looked impossible. This is how it works in Singapore. All parcels of land for church use are controlled by the government. In those days, the government would release one or two lots of land every few years. Many land-starved churches would tender for it, with the land going to the highest bidder. Singapore is blessed with many growing megachurches with strong financial muscle while HOGC is a youth church. There was no way we could go head-to-head with other megachurches in a tender. It would be like bringing a knife to a gunfight. At the time, each parcel of land was going for $20 million upwards. That's only for a 30-year lease and we had not even accounted for construction costs yet. So most church building projects were costing $40 million to $50 million plus (US$30–US$40 million) upfront. $40 million would be pretty basic, certainly not Solomon's Temple. Even though we raised a Building Fund every year to prepare and save up, we only had a fraction of that cash in reserves. We were thousands of schooling youths and only a few hundred working adults. We could not come up with the huge upfront cash and the banks definitely would not lend to a youth church with zero assets. I had to find another solution around this.

Fast outgrowing our venue – the snaking queue for the lifts that led to our SingPost auditorium.

The Building Committee scoured the whole country for land, buildings, and properties of any kind that could suit our needs and most importantly, that we could afford. Everything was out of our league. I felt like Moses standing at the edge of the Red Sea. I was facing a dead end with thousands of refugees looking for the promised land.

As Lia wrote earlier, we ran into His provision again. One afternoon, I got a phone call from Pastor Vincent. He is the nicest human being I know and a man of character with the biggest Kingdom heart. (Till this day, I am eternally grateful to Pastor Vincent.) He introduced me to a friend of a friend who owned a piece of land and wanted to develop it. And this is the part that is miraculous – it was a seven-minute walk from our current location, SingPost. Pastor Vincent told me, "As soon as I knew the location of the land, the Holy Spirit shouted to me: 'Call Pastor How!'"

We were searching for land for years and nothing. That day when Lia and I went to see the parcel of land for the first time, the Holy Spirit reminded me of Bishop Bronner's prophecy years earlier. He had declared: "The land is not hidden from you. It is hidden for you."

Amen.

We were looking around the whole country while the land was just sitting a seven-minute walk away. It was hiding in plain sight. It was hidden from others, until HOGC needed it. Again, we ran into His provision.

So in 2012, I started the long and draining process of negotiating the deal. In the same year when Lia was going through her cancer treatments, I was also in the midst of tough negotiations for our new venue. As a pastor, I operated in the "innocent as dove" zone, but now I had to step out of my comfort zone and navigate in the "wise as serpent" zone. After another two years of board meetings, AGMs and EGMs, legal and expert consultations, hammering out the contracts, back and forth, we finally came to an agreement.

Then another two years of design and planning. People who visit Imaginarium ask if we engaged an architect and I tell them, "Everything is done in-house." My team and I planned the structure and space of every room. One of our adult connect group leaders, Mr. Sim, is the owner of a major construction company. He and his wife Khim supported our fledgling youth church in the pioneering years when we needed it most. They continue to be pillars to this day (HOGC youths, you need to be grateful to people like them). For the Imaginarium project, he vetted every contract, quote, and timeline to ensure that our young team was not defrauded. Mr. Sim would come every week to supervise the construction. Lia and her young team came up with the interior design, coordinated with vendors, and sourced for furniture and even our chandeliers from China (cutting our costs by 70–90%). We used to say, "In the beginning God created the heavens and earth, but after that, everything else is made in China."

Pastors and leaders who visit us are always intrigued by our Cross Stage. I joke that I have always secretly wanted to be a supermodel, so I built that long catwalk runway. But here's how the idea originated. In the early days, the church was still a bunch of passionate kids giving concerned parents the cultish vibe haha. Some were distressed that we didn't have a cross in the premises. They said, "Are you even a real church? Your church doesn't even have a cross?"

So around 2007, when I was designing the stage for SingPost, a thought came to my mind: *If you want a cross, let me give you a CROSS!*

So I made a cross stage.

The next time anyone asks, "Where is the cross?" I will ask them to check their eyes.

HOGC Iconic Cross Stage at SingPost worship venue (2007).

When I was designing the Imaginarium stage, I wanted the preacher to be as up close and personal with the people as possible, especially the back rows. It's always the back rows that need the interaction and engagement. We had a design principle – No Bad Seats. At first, I wanted raised seats at the back but the low ceiling put an end to that idea. Then Lia and I were at the U2 iNNOCENCE concert tour in Chicago. It was held in a rectangular basketball arena, the same shape as Imaginarium. They had built a long stage that the band walked to both extremes, allowing the fans to be up close.

Lightbulb moment!

What if we flip the SingPost cross around and extend the vertical of the Cross right to the back of the hall?

After the concert, I immediately sketched out the design on whatever I could find. And that's how our Cross Stage became an HOGC trademark. Since 2007, the HOGC Cross Stage has influenced and shaped the stages of many churches and conferences all over the world.

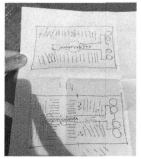

Pastor How's first sketch of the extended Cross Stage 2.0

HOGC Iconic Cross Stage at Imaginarium (2016).

By the end of 2015, the project was steadily coming to the finish line.

There was one final hurdle. The biggest and one that was outside my control.

Like I mentioned earlier, all land permitted for church use must be zoned specifically for that purpose. As HOGC did not have the upfront cash, the solution was a long-term lease model on industrial land. In order to use industrial land for church, we needed a special permit from the government. Here is the catch-22 situation: We could only submit for approval *after* it was built. So we literally had to sink in $15 million (US$11+ million) by faith and pray that we'd get the permit.

Those months from application to approval were some of the most anxious waits of my life. It's almost like sitting outside the operating theater waiting for Lia to finish her cancer surgery. My mind was thinking – *What if we don't get the approval? How am I going on stage to tell the church, "Sorry guys, we have lost your $15 million... Oops. And we are back to square one"?* All my life, I have slept really well. When my head hits the pillow, I am out within five minutes, and when I open my eyes, it's morning. During those months, I started waking up in the middle of the night. At first, I thought the Holy Spirit was waking me up to pray. So I was very spiritual about it. But as weeks passed, I knew that God was not that cruel. Those months, I lost a lot of sleep and hair haha.

I will never forget the moment. I was driving on the highway from my home in Woodlands to church. I got the call that our permit for church use was approved.

Imaginarium is our new Home.

God did it!

I stopped my car on the side of the highway. And I teared... Then I shouted in victory... and thanked Jesus.

That night, I slept through the night.

SingPost, 23 December 2015 – Approved! That weekend, we announced the long-anticipated approval for Imaginarium. Upon hearing the news, the entire church erupted in cheers and tears... we were finally going into our new Home!

The real heroes of this building project are the sacrificial givers of HOGC. The youths gave their five loaves and two fish. The young working adults gave months of their salaries. And the few older adults we had gave their savings. Imaginarium is an altar because it is built on the sacrifices of the people. That is why every time you worship there, you can feel the presence of God.

Who would have thought that a youth church could commit to paying $50+ million (almost US$40 million) over a 25-year lease? That's a major long-term commitment from our people. If our youths were 15 years old then, they had to be faithful to giving their Building Fund till they were 40. But these kids told me they were happy to do it, because they are giving to build a church for their future kids. HOGC now has a new home, debt-free, because our people have long-term vision and can be relied on for long-term commitment.

Heart of God Church is the story of the kids who built a world-class church.

But Imaginarium is the sacrifice of the kids who financed a world-class church.

DIVINE EXPERIMENT

When we celebrated our 20th anniversary, people asked Lia and me how we felt about our so-called "success."

Happy? Grateful? Fulfilled?

Of course a little of everything but the word that immediately came to mind was "relief."

Relieved that we survived.

Relieved that we didn't mess up so badly that we caused people to stumble.

Relieved that we didn't fail so spectacularly that we brought shame to Jesus.

Lia and I sincerely believed that we were a divine experiment, heaven's pilot project and earth's guinea pigs. It took a lot of stupidity and insanity to believe that we could build a youth church, especially without financial backing or a branded movement's endorsement. If there were a vote on the potential of new church plants, we would probably be voted most likely to crash and burn. In fact, during the early years, we had two pastors who told us so. One was a New Zealand preacher. After preaching to our zombie-like youths and corpse-like adults, he tried to subtly hint that we should think about quitting. He kept consoling us that there was nothing wrong or shameful if we quit pastoring... at least we tried. And God might have called us to serve Him in a different way. It felt like he was comforting us at our own funeral. I don't really blame him, the 50-year-old me might have given that 30-year-old me the same counsel. After all, we were like Lazarus in the tomb for four days and we had a stench of death.

Another local pastor who graciously walked with us in the first few years, finally told us what he really thought. We had no breakthroughs in those early years and really struggled. He probed, "Have you ever considered that you are not a number one guy?"

He went on with the verbal surgery: "Maybe you are a number two or number three guy. You can either continue as a number one guy and fail or..."

Here it comes...

"... or you can be a successful number three or four guy by joining me. Close down your church and bring all your members to join my church."

They all had good intentions and probably wanted to save Lia and me from more pain and disappointment. So they decided to perform spiritual euthanasia, mercy killing to put us out of our misery.

So yes, the word is "relief."

It was "Whew! It actually worked."

It was a long, long shot. We threw a Hail Mary pass and Jesus caught the ball for a last-second touchdown. Truly unless the Lord builds the house, we labor in vain.

UNKNOWN ON EARTH BUT KNOWN IN HEAVEN

People talk about humble beginnings... For us, it was more like humiliated beginnings. Not only did we not have money, but we also lacked credibility. Nobody had heard of Heart of God Church, so both Christian and non-Christian parents were very skeptical about sending their kids to our church. Some of the kids who were ignited for Jesus in HOGC wanted to attend our services regularly, so naturally the parents did a deep dive into HOGC. They inquired from friends and family who are pastors or church leaders. Most had never heard of us, the few who did said we were a bunch of kids, not a real church. They said HOGC was more like a big children's church, not very deep in theology, so it had the potential to become a cult. It didn't help that I overheard one of our youth leaders teaching the genealogy of Jesus. He confidently proclaimed that Jesus' father was Joseph and Joseph's father was Jacob, whose father was Isaac. 🙇🤢😅 No wonder his Bible looked a bit thin. He just conveniently cut out Exodus to Malachi from his Bible.

There was a pressure to build a more credible church, meaning focus more on adults and business people. In essence, go legit... go mainstream and do what other churches were doing. But God encouraged us to keep on building a youth church through a 14-year-old girl.

Meet Stephanie.

When she was four, her dad left her. Home was messy and often violent, so she poured all her energy into doing well in school. Despite scoring straight As and winning many awards in national track meets, she still felt empty on the inside.

When she was 14, on an ordinary morning, she woke up and heard a clear voice in her heart that said, "Go to Heart of God Church."

It was so distinct that she remembered thinking to herself, *Church? Why would I go to church? I'm not even a Christian! But no harm, just Google it.* To her shock, there was really a church called Heart of God Church.

So she clicked into the website.

Next shock.

It's in Singapore!

Doubts turned into curiosity and now curiosity turned into a holy fear.

Stephanie, who had never been to church, never prayed to Jesus, was not even a Christian, was thinking, *Was that really God?*

So she emailed the church – info@heartofgodchurch.org.

Our staff replied. She came to service, got saved, and was planted in church.

When I first heard this story, I had to check if Stephanie had hidden wings behind her back. She is a godsend. A message from heaven: *Heart of God Church, unknown on earth but known in heaven.*

And I felt that God was speaking to Lia and me: "Even if no one will recommend youths to go to your church, I will personally speak to the youths directly to go to HOGC."

Thank You Jesus.

He knows exactly when to send a raven to feed us (1 Kings 17:2-6), when to speak in a still small voice, and when to send a 14-year-old girl.

God continued to use Stephanie to encourage us. She brought her younger brother, Sylvester, to church too. They both became on fire for Jesus and started serving in church.

We found out that they were skipping meals because they didn't have enough money. So we put them on our church's Scholarship and Opportunity Fund, making sure they had pocket money and could live like normal teenagers. They had no father to guide them about finances, so I taught them about the importance of savings. For six months, I challenged them that for every dollar they saved, I would match it dollar for dollar.

Young Sylvester and Stephanie.

Stephanie rose up to become a leader in church and served in many ministries. In university she was leading over 20 youths and interning in church. When she was 19, she went for the funeral of a relative and saw her father there. The last time she had seen him was when she was four years old yet somehow she could still recognize him. I guess runaway fathers will never know the vacuum they leave in their little girls.

In that awkward moment when he also recognized her, the seconds felt like an eternity.

What would he do?

What would he say?

What should I do?

What should I say?

But he broke the eyelock, turned around, and walked away.

In that moment, her heart broke... again.

To be abandoned once... maybe you can really stretch it and give the benefit of the doubt.

But twice?

This time she had God and His voice assured her, "From you and your generation onwards, it will be different."

Stephanie is a brilliant young lady. She would go on to secure an internship in San Francisco. She did so well that they offered her a full-time position. For most Singaporeans, this is a dream come true – fresh grad with a job in SF. But she turned it down and came home to work full-time in HOGC. Now she co-heads the Events Department, leads 30 youths, and is also our PA.

Sylvester and Stephanie all grown up.

Stephanie's story is just one of many. There are so many kids who came from broken families but God healed them. HOGC gave them a spiritual family and a home. And they have grown up to become doctors, lawyers, bankers, and entrepreneurs. More importantly, this army of the best and brightest are serving in church and building His House. They have grown up and are now like Abraham's 318 trained men who were born in his own house (Genesis 14:14). Recently another young lady just joined our Communications team. She read Linguistics at Cambridge University. She understands six languages: English, Mandarin, Cantonese, Japanese, Korean, and Spanish. She is translating, copywriting for our Hong Kong and Mandarin materials, and is an interpreter too. We also hired seven top IT developers, who worked for top companies or the government, for our online church.

When people see the army of brilliant young adults and the caliber of young leaders and staff in HOGC, they often comment that we are so blessed. I just smile and thank God. And my mind goes back to the story of Stephanie. There was a time when HOGC was full of kids... they were nobodies, neglected, marginalized, and insignificant. Stephanie is just one story out of hundreds. When she was a kid, nobody wanted her... not even her own father. Now everyone wants her – top companies offering her top money. But she chose to work for HOGC.

How did all this happen?

Many years ago, in those humble times of discouragement, lacking credibility and money, God made Lia and me a promise: Love the people nobody wants and God will give you the people everybody wants.

Love the people nobody wants and God will give you the people everybody wants.

I believe the same promise still holds true today for everyone and anyone who is willing to give their hearts and lives to young people.

"Some people say HOGC is an overnight success..."
What's the next line? Every true-blue HOGC member knows this. Scan to watch HOGC's history and heritage.

Matt Redman

Two-time Grammy Award winner,
singer-songwriter and worship leader

It's a little tough to sum up what I love best about Heart of God Church –
I have quite a long list! Maybe it's the wholehearted worship or the
warm-hearted welcome. Or perhaps the sense of joy that seems to be a
thread running throughout the church. Or maybe the kindness that you
find radiating from the most senior leadership levels right down to the
volunteers. All of these things have made a marked impression on myself
and my team as we've spent time there. But perhaps what has impacted
me above all is Heart of God's passion for young people. It is the most
exciting expression I've ever seen of a church body who sow vision, time,
money and energy into reaching, keeping and growing the young people
in their community.

Heart of God's holistic approach to discipleship among this young
generation is so refreshing. In some examples of youth ministry, the
approach to reaching young people ends up becoming something of a
'spectator sport'. We try to wow them with visuals. We attempt to impress
them with cultural relevancy – and give all sorts of gifts or perks to keep
them coming along each week. They get to watch us doing ministry –
while they eat candy – kind of like spectators at a sports game! All this
approach seems to do is raise a passive kind of Christian. It's not really
discipleship – it's just building a crowd.

Heart of God take a completely opposite approach – involving teens
(even young teens) from day one – and helping them find out where their
calling might be, in serving within the church community. It's so dignifying
and it's so welcoming – and ultimately it's the Jesus model of discipleship.
If anyone ever had reason or right to do all of the ministry themselves,

it would have been Jesus. But instead, as He walked this earth, He involved his (underqualified) disciples. Sometimes it was mundane tasks, like organising the distribution of food (though even then a miracle happened!). At other times He sent them out on ministry trips of their own – where they were presumably way out of their depth (in their own eyes, at least). Christ trusted His disciples with responsibility and wouldn't allow them to just remain spectators. I've seen that very same dynamic in play at Heart of God – and it's so refreshing to be around.

On my most recent visit one of my band was so wowed by the environment of the visual/video tech room – where he saw not just one operator at each station, but three. He was confused by this and asked for someone to explain it to him. The answer was so impressive – there was one operator, one trainer and one trainee. At most stations these were people in their mid to high teens, and some of the trainees were as young as 12 or 13. Considering the amount of responsibility a video/visual team carries in a large service, and how much specialised technical skill there is to learn in these roles, he was amazed. There was a beautiful trust being placed in these young people – and such a sense of the values of the Kingdom of God about the whole operation.

One reason why my heart resonates so much with Heart of God in Singapore is because I was also blessed to grow up in a church that really valued young people – and trusted us with ministry opportunities early on in life. At St Andrews Chorleywood in the UK, I was strongly encouraged to jump into worship leading at the age of 13 – much to my annoyance! I was hoping to just play these worship songs on my own at home, but the leadership had different ideas – and practically forced me to start leading the youth group in worship, ha! I'm so glad they did – and from that moment on they encouraged, edified, challenged and stretched me. Time after time they put me in ministry situations that seemed to be just that little bit out of my depth – helping me grow further, and letting me learn what

IN HIS OWN WORDS....

it looks like to live in dependence upon God. To this day I'm hugely grateful for this.

Heart of God take the very same approach to ministry, but have elevated it to a whole different level. Each week hundreds of young people in Singapore get not only to belong there, but to build church together. I wholeheartedly encourage you to follow their example, as they follow Christ!

 Watch: Matt Redman's LIVE RECORDING in HOGC! Also, what's this Englishman's favourite tea – Earl Grey or Boba? Scan to find out.

Imaginarium

Imaginarium: an incubator for the
imaginations and idealism of young people.
Heart of God Church is a spiritual Imaginarium.

How and I named our 2,000-seat auditorium — Imaginarium.

> Ephesians 3:20 (NIV)
> Now to him who is able to do immeasurably more than all
> we ask or *imagine,* according to his power that is at work
> within us,

Heart of God Church is a spiritual Imaginarium.

We want Imaginarium to be an incubator for the imaginations and idealism of young people.

HOGC is a place where young people can imagine what God can do through them. John Lennon famously sang, "Imagine there's no heaven..." Well, he hasn't been to Imaginarium. Imaginarium is a place where the Holy Spirit can birth and accelerate the young people's dreams to impact the world.

Since day one, it has been our modus operandi to get young people to listen to God and to dream how God can use them to do mighty things.

Then we ask them to tell us their dreams. We take their dreams seriously and do everything in our power to help make their dreams come true. Without fail, God shows up and phenomenal things happen.

Now, we are not talking about your garden variety of dreams and visions. Youths, when they dream, sometimes they dream bigger than us adults. Some of our youths imagined that they would serve God on the worship team — even though they had zero music skills and no prior experience! But, no problem. We trained them from scratch in our School of Worship. We discipled them to have the right heart and attitude of worship.

One of our required readings is a book by our dear friend... a relatively unknown worship leader and songwriter called Matt Redman, maybe you have heard of him. 😜 Through the years, Matt's teachings set the foundation for hundreds of raw young people entering the worship team. Amazingly, the young people are not afraid to reinforce their Imaginarium-sparked-off dreams with sweat.

Others dream of one day becoming the chief usher. So we put them on the Guest Experience training track and teach them about excellence, serving and systems. Most importantly, we start to renew their mindset that they are not merely ushering people to their seats but actually ushering them into their destinies. We teach them to pray for every chair they lay out because someone is going to sit on it and encounter God.

How

Talking about getting young people to imagine...

One of our youths who grew up in church went on to work in the hospitality industry. Her attitude and excellence were so impressive that she was noticed by her boss and boss' boss. So when her biggest boss came to visit the hotel, Cheryl was assigned to work with him. Cheryl was so outstanding that this head honcho who is a guru in customer service wanted to know what made her so remarkable. As they got talking, Cheryl started talking about church and how church had prepared her. He said, "I gotta see your church."

So I got a text message from Cheryl saying, "My boss wants to see our church."

"Who's your boss?" I asked.

Horst Schulze, Founder of Ritz-Carlton and Capella Hotel.

The guy is a legend.

He came to visit and I asked him if he could train our Guest Experience team. He agreed and his training has been used as part of our training syllabus since.

This story is heartwarming for Lia and me because HOGC-born-and-bred Cheryl brought her training and testimony to the marketplace and she stood out.

Truly, Imaginarium is a place where imaginations can come true.

The formula of Imaginarium is simple:

1. Create a *spiritual environment* where youths can catch a vision of doing something great for God and in life.
2. Then build a *systematic yet personalized training process* to help them fulfill their dreams and walk into their destiny.
3. At the same time, immerse these youths in a *culture* of faith, encouragement, belief, and discipleship.

Think of soccer clubs like Barcelona. They have a youth academy called La Masia. They recruit youths with potential and passion. Every year 200 boys aged 6 to 8 join the club. Read again... yes, 6 to 8 years old. They put them through their training system and infuse into them the club's culture and a winning mentality. Out of La Masia (The Farmhouse) emerged some of the greatest players in the world: Messi, Xavi, Guardiola, Iniesta, Busquets, and many more.

The golden generation of Spanish football that made history by being the only national team to win three consecutive major titles – the 2008 and 2012 European Championship and the 2010 World Cup – is made up of a core of La Masia graduates. In 2010, La Masia became the first youth academy to have trained all three finalists for the Ballon d'Or (the most prestigious award for an individual player) in a single year – Andrés Iniesta, Lionel Messi, and Xavi.

Churches should have our own La Masia.

Lia and I built HOGC like La Masia... producing spiritual champions. When we see youths, I am looking for the spiritual Messi. We will regularly meet up with 10 to 12 young people and ask them about their dreams. They would share with us that their vision is to lead and influence others. This excites us tremendously because we see the next generation of pastors.

I recall a 13-year-old boy who shared with Lia and me that his vision was to lead 1,000 people by the time he turned 21. Now that's a kid who dares to dream *big*, especially considering our entire church was not even 500 at the time. Lia and I didn't laugh off his teenage dreams but we nurtured it. Through the years ahead, we discipled him in every area of his life – leadership, pastoral care, character, decision-making, organization, prayer, preaching... basically the full works.

As he grew in maturity, his connect groups multiplied into zones. And on his 21st birthday, he became a leader of 1,000. His imagination became reality. Now his story is an inspiration to new generations of youths in HOGC.

Today, our church knows him as Pastor Charleston. He graduated with a Master of Divinity (MDiv) from Oral Roberts University (USA) at 29. He is overall in-charge of all pastoral zones, responsible for church growth, and leadership development. Did I mention he was our first Chief of Staff, HR Director, and drummer as well?

Charleston, homegrown pastor: From a 13-year-old boy, saved in HOGC, to MDiv graduate from Oral Roberts University. He preaches, oversees all pastoral zones with his wife, Pastor Lynette, and is responsible for leadership development.

Pastor Charleston's dream came to pass.

It is prophesied in Acts 2:17 that in the last days, "your young men (and women) will see visions." That means a kid's dream is a Kingdom dream.

Just think of Joseph and David. God birthed dreams in them when they were kids. Don't be like Joseph's or David's brothers. Don't rubbish their dreams.

This verse in Acts 2, speaks about how the young will see visions and the old will dream dreams. I can't help but wonder what happened to the middle-aged people? Why are they not mentioned? Could it be that the middle-aged are too busy with life or are already pursuing their own dreams? I don't have the stats, but most of the great men and women of God I know had their dreams birthed at a very young age. The Holy Spirit has a track record of birthing dreams in young hearts. So it pains me to see their embryonic dreams aborted when it is ignored, ridiculed, and rubbished. The consequences are just heartbreaking. Just because the Church marginalizes them, does not mean their idealism and gifts are dead. No, they are still dormant inside. But the world comes and captivates their imaginations and rechannels their dreams. Now instead of giving birth to Isaac, they give birth to Ishmael. To rub salt into their wounds, church fathers who ignored them in the first place now judge them to be worldly and send them away to the wilderness. That's a page out of Abraham's playbook. There is a lot we should learn from Abraham but the birth and fathering of Ishmael isn't one of them. This is a tragedy played out for generations.

Let's take the dreams of young people seriously.

Meet Russell.

His family was saved and joined our church when he was 11 years old. He loved children's church. Even at a young age, you could tell he was different. His idea of fun is building Tesla coils and using sound waves to levitate objects. His hobby is publishing scientific papers and he just submitted one for peer review. At night he watches statistical mechanics videos before falling asleep. He says it's like Netflix to him.

At 17, during a service in Imaginarium, he saw two of our youngest board members on stage. John is a lawyer, Leonard is a doctor. They were in their 20s.

In that spiritual moment, sight turned into vision. God planted a seed of a dream in Russell. He thought to himself, *What if I could be a board member too?* Which 17-year-old dreams of becoming a board member? Surely it must be God.

Russell was not thinking about the title but how he could serve and build the church in this way. Russell has a burden for HOGC. Being a youth church doesn't rank us high in terms of credibility. Some non-Christian parents still think we are a cult. Some Christians condescendingly dismiss youth churches as hype and shallow. Russell grew up in HOGC under this shadow, so in a moment of epiphany, his burden crystallized into his mission. He wants to use his credentials to bring credibility to the church he grew up in and to the Jesus he loves. This is his reasoning: "When a youth says that HOGC is a good church, skeptics will say they are brainwashed. But when a scientist says that HOGC is a great church, it is much more convincing." With the same logic, Russell wants to testify about Christ too.

Russell told his friends, "I want to grow up to defend our church, defend Christ, and speak the truth." 17-year-old Russell came up with a plan. He is going to be a scientist.

I will interrupt the story here to point out a few things...

Lia and I regularly share the problems and burdens of our church with the youths. We don't whitewash it. We realized this a long time ago. If we see the youths as mature, capable of processing bad news and troubles, then they will grow up and rise up. But if we see them as "too young" and sideline them, then they will remain irresponsible and disengaged. You have probably observed this in families too. Kids who are sheltered and shielded tend to be less mature, while kids exposed to difficult situations tend to be more sensible and responsible. For HOGC, youth ministry is not just fun and games. We share transparently about the pressure to pay rent or frustrations with internet attacks.

Try it. Your young people will surprise you by their maturity and support.

Bishop Dale Bronner shared with me this: "A calling is always first conceived with a burden or problem, then it is birthed into a vision."

If you have a vision without a burden, you are answering questions nobody is asking.

So if a person has a vision without a burden, then it is just ambition.

David met a problem – Goliath.

Nehemiah had a burden – the broken-down walls of Jerusalem.

Moses saw an injustice – slavery.

Esther rose up in a crisis.

> **A calling is always first conceived with a burden or problem, then it is birthed into a vision.**
> - Bishop Dale Bronner

It always begins with a burden or problem.

Lia had a burden for youths and children.

I saw problems in the organization and operations of the Church at large.

Out of that burden, came the vision.

For Russell, this burden became his vision.

Our cause became his crusade.

The first step to fulfilling his vision was to be a scientist.

This young man was a man on a mission.

At 17, he did a one-year research internship with A*STAR, Singapore's top research organization. Then he went for an International Science and Engineering Fair (ISEF) physics competition. Only the top nine science students in Singapore get to go to this international competition to represent the country. His research and project was condensed matter physics. (I thought only Tony Stark and Bruce Banner talked about this kind of stuff.) A group of scientists won the 2016 Nobel Prize for achieving a breakthrough in this area. They had success in an experiment that cost millions of dollars for this breakthrough. Russell recreated their experiment using electrical circuits for $100. In doing so, he accessed "a new way to study the field, shedding light on quantum edge effects. This allowed new exotic materials to be simulated by introducing dissipation into a material's bulk, implying a new state of matter." (If you don't understand a word of what you have just read, don't worry, neither do I. I just copied and pasted those words from Russell's text to me.) He won an award for his research and also received an award for the Most Outstanding Junior College Science Student in Singapore.

At 18 years young, he was invited to represent Singapore at the Nobel Prize ceremony in Stockholm. Each year, Singapore selects only one person to go. For a scientist or physics student, it is like a sportsman going to the Olympics or an actor invited to the Academy Awards. Many professional scientists never get invited, but Russell doesn't even have a university degree yet. On top of this, Russell was also invited to give a talk to 1,000 of the top high school students in the world to inspire them to pursue science.

A year later, he went to phase two of his plan. He was accepted into Oxford University to read Physics... full scholarship... full ride. And just to assure us, he said, "Even though I am away for a few years, the number one thing on my heart is HOGC. Being overseas is just temporary. In the future, it's always about serving in the House of God."

Why?

He says what makes him so grateful is that the church would believe in him as an 11-year-old kid and as a youth, even before he had any achievements. Usually in the world, they only believe in people after they have all the achievements and accolades. For that, "HOGC will always have my allegiance and I will use my achievements to protect my spiritual home."

11-year-old Russell.

Russell at the Nobel Prize ceremony in Stockholm as an 18-year-old.

After hearing the stories of Russell, Cheryl, and Charleston, you get a sense that it's about the dreams and destiny of individuals.

Here's the paradox: Imaginarium can hold crowds, but it is not built for crowds. It is designed for individuals.

Imaginarium is not about fancy lights and screens. It is not about state-of-the-art equipment.

It is about young people free to imagine and encouraged to live out their godly imagination.

A WORD TO HOGC MEMBERS:
LET US BE THE CITY ON A HILL

What's next?

That's the question Pastor Lia and I asked ourselves.

As we are writing this book, we have just celebrated HOGC's 20th year. We watched the first few generations of youths grow up, make their impact in society, get married, become parents.

So what's next?

My mind went back to a dinner with Bishop Dale Bronner. It was in 2012, amidst jokes and laughter, I could feel the anointing hit. That's the cue to put down the fork and pick up a pen. He started to speak life and wisdom to us. He said:

> "God always develops something in obscurity, but it will not stay in obscurity. When He uncovers something, the world will discover it... because beauty is not meant to be hidden.
> Whenever something is done well, God will reveal it.
> God develops a carrot underground, but when it is full-grown, God will serve it to the world – He pulls it out and exposes it.
> (Author's note: We were not eating any carrots for dinner.)
>
> "The influence is not to be contained in a city.
> God will never keep a good thing only in Singapore.

A city on a hill is not hidden. A light is not hidden under a bushel. He develops it under a bushel, but it will not stay there.

"You cannot export what is not homegrown.
But because HOGC is not an imitation or copy of other ministries. You and your young people are homegrown, you can export it."

Boom! And then we were back joking. That's what I call being naturally supernatural and supernaturally natural.

Export HOGC?

How do we do that?

Plant churches?

I remember being in prayer and having an exploratory conversation with God. "God, where do You want us to go?" I felt very noble because I sounded like Isaiah: "Here I am, send me."

It was months later that the Holy Spirit dropped a thought in my head: *the 10/40 window.* It is a missional definition of nations located between 10 and 40 degrees north of the equator.

I thought I finally got a location.

But God said clearly: *"Lia and you are not called to a 10/40 geography but the 10/40 demography. HOGC is not called to an area but to an age group."*

Our vision is not geographical, but generational.

We are called to anyone who is between 10 and 40 years old and any pastor or leader who works with 10 to 40-year-olds.

Woah!

It was around this time that God was speaking to Pastor Lia too.

HOGC is not called to an area but to an age group. Our vision is not geographical, but generational.

This was a time when the phrase "act local, think global" was popular in the business world and even in church circles too. I am sure it was well-intentioned, but it kind of evolved into a negative connotation implying that "acting local" was too small-minded and "thinking global" was having a big vision. The vibe at the time was that a pastor who is faithful to his local church is insignificant, while a pastor who has a global ministry is "the great man of God."

At this time, God spoke to Pastor Lia: "Don't think that being local is small-minded or thinking global is big-minded. Let Me tell you what's big... it's thinking generational. I am a God of the generations. I think in 1,000 years and 1,000 generations. Thinking global is good but thinking generational is God."

Boom!

That's the sound of God's mic drop.

If you think about it, going global is relatively easy in this age of social media and air travel. But going generational, you would need a time machine. In other words, without God it is impossible. Going generational means that we will have to be like Abraham, raising up spiritual sons and daughters, and having faith that God's promises will come to pass.

This is how we coined the phrase: "Don't just think local or global, think generational. Think GenerationS."

Don't just think local or global, think generational. Think GenerationS!

For Pastor Lia and me, it is an honor to be called to the local church. We would die happy if we did not do anything globally. It is our greatest privilege to be pastors of Heart of God Church. We are local pastors with a generational vision.

So if we combine local and generational, what do we get?

Heart of God Church.

A missionary once said his vision was "Every nation in my generation."

Praise God for missionaries.

But for HOGC, it is "Every Generation in my nation."

Going beyond "Every nation in my generation" to "Every Generation in my nation"

We are local and generational.

So what about global?

Didn't Bishop Bronner prophesy that God wants to export what we have grown?

Pastors from all over the world who come to visit often comment, "How come we have never heard of you? The world needs to see this. You are God's best-kept secret." Their words, not mine.

And suddenly it all makes sense. Let's connect the dots.

HOGC, you are the City on a Hill (reread Bishop Bronner's words).

The world will come and see this youth revival.

They will come and see the kids who built a world-class church.

And they will take the heart and spirit of HOGC back to their local churches and bring a revival to the GenerationS.

And that's how it will be exported.

We open our doors and arms and welcome our global friends to visit us.

So Imaginarium will not be just for young people, but also an incubator for the imaginations and idealism of pastors and leaders globally.

HoGcX – THE HEART OF GOD CHURCH XPERIENCE

To all our friends globally, Lia and I would like to extend an open invite to come visit us in Singapore. As hard as I try, all that I write in this book and all that I can share in your conferences will only be 10% of what you will experience when you come visit personally. The magic of HOGC is not Lia and me, but the youths. We try to bring as many of them as we can when we preach in overseas conferences. We always share the stage and airtime with them so that the world can hear the real heroes. Not surprisingly, the pastors and audiences love them and their stories. In that moment, Lia and I are relegated from invited keynote speakers to chaperons of child stars. And we love it.

When you come to Singapore for HoGcX, you will see all these kids who built a world-class church. Hundreds and thousands of them.

12-year-old keyboardists on the main worship team.

13-year-olds planning church-wide events.

14-year-olds preaching in connect groups.

15-year-olds serving as Events Coordinators for a main service of 2,000 people.

17-year-olds leading the entire church during prayer meetings.

At the point of writing, our average age is now 22. It used to be 16, then 19. It takes a mammoth effort to keep our average age down. Why do young people have to keep growing up? Sigh. We have already banned birthday celebrations. So as hard as we are working to raise up 12-year-olds, there is no guarantee that we can keep unearthing these gems. So come quickly to experience this youth revival.

We try to run Heart of God Church Xperience twice a year.

HoGcX is not a conference. A conference typically showcases the best the church can offer... all the bells and whistles. While it is inspirational, we want HoGcX to be real and practical. We want to remove the cosmetics and show what happens on a regular weekend in HOGC. We also want to give pastors a behind-the-scenes look at what is happening, pull back the curtains, and show them what's under the hood – not just the good but also the bad and the ugly.

It is an all-access intensive training course for pastors, decision-makers, influencers, and implementers. Each intake for HoGcX is relatively small at about 200 people (that's why there is a waiting list). We limit it to key decision-makers so that we can keep the experience intimate and narrow the program to what is relevant for senior pastors and senior leaders. The participants so far are pretty diverse. We have had pastors and their teams from Australia and America, Barcelona and Brazil, China, Hong Kong, Taiwan to Zurich. What encourages us is that now many are inspired and practically equipped to build Strong GenerationS Churches in their cities.

Lia and I hope that Imaginarium can also help you imagine the youths in your church rising up and the young people in your city in a revival.

HOGC can become your Imaginarium too.

- Must-see! Hundreds of youths lifting hands and responding to Jesus at Imaginarium.
- Check out a virtual walk-through of Imaginarium and more!

Dr Robi Sonderegger

Renowned clinical psychologist, church consultant
and sought-after international conference speaker

Every now and again, you discover a treasure so valuable that you'd
give everything you have to pursue it – whether it's a newly found love
that you forsake all others for, or a treasure hidden in a field that's worth
selling everything you own to acquire (Matthew 13:44). The Bride of
Christ, expressed in the form of Heart of God Church (HOGC), is one
such valuable treasure. It is no exaggeration to say people from around
the world who've had the privilege of visiting HOGC, have been totally
captivated by what they've seen. However, the real treasure is in the
'unseen' or 'behind the scenes'. This book pulls back the curtain to
reveal the mindset and methods used to build what is arguably one of
the most innovative churches in the world today.

The hidden treasure I speak of is not the state-of-the-art auditorium,
dubbed 'Imaginarium' (although it is amazing); it's not the vibrant
'sound of revival' worship, the high-tech digital lighting, creative graphic
displays and innovative stage presentation (although mind-blowing to
say the least); it's not even the world-class teaching by Senior Pastors
How and Lia (although, I can personally attest, it's truly compelling).
The real treasure is the 'heart of God' embraced by thousands of young
people that call HOGC home – youth and young adults, many of whom
came into church as lost, but who subsequently have been (or are
being) transformed into leaders. With the overarching philosophy that
'young people are not just the leaders of tomorrow, but indeed, leaders
of today', HOGC has set about to create highly disciplined 'special
forces'. They're not mere members, they're 'marines' – young people
who are committed to the cause of Christ, compelled by their calling
and commissioned to be the church (not just attend it).

As a people-systems consultant, I've had the great honour of working with HOGC over the past decade and have witnessed first-hand the growth and development of these leaders. I don't write as someone who has been impressed by what I've witnessed, but rather, someone who has been 'in-pressed' by what I've experienced. The impact HOGC has had on my own life and leadership cannot be understated. For this reason, I am excited for the heart-and-mind-explosion you too may have as you peel through the pages of this book.

GenerationS lays out a practical pathway to building a Strong Church. If you are the right person (a church builder, pioneer or decision-maker) reading this book at the right time, let me encourage you to focus on the right things. It's not the bells and whistles, the screens, the multimedia, lights or the worship team that makes for a great church. Those things are trivial. You can hire or buy most of what you need to present well. But you cannot lease or purchase the presence of God, the heart of commitment and the vision required to build something truly great. Focus on the strategy, not the strobe light. Give your attention to the systems, not just the slick slogans.

Unfortunately, we are living in a day and age where churches have become competitive. To fund the latest innovations, there are key demographics (other than youth) that better serve to 'finance the ministry'. Consequently, instead of being the priority, youth become the minority. Instead of mobilising young people, churches around the world often invite experienced experts and leaders in business to serve, build and advance the church. However, HOGC does this in reverse. They train up young servant leaders who go on to become experienced experts, start businesses and become leaders in every aspect of society so as to advance, impact and transform their nation. It's almost always encouraging to see a church doing amazing things with, for and through young people. Yet for some, it may also be intimidating (especially if you're part of an ageing church). However, you would be misguided to minimise the impact or transferability of HOGC, dismissing it as 'a Singapore thing that wouldn't work elsewhere'; or perhaps downplaying its authenticity, suggesting 'a youth church is not a real church'. According to Jesus, the humble who become just like the youth, are considered to be the greatest in God's Kingdom (Matthew 18:4). Therefore, if God takes young people seriously, we as Christian leaders would do well to adopt the same attitude. Nevertheless, a competitive spirit still exists within the church today.

Many churches are in the habit of comparing, critiquing and copying. A competitive spirit typically rejects in public yet adopts in private. Typically, it's the insecure that attempt to disparage then duplicate. So, rather than feel excluded, get excited. Rather than be covetous, stay curious. How do they disciple and develop young people to be the leaders of today? What was the process? How can we achieve the same results? HOGC is not in competition with your church. Despite the genuinely warranted admiration and accolades I've offered so far; this book is not a thesis on how good HOGC is compared to others. Rather, the goal of this book is to illuminate a path for your church to become strong and influential in ways you've most likely not previously considered.

Everything you read, learn and receive from this book is free for you to use. But there is an important difference between using and copying. Everything HOGC does is educational in nature. Every policy is carefully designed to teach and model to young people. Likewise, this book invites you to join HOGC and model well to the next generation – this is something we can do together. Despite the cultural myth that 'copyright is the right to copy', when churches try to rip off and then re-package as their own, authenticity is lost, and a lack of integrity is modelled. HOGC wants to create a culture of honour. So, if you see a new idea, strategy or quote, feel free to use it and practise honour by acknowledging its source. And if you need to adapt, modify or build upon something to make it work in a brand new context, be sure to provide feedback so everyone can learn. Remember, as the Body of Christ, we are all in this together.

Dr Robi Sonderegger

Watch Dr Robi @ HOGC: Every youth church needs an appointment with a clinical psychologist.
Scan to find out why!

One Generation From Extinction - Christianity in Crisis

Legacy is not what you leave behind.
It is who you leave behind.

We have all heard about the great South Korean revival. My jaw dropped when Lia and I attended the 50th anniversary celebration service of the world's biggest church in the Seoul Olympic stadium. 80,000 South Korean Christians, worshipping and praying. And that's just a small portion of their members allowed to come. If they all came, they would fill the stadium ten times over. The massiveness of it all made me think that maybe this is how heaven is going to be like. I was convinced that we will be speaking Korean and eating kimchi in heaven. When they started praying, it was probably the closest thing to

> Acts 4:31
> ... the place where they were assembled together was shaken; and they were all filled with the Holy Spirit, and they spoke the word of God with boldness.

Before the Korean War (1950–1953), only 4% of South Koreans were Christians. By 1985, that number went from 4% to 34%. Literally one in three South Koreans was a Christian. Now that's what I call a revival.

By 2015, it had declined to 22%.

This is not the bad news yet.

In the same report, the number of South Korean youths between 10 and 19 years old, who professed to be Christians, had plunged to 3%.

Oh how my heart sank when I read these statistics.

3%!!!!

This is even lower than the 4% before the war.

The great Korean revival only lasted one or two generations. In another 20 years, when the post-war, pioneering, and praying generation passes on, Korean Christianity will be worse than before the war.

If nothing miraculous happens to pull back this nosedive, by the next generation, the Korean revival is over. I can imagine the demons in Satan's war council high-fiving each other and saying, "We let them have their revival for 50 years, but we played the long game. We couldn't stop them from building their cathedrals but we targeted their children and grandchildren."

While the Korean Christian leaders were good at growing big, far, and wide, they didn't grow younger.

Legacy is not what you leave behind but *who* you leave behind.

Legacy is not what you leave behind but *who* you leave behind.

The massive church buildings with the neon red crosses that dot the Korean night skyline will be empty in the next generation. They will be like the cathedrals in Europe, sold and turned into restaurants and clubs. I finished reading Robert Schuller's autobiography with a bittersweet feeling. I was in awe of how God could use one man's faith to build a monumental, awe-inspiring building like the Crystal Cathedral. Yet I know that it went bankrupt and was sold. I can't help but imagine how I would feel if this happened to my church when I am in my 80s. All my life's work gone. It didn't even last till the next generation. That is why for Lia and me, our priority is to grow our church younger and stronger. If pastors are impatient to grow their church big, they will certainly not be patient enough to grow their church young. It takes patience to build your church for the next generations. So let's play the long game and outlast and outsmart the devil's endgame.

Sadly, the graying church is not limited to South Korea, but it is a global pandemic.

Take Indonesia for example. Similar to South Korea, in the '60s and '70s they experienced a revival and the Christians doubled from 6.7 million to 12.8 million. Their churches were experiencing growth rates of about 15%, believed to be the highest in the world. But today, like Korea, unfortunately they are also losing their next generations. An Indonesian pastor told me that his denomination, which has over 100,000 churches, is seeing 85% of their youth ministries declining or closing down.

In America, the average age of a typical church is 53. Millennials are leaving the church – 6 out of 10 young people who grew up in church end up walking away. Those youths 13 to 17 years old who are attending church are only tagging along because their parents are going. The day they gain their independence, they're out the door faster than Usain Bolt on steroids.

We don't even need to talk about Western Europe. Everybody knows the traditional European churches have already lost their youth. The continent that was once a bedrock of Christianity is now left with empty cathedrals filled with more tourists than worshippers.

Australia is blessed with many famous churches like Hillsong, Planetshakers, and other global ministries that have impacted the world. It is easy to assume that the rest of the Aussie churches are overflowing with young people. Yet the average age of the church there is 53. While 53% of Australians call themselves Christian, only 38% of those 13 to 18 years old do so. Based on trends, it is projected that by 2050, the percentage of Christians in Australia will drop by 20%.

This is not merely a problem plaguing Western churches. In Hong Kong, churches are also seeing an exodus of their youth. Millennials and Gen Z, even those who claim to be Christians, are moving away from church. They view the church as irrelevant and they direct their idealism towards political and social justice causes instead. One survey confirmed this when 58% of Hong Kong churches reported that their youths were dissatisfied and found it difficult to fit in. Heart of God Church has run Strong Church Hong Kong conferences for a number of years to inspire and equip local churches to win their youths. When we talk to local pastors, many have echoed these sentiments.

There may be a few bright spots in the world, but they are the exception rather than the norm. Walk into churches all over the world, and it is a congregation of faithful attendees whose haircuts are more ceremonial than necessary and the saints serving have the metabolism for salads and porridge.

Where have all the young people gone?

What the church world is going through is akin to the World War I and II scenarios, when all the young men became casualties and didn't come home. And entire towns were left with kids and old people. Our young people are casualties and we have lost a generation.

This is not a criticism but a concern.

This is not a judgment but a warning cry.

Christianity is one generation away from extinction.

RUNNING DOWN AN UPWARD ESCALATOR

People say that "everything that goes up must come down." But what is one thing that goes up and never comes down?

Age.

In 2019, we celebrated our 20th anniversary as a church. Lia and I were seeking God for His plan for the next 10–20 years for HOGC.

Is it to plant churches globally?

Host a mega-conference in stadiums?

I mean that's the usual route and typical next step for most megachurches.

Then God asked me a question: "What is the average age of HOGC now?"

When God asks a question, He isn't asking for information. He knows everything. When He asked Adam, "Where are you?" it wasn't because He misplaced Adam and couldn't locate him. It was a probing question.

I didn't know exactly. So I got my team to calculate.

Our average age was 22.3.

I was unpleasantly surprised, because we used to be 16 or 19.

We are no longer a youth church. Ouch!

Then God spoke: "For the next 10–20 years, the vision of HOGC is to bring down the average age."

Honestly, I was thinking, *God, that's not very spectacular. Other megachurches are running conferences and planting churches. But bringing down average age is not exactly an impressive vision.*

Nevertheless, we attempted it. Lia and I shared the vision with the whole church. We called it HOGC21: Bring down our average age from 22.3 to 21.

Sounds easy right? Well, until you try it.

So we mobilized the entire church to bring youths. For a whole year, our church brought 4,147 unchurched youths to our service.

1,528 of them made decisions for Christ.

379 of these youths stayed and are now planted.

It's fantastic... I mean youths are getting saved and planted in church.

So a year later, I was excited when the team presented to me the latest stats.

Are you ready?

Drumroll...

Our average age now is 22.17.

WHAT!!!!

After all the hard work... so many youths saved and planted... we just managed to bring it down from 22.3 to 22.17?

That's a meager 0.13.

I was demoralized.

Then I realized the difficulty of bringing down a church's average age.

In order to bring it down by just one year, you actually have to bring it down by two years, because every year the church ages by a year.

It's like running down an upward escalator.

So with all the effort and focus, after 4,000+ youths came and 1,500+ decisions, we only managed to stem the tide.

We kept our average age at 22.

If we had gone on with business as usual, it would have been 23.

And we cannot rest on our laurels, because if we do not add another 400 youths this year again, we will inevitably age to 23.

To make it harder, HOGC now has thousands of *vintage youths.* They include the first few generations who are now in their 20s and 30s. They are still as on fire as ever, so they are reaching out to their friends of the same age. So they are growing this age group. Therefore, mathematically, in order to bring down our average age, the youths have to outpace the adults' growth.

Now you understand why I am unapologetically proud to proclaim that HOGC's average age is 22, even after 20 years as a church.

Most pastors and churches are not monitoring this number. While we want to grow bigger, we must not neglect growing younger. We don't realize how time flies. Many churches started with pastors in their 30s and a congregation around the same age. Typically, the church will grow old with the pastor. By the time the church is established, everyone will be in their 40s or 50s. This is when pastors realize that they have been blindsided. I strongly encourage pastors to take the first step. Start by calculating the current average age of your church. Then make a simple mathematical plan to maintain or lower this average age.

This "average age down" exercise has shown me that it is much harder to grow younger than grow bigger. If the majority of the church is in their 40s, the friends they reach out to will naturally be around their same age. So even as the church is growing bigger, it is growing in the same demographic group. Furthermore, when a 60-year-old is added to your church, you need to add 4 more 15-year-olds just to average out to 24 years old. Don't get me wrong, we love old people in our church. Our young adults are bringing their parents to church and getting them saved. Our joke is that if you want your parent to be planted in church, you need to bring four more youths to balance out their age. So eight youths to offset both mom and dad... haha.

Now I know why our God is a genius. In my ignorance, I thought planting churches and growing bigger was the next step. Now that I realize the enormity of the task, I understand what God was teaching Lia and me. Now I get it – growing the church younger is infinitely more difficult than growing the church bigger or planting new churches. For most successful churches, they have already discovered their growth formula. Therefore, growing bigger or planting churches is essentially replicating the template, kind of like franchising. On the other hand, reaching the next generation is ever evolving. Every ten years, the youths of that generation are different. It is a moving target and the leadership has to figure out what works. A youth church needs to be constantly reinventing itself and finding new methods. Strong GenerationS Churches do not fight tomorrow's war with yesterday's strategies.

Just think of the megastar rock band U2. They mesmerized an entire generation with hypnotic guitar riffs and Bono's anthemic voice. Lia and I watched them three times in Chicago, Santa Clara, and Singapore. Their last concert in Singapore, I was so excited I asked my daughter if she wanted to go. She replied, "It's OK dad, I will give it a miss."

Give it a miss?!!!

U2 concert is like on the bucket list of many people and you want to give it a miss?

Then a few days later she asked if the money I saved from her U2 ticket could be used for a Khalid or Billie Eilish concert instead.

Lesson learned – U2 may be the biggest band in my generation, but they are not reaching the next generation. So it is much easier for U2 to pack stadiums and go for a world tour than to reach the next generation. For them to reach the next generation, they have to reinvent their music and even themselves.

Strong GenerationS Churches do not fight tomorrow's war with yesterday's strategies.

This is what I see for churches. For the big brand name megachurches, it is much easier for them to plant more churches and pack their conferences, but much harder to reach the next generation.

Oh, we have the coolest Christian band and the most famous and anointed preacher headlining this year's conference.

The youth's reply, "It's OK dad, I will give it a miss."

That is why for HOGC, it is not about going global but going generational. Lia and I want to build to last.

Why are we obsessed with reaching down to the next generation?

Two reasons.

Firstly, once you lose the next generation, it is 100 times more difficult to restart. As I have explained earlier, church members typically reach out to people in the same age range. It is uncommon for a 40-year-old guy to invite 15-year-old youths to church. With the exception of his nephews or nieces, he really does not know many youths. It's the youths who bring youths. So if a church has lost its youths or they are not on fire but merely dragged to church by their parents, that church has effectively lost its foothold and reach in the next generation.

Secondly, a church that has lost the next generation will suffer from the Family Church Syndrome: a church condition that I coined from observing the first church I attended.

FAMILY CHURCH SYNDROME

When I talk to pastors about bringing down the average age or reaching the next generation, they ask a very good question. "When the married couples give birth to kids, wouldn't it naturally and mathematically bring down the average age?"

True.

But while the average age may seem lower, there is still a camouflaged problem.

Look at Diagram 1.

A lot of pastors plant their church in their 30s. Naturally and typically their congregation will be around the same age or slightly younger.

Diagram 1. Church ABC's Demographics Now

Fast forward ten years. See Diagram 2.

The pioneer congregation and members who subsequently joined would be in their 30s and 40s.

Diagram 2. Church ABC's Demographics in 10 Years

≤ 9
10 - 19
20 - 29
30 - 39
40 - 49
50 - 59
60 +

Look at Diagram 3. People in their 30s and 40s have children who are in their teens or younger. So now your church is in its "cute stage" – the baby boom. HOGC went through a similar phase of conducting weddings every week. Now, it's like raining babies.

On the surface, all seems fine at the family church. The church is teeming with the pitter patter of little feet and your children's ministry has their hands full. And you will also have a youth group of kids who grew up together.

Diagram 3. Church ABC's Demographics in 10 Years (Youth Highlight)

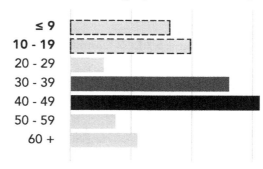

≤ 9
10 - 19
20 - 29
30 - 39
40 - 49
50 - 59
60 +

But look carefully, do you see the problem?

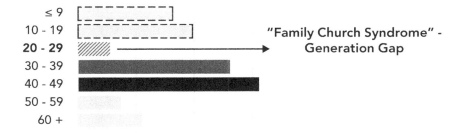

Diagram 4. The Family Church Syndrome - Generation Gap

This church will have a generation gap. It is missing a generation in their 20s. And the repercussion is that it is exactly these young men and women who typically power the volunteers in a church. This is typical of a family church. I know because I was a university student when I saw my former church suffer from the Family Church Syndrome. My former church lost a whole generation of youths and young adults. Most of my peers have either left church or are now backslidden. It was sad to see the children's church segment of fast-paced praise songs and high energy dance led by grandmas and grandpas. Now, I love these G-Pas and G-Mas. They are the nicest and most faithful people. God bless them. But where are the young guys and gals? The kids should be hearing grannies' miracle tales and grandpas' wisdom, not their creaking knees and gasps for air.

Most churches do not intentionally focus on retaining and reaching the youths and young adults. They just leave it to the organic cycle of life. The problem is that the gap between parents and children is typically between 25 to 35 years. However, the church cannot afford this time gap. A Strong Church needs a cohort of leaders and church builders every ten years. If the church is big, like in the thousands, then you may have a spread of age groups and it might mitigate the problem. But if your church is in the hundreds, you will feel the adverse impact of this gap. The lack of manpower will be felt even more if your church is located in places where your young people move away for university or work.

So what is the stopgap measure, literally?

GenerationS.

Every three to five years, we reach out to a new generation of youths. Not just the homegrown ones, but we also need to reach new, unchurched ones.

Lia is a futurist. After she raised up the first generation of youths, she prophetically told me, "We need to start a new youth group for a new generation."

And so in 2006, she started Zone F. F for Future. They were 13–14-year-olds. At the time of this writing, these Zone F "kids" are already almost 30 years old. All young working adults and some are even married.

In 2013, Lia launched Zone M. M for Millennium – those born after the year 2000.

In 2016, Pastor Lynette launched Zone Z for Gen Z. Their average age was 12.9.

In 2021, Ee Loo and Pastor Lynette launched another new generation – Zone A for Gen Alpha. 200 youths with an average age of 13.4. Out of them will come our 7th Generation of youth leaders.

We need to repeat this in 2025 and beyond. The pipeline must keep flowing.

Only with this relentless commitment to raise GenerationS, can our church ensure that each five-year cohort will have hundreds of leaders and church builders, resulting in a Strong GenerationS Church.

So how do you grow your church younger?

There is no quick fix.

Being aware of this problem is a start.

Find out the average age of your congregation.

Find out the demographic breakdown of your church.

Analyze the numbers. Project ten years ahead.

Realizing the seriousness of this aging issue and the enormity of the task ahead is critical. It pushes the church leadership to throw all its resources and support to reach young people. The graying of the church is quite similar to climate change. The future is at stake but everything seems good now, so there is no urgency to take drastic action. So we kick the can down the road until it's too late.

We have to stop the rot now. We have to ignite and involve the existing youths in our churches. Many youths are just attending church as a routine. Pastor Lynette told me that when she was in her former church, she was just eight years old but she already told herself that the day she gets her independence will be her last day in church. Parents have thanked us saying, "Before HOGC, it was easier to get my kids to the dentist than to church." In Chapters 9 and 10, we will talk about how you can turn your church around into a home for youths.

Hiring a youth worker or having an occasional youth takeover is not enough. It is like your family changing to metal straws and stopping the use of plastic bags. Commendable but it will take an industry-wide and society-deep transformation to even make a dent. The top leadership of the church must lead the way. The entire church must be mobilized to reach young people. Just the youth ministry reaching youths is not enough to stop the rot. For HOGC, Lia and I had to rally the older people to turn their hearts to young people. We challenged them to bring their nephews and nieces and younger cousins. We told them, "If your grown-up children do not want to come, you bring your grandchildren. If your colleagues or friends do not want to come, offer to take their children instead." Most parents won't pass up on free babysitting for a few hours on Sunday. We send buses to the four corners of the island to pick up youths to come.

Let me tell you how our vintage youths are reaching out to the youths.

One mother personally grew a HeartKidz connect group from 2 to 12. She has two amazing daughters, Janelle, 12 and Rachel, 10.

She is smart and saw immediately that they were her way into a pool of youths. So mom and daughters tag team: daughters will invite their friends to church while mom will persuade their parents to let them come. She even offers to drive their kids and send them home, just to seal the deal. Another inroad – all the parents in her daughters' classes have WhatsApp group chats together. So she sends in the promo materials of our HeartKidz events into the chats. One parent replied and just like that two more kids added to church.

There is another supermom. She is always texting and calling up our youth leaders to enquire about what is happening in the youth

One supermom always has brochures of youth and children's church events, ready to hand out to the parents of her daughter's friends.

zones. And it isn't to track her kids. She keeps a plastic folder of brochures of youth and children's church events in her bag. Every time she meets the parents of her daughter's friends, she will hand out the brochures and convince them to allow their kids to come. She has a list of the names of the people she is reaching out to and the events she thinks will be attractive and relevant: Youth Big Day Out, Children's Carnival, Academic Excellence weekend, etc. She deliberately and meticulously plans her evangelism, so that it is effective. This supermom single-handedly brought over 50 youths to HOGC.

Mother and daughter prayed over this list of names. Together, they brought over 50 youths to HOGC!

You need to mobilize people like these supermoms in your church. They will bring the cure to any Family Church Syndrome and personally lower the average age of your church. And how appropriate. The ladies spend a lot of money buying anti-aging products. Well, the Bride of Christ needs the same resources and focus to fight aging too. Cosmetics will not help. The church needs all hands on deck to reach youths.

Watch: It started in Singapore. Today, the GenerationS Movement has caught on in churches and conferences all around the world.

John Bevere

Minister and international speaker
Best-selling author of *The Bait of Satan*
Co-Founder of Messenger International

THE YOUTH ARE THE CHURCH OF TODAY

One of the most profound revelations I had as a young minister was this: the youth are not the church of tomorrow; they are the church of today. When God spoke these words to me in the late '80s, I had just become a youth pastor at one of the most influential churches in America. At that time, and still today, the common mindset toward youth is they are in their own class, separate from adults. What creates this ideology? The world categorizes people into four age groups: babies, children, teenagers, and adults. When a person reaches the age of twenty-one, they are recognized as an adult and can enjoy the privileges of being identified as one. However, according to Scripture, God recognizes only three categories: babies, children, and adults. If you consider a young Jewish man, he goes through a bar mitzvah at the age of thirteen, in which he's publicly recognized as an adult. When does a man or woman reach adolescence? When does a young man's voice change, a young woman begin to have menstrual cycles, etc. At the age of twenty-one? No, rather in the neighborhood of thirteen. With these conflicting perspectives, especially in the West, we find the reason why our attitude toward the youth has been incorrect all along.

Throughout the Bible, you'll find "teenagers" treated like young "adults." If you look at Jeremiah, he was called as a prophet at the age of sixteen. David was called to be the king of Israel at the age of seventeen. With the exception of Peter (who was twenty-one), Jesus' disciples were all teenagers when he called them to follow him. This clearly shows the window of opportunity we have from the ages of thirteen to twenty-one is pivotal for the development of leadership. After God had spoken to me, my mindset as a youth pastor shifted. As a result of this new attitude, my youth group multiplied greatly, and many of them ended up in ministry and were successful.

Sadly, many people's idea for ministering to youth is more like a club where those who attend are entertained with a lot of hype, games, and cool pyrotechnics. These are great tools, but if all we do is entertain our youth, they'll lack the spiritual nourishment needed to realize their God-given potential. So when I first met Pastors How and Lia from Heart of God Church, it felt like I had connected with kindred spirits. Because what stood out to me the most about their church was that they didn't need a youth group; the whole massive church is basically led and run by young people—with the average age being twenty-two years old.

Whenever I've ministered to them, which has been often, they're leaning off the edge of their seats, taking copious notes, responding eagerly to God's Word, hungry for the presence of the Lord—and if you know me, these were messages on holiness and the fear of the Lord. After a decade of regular visits to their church, I've seen them grow from 1,500 members to well over 5,000 members—with the average age still being twenty-two years old!

This is mind-blowing! Pastors in the West go to great efforts to cultivate the type of atmosphere and culture that Pastors How and Lia have built. At Heart of God Church, things are different. Their commitment to discipleship is the distinguishing factor for their rapid growth, especially with the younger generation. Their mantra has always been, "Generations are not replacements. Generations are reinforcements."

Everywhere you look, you'll find fifteen-year-olds running the soundboards, sixteen-year-olds operating the screens and cameras, seventeen-year-olds leading connect groups, twelve to eighteen-year-olds leading worship, and teenagers discipling teenagers on a variety of levels! That's because they've caught something many churches in the West have not. By viewing the youth as the church of today, not only have they provided them with a higher vision and purpose for their lives; they have also positioned them to become actively engaged in it, right now!

After ministering in the biggest churches and conferences all over the world, what I've witnessed at Heart of God Church is unlike anything I have experienced before. That's why I'm so thrilled that you hold this book in your hands. The wisdom and insights contained within these pages are not only applicable in Asia; they're especially relevant for the church worldwide. What Heart of God Church has wonderfully modeled for us all should not only be applauded and admired; it should also be reproduced everywhere. So let these words sink deep into your heart: the youth are not the church of tomorrow. They are the church of today!

John Bevere

- Who says youths cannot handle deep truths and have short attention spans? Watch John Bevere teach HOGC youths!
- Also, don't miss this conversation between Pastor How and John Bevere!

INTRO: MINDSET SHIFTS

How

This is where our journey will begin...

The great evangelist D.L. Moody once came back from an evangelistic meeting. His friend was waiting for him at his home. When his friend asked him, "How many people got saved today?"

D.L. Moody replied, "Two and a half."

His friend was puzzled. "Hmmm... two and a half? You mean two adults and one youth?"

D.L. Moody answered, "No, two youths and one adult. The youths have their whole lives ahead of them, while the adult has only half a life left."

That's another mic drop moment. Now that's what I call a paradigm shift. If we reach out to youths, the impact of Christ on them is for a whole lifetime. Furthermore, they have a whole lifetime to impact others. (Apologies to the adults reading this. I feel you... according to Moody's math, I am about a 0.35 now.)

Our good friend, Pastor Bill Wilson (Metro World Child), who runs the world's largest Sunday School with 200,000 kids, puts it this way: "It is better to build boys than repair men." There is a lot of truth in this statement. By the time people become older, they may have a lot of baggage and issues, so there is a lot of "repair" work to be done. Yes, of course God can redeem, but isn't it better and easier to preempt the mess? I definitely prefer less pain and detours. This is surely a case of "prevention is better than cure." *It is better to build schools than prisons. Good foundation and formation is always smarter than rehab and reformation.* We are all familiar with the verse:

> Proverbs 22:6
> Train up a child in the way he should go,
> And when he is old he will not depart from it.

Mindset Shift #1
Youth Are Leaders TODAY, Not Just Tomorrow

Youths need to be invited, included, involved, before they can be influenced and impacted. But we try to impress... in vain.

If you BABYSIT the youths, you will get BABIES.
If you LEAD the youths, you will have LEADERS!

Lia 🎾

I have spoken to countless pastors, politicians, business leaders about youths and every one of them has agreed with me enthusiastically about their importance. Many tell me that 'Youth are the future' and 'Youth are the leaders of tomorrow'. And here is where our road diverges. Yes, it is obvious that youth are leaders tomorrow but for How and me, our crusade is that – youth are leaders *today*!

Youth are leaders TODAY, not just tomorrow!
- Pastor How & Pastor Lia

Let the 14-year-old lead.
Let the 9-year-old serve God.
Let me tell you about this boy Wei Ze. He is a legend in our church.

He was nine years old when he first came, and he requested, "I want to play the drums." When he said that, he looked self-assured but not arrogant, vulnerable but not feeble.

Everything in our hearts wanted to say yes. But there was just one problem. He was nine. It took all of two seconds to glance at him from head to toe. Immediately you knew that his foot could not reach the kick drum pedal. On the drums, he would look like a kid driving his dad's Honda. You could only peek at his forehead through the steering wheel.

Ah. We told him, "You cannot play the drums *but* you can play the bass guitar *now*!" (Note to self: bass guitar no height requirement, no length of limbs limits. Another two-second glance at him. Yes, it will work.)

Wei Ze thought about it and being the smart boy he was, he said *yes*! He learnt the bass guitar from scratch in our School of Worship (SOW).

Then at 11, he started playing the bass guitar on the main stage. And this is not the children's church team or stage. But the main service platform with a thousand people in attendance!

Now, Wei Ze is all grown up. He's 23 years old, and he has more than 10 years of bass guitar experience under his belt!

11-year-old Wei Ze debuts as a bassist, not in children's church but in the main service.

23-year-old Wei Ze now has more than 10 years of experience playing the bass guitar.

*Let your young people rise up now to serve God **now.***

Don't wait till they are older and more experienced.

Youths are leaders today!! Not just tomorrow.

I thank God that we did not say to him, "Tomorrow, later, then you can serve God." We did not send him away by telling him, "Wait, wait till you are older and taller, then you play the drums for God."

Today, Wei Ze has remained as our legendary bassist. And he has become a worship team leader who puts an entire band together for weekend services. More than that, he has trained up many younger bassists in our SOW because he has tasted our belief and wants the next generation to experience it as well. And this is how it becomes a culture. We are so proud of Wei Ze. He is now our volunteer staff, leading 55 young people and also heads a department in the Social Media team. But his story doesn't stop here. The colourful journey of discipleship and growing in leadership continues for him. Watch out for the next part of his story in Volume 2.

Let the 14-year-old lead!

Let the 9-year-old serve!

How

I wonder how many youths we let slip through our churches because we told them to wait... to come back when they are older. And the tragedy is that when they are 16 or 22, we cajole, beg, and bribe them to serve, but it's too late. They have found another vision.

Youths need to be invited, included, involved, before they can be influenced and impacted.

But we try to impress... in vain.

Youths need to be invited, included, involved, before they can be influenced and impacted.

A nine-year-old coming up and volunteering to serve God is as rare as a kid asking for a kale salad for lunch. Almost all the time, we got to approach them first.

How did Lia and I raise up thousands of young people to serve God?

It is not rocket science. It's also not some special anointing that we have.

Just invite, include, and involve youths in ministry. Let me throw you a simple question. Ask any 10-year-old boy, "Would you rather play soccer or watch soccer?"

Without a second thought, he will be off the couch and kicking the ball around.

"Oh, but Ronaldo is on TV..." or "Liverpool is playing live..."

Nah... Most kids will still prefer to play soccer than watch soccer. Therein lies the problem with the church. Traditional youth ministries are set up for the kids to "watch soccer" rather than to "play soccer." This is essentially what we do: "Come to youth, we have a really cool band, brilliant lights, and funny preaching. Join us, we have fun and crazy games." Think about it. The games are played on stage with a few participants and everyone else is "watching." The band, lights, screens, preaching are all on stage. The youths are just "watching." They are spectators while we "do" church. And we are trying so hard to impress them with what's going on on stage.

Here's HOGC's secret: Let the youths "do" church, while we "watch."

Turn it around. Let the youths be on stage. Let them run the whole show. Let them impress and we celebrate them. Isn't it more normal? Parents go to school to watch their kids act in dramas, compete in sports, or perform in arts. The church is the only youth organization that does it the other way round. Imagine if the schools did it like us, the parents in school play soccer and then invite their kids to watch. (You are laughing now.) Imagine the 40-year-old

Let the youths "do" church, while we "watch."

dad acting in the school drama or the 40-year-old mom dancing ballet, and then try to get their kids to come watch. (It would be a ridiculous sight. Actually, it would be so hilarious that I might just go watch.) The kids will never come watch the adults play.

It is no wonder that youth ministry is not working. Again, it is as simple as getting the youths involved. Stop putting on a show and trying to impress them. You will never beat Hollywood and pop culture.

This brings me to the next benefit of involving youth and not impressing youths. Good news for smaller and less-resourced youth ministries – you don't have to compete with Hollywood or the big churches. When you involve the youths, you don't need big budgets or big productions or big names. The first ten years of HOGC, Lia grew the youths from nine to hundreds with a guitar, an overhead projector (if you even know what that is), and simply involving the youths in ministry.

Once they are "in the ministry," then you can influence and impact them. That is where discipleship begins. It's always on the job, on the go, not a lecture-style Bible study. Again, isn't that how it works in school? When teachers try to get the kids to run during PE lessons, they are lethargic and disinterested. However, when they sign up for the school basketball team, then the coach can push them to train hard. When youths are "in the team or ministry," then you can influence and impact them.

Lia ⚾ EMPOWER, DON'T ENTERTAIN

The problem with most youth ministries is that they are built on entertainment. Most youth pastors feel a great need to be the clown, fire-eater and juggler all rolled into one. Empower the youths, don't entertain them!

Empower the youths, Don't Entertain them!

This is good news for pastors who know they can never be a Jimmy Fallon or a James Corden. Don't get me wrong. Xbox, basketball, games – they all have their place.

There is nothing wrong with all those. In fact, we need those to attract new friends who are not yet Christians. But we cannot *build* a youth ministry purely on entertainment. Empower your youths, don't entertain them.

In our services, the Word is never watered down. The message is tweaked to be relevant, yes, but never diluted.

I always tell our youth leaders:

If you babysit the youths, you will get babies.

If you lead the youths, you will have leaders.

Don't just love them. *Train* them, *lead* them, *guide* them.

Give them a vision for God and train them towards fulfilling that vision.

If you BABYSIT the youths, you will get BABIES. If you LEAD the youths, you will have LEADERS!

So if you come visit Heart of God Church, you will see youths running the weekend services for youths. They are trained to be leaders. They are trained to handle the operation of the services – screens, cameras, lighting, sound, music.

You might spot a nine-year-old photographer zipping through the congregation, stealthily capturing moments in the service. You'll see 16-year-old leaders boldly praying for other pastors to have the same anointing for reaching youth. During 'Reinforcements Weekend', we up the ante. The entire service in all its departments is run by those 16 and below!

When the recent COVID-19 crisis hit and the church went into online mode, we did not lose the momentum. The youths made the jump to online with such finesse because from day one, it has always been about training and empowerment. So when COVID-19 descended, the youths didn't just wait around to be entertained by church online programming. They knew it was not about entertainment! Instead they jumped onboard to create captivating content for our online services. It was so surreal watching them make the digital plunge! *During COVID-19, the youths used technology for* **empowerment and enrichment, not entertainment!**

But sadly, we live in a world that has a consumer mentality. In the end times, there will be a consumer mentality.

> 2 Timothy 3:1-5
> But know this, that in the last days perilous times will come: For men will be *lovers of themselves, lovers of money,* boasters, proud, blasphemers, disobedient to parents, unthankful, unholy, unloving, unforgiving, slanderers, without self-control, brutal, despisers of good, traitors, headstrong, haughty, *lovers of pleasure* rather than lovers of God, having a form of godliness but denying its power. And from such people turn away!

People will live for themselves. They will live for pleasure and enjoyment. Sometimes Christians will have a consumer mentality too.

But Christianity is not a consumer religion. It is a producer faith!

The church is not an amusement centre. It is a training centre.

The church is not a shopping centre. It is a giving centre.

The church is not a nursery or a childcare. It is a gym.

The church exists not to solve your problems but to help you grow to become a problem solver.

Remember this: Empowered youths become producers. Entertained youths become consumers. Empower, and don't entertain your youths today!

> **Empowered Youths become Producers.**
> **Entertained Youths become Consumers.**

EMPOWER, DON'T OVERPOWER

This next principle highlights a gap that adults like us can fall into unwittingly when we work with youths. We can easily overpower a room filled with young people.

Perhaps we feel a great need to constantly lead, being the older and more experienced ones. I have seen too many interactions between young people and older people taking a hazardous direction – the top-down approach.

Don't talk down to young people or speak condescendingly. Whenever you step into a room filled with young people, take a deep breath and tell yourself – *empower, don't overpower!*

I have been in too many rooms with too many young people and so I have seen the effects of an overpowered room.

There was once I was hanging around with 20 youth leaders. A famous visitor dropped by our room on her way out of the office. The moment she entered, the atmosphere in the room changed. No kidding.

This dignitary, excited by the sound of her own voice, went on to lull the crowd about her accomplishments. There was no contributor in the room but her. She asked the questions and answered her own questions. She was the comma, semicolon, quotation marks and the full stop. Finally, she left with the swiftness of a woman who was late to her own coronation.

And the youths? Well, they looked like fish temporarily tired of water, till she walked out of the room. And they swam again!

Lesson for us all? Never suck the oxygen out of a room! Never overpower a room! Bridge that generation gap carefully.

Instead of laying a red carpet for yourself to walk on, lay a bridge and let the young people walk over to you.

Empower the room. You do that by asking them questions. Get to know them better. Draw their thoughts out of them. Find out what their dreams are. See whether you can make that dream come to pass.

Instead of laying a red carpet for yourself to walk on, lay a bridge and let the young people walk over to you.

Stop forcing our man-sized armour on them. Instead, let them tell us about their five stones and a sling. Let them tell us about the lion and the bear they killed. Let them tell us about the songs they wrote while they turned a desert into a spring. Coax them to share with us how they are coming out of the backyard to the frontline when the prophet is ready to anoint the next king.

Believe me, the young people will let us dominate a room because youths can be very polite. They will let us be the brightest ones in the room. But when we walk out, we will be the ones with the most to lose. We would have just lost out on a golden opportunity to listen to what is vibing with the current generation. We would have lost the chance to spot leaders. We would have missed the moment to empower the next generation of world changers.

In other words, we would have missed out on spotting the next anointed king.

Don't just invite youths to the party, give them a seat at the table.

Don't just invite youths to the party, give them a seat at the table.
- Pastor Lia & Pastor How

Heart of God Church is not perfect. You probably think after 20 years, we have got our mantras down to a science. That is not the case. With every new generation of youths coming through, we still have to keep ensuring the older youth leaders are still empowering the young ones! Sometimes, How and I sound like a vinyl record stuck in its groove.

Empower, don't entertain...

Empower, don't overpower...

Being the empowering pastor he is, How had to intervene in a recent episode in our church. He was asking the Communications team to let the young people take over his Instagram Stories permanently. He told the team, "It is just an Insta Story, it's not a press release. It goes away in 24 hours, it's alright. We can give this opportunity to the youth." He spoke to the youths and asked them to come up with Instagram Stories and send them in. He spoke to both sides... but for a few weeks, nothing happened. He thought to himself, *I have engaged the Comms team, I have engaged the young people, what's happening?*

Asking became pushing, still there were only one to two dated stories a week appearing. At that point, he sighed. Whether he liked it or not, he realised that some of our 'professional' staff had lost the heart for youths. It is easier to play it safe by subjecting the youths' ideas and inputs through a bureaucratic labyrinth of 'nos', 'this will not work' and 'we don't like that'. That day How realised that HOGC was no longer youth-friendly. The youths who were once believed in and given opportunities were not passing it forward.

How went directly to the 14-year-olds and asked what happened. They explained, "We submitted our work but it was seldom approved. A lot of it came back to us, we were asked to change a lot, a lot of things. A simple Insta Story that we could have posted in five minutes, took many many revisions and days to be approved."

Apparently, the youths' stories were remodified, reedited, revamped. And not for the better, but just to line up with the older leaders' taste and fancy. It did not look 'youth-y' anymore. It looked like an... older person's Instagram Story – black with white, Times New Roman font compared with the vibrant and gritty colours of a youth Instagram Story. The 'adult' Communications team had successfully filtered out the creativity, spontaneity and freshness of the youths. Beyond the work, they also stifled, stymied and suffocated the enthusiasm of the youths. This is the opposite of 'empower'. To How, that was it. He knew there was a problem with HOGC. He had to restructure and filter out the 'adults'. Look, we are not bubble wrapping things here. After 20 years, we still have to fight against people despising youths. It seems like it is an age-old prejudice that even Paul had to tell Timothy to stand up against (1 Timothy 4:12). We feel like marching with placards that say #YoungLivesMatter in our own church.

To all the HOGC people, especially staff and leaders, reading this, if that is you we are describing, that means you have become an old wineskin and are no longer carrying the HOGC DNA. Our concern is that there are leaders and staff in our church who have lost the youthful spirit. They are no longer championing the cause of young people.

Let's continue to empower youths. Pastor How and I are the watchmen, guarding the heart and soul of HOGC.

If you really respect youths, *don't just invite them to the party, give them a seat at the table.* Give them a voice and a vote. Implement their inputs, let them make decisions and make changes.

In many churches, youths are great for optics but never invited to have a substantial voice. A once-a-year youth takeover is a start but we need to let them input into all the other areas of ministry. Don't just limit them to the band or dance items. In fact, here is what we are implementing in HOGC as we are writing this: *Every department and ministry must now have a Gen Z voice.* (By the way, at the time of writing, the oldest Gen Z is already 23.) *Every project and idea must pass through their lens and get their vote or veto.* Yes, we will be ruthlessly enforcing this.

After 20 years of building youths, we are still finding ways to give them a voice today. Young leaders below 16 years old run our entire youth camps. Youth interns boldly speak up at senior leaders' meetings. Young singers push for younger sounding songs to be used on the worship team... and younger movements on stage. (Hmm... Hammer Dance, anybody?)

Besides letting 14–15-year-olds take charge of our Insta Stories on our personal accounts, I also conduct many surveys via phone to ask the youths what message titles work. My discipleship message *One Conversation Away From Success* was originally *One Conversation Away from Growth.* Being the spiritual pastor I was, I thought the word *success* would throw my holy message into the mire of the shallow motivational talks category. But the youths convinced me that the word *success* would draw interest especially from their unsaved friends whom they intended to invite for service! They reasoned, "Pastor, our unsaved friends won't look at 'growth', they want 'success'!" Ok, ok, forgive me for being too religiously holy and exclusive.

Sometimes youths do not rise because they see you have got it all covered. You are doing so well without them. My solution? Well, pretend to need help if you must. Just so that the youths must rise up to lead!

How  WE NEED <u>YOU</u>TH! WE WANT <u>YOU</u>TH!

We need YOUth! We want YOUth!

We need you! We want you!

YOUth can do it.

You can do it.

As a rule of thumb, within six months to one year of a youth getting saved or joining your church, you've got to get them involved. In HOGC, when a youth gets saved, they go through eight lessons of one-on-one follow-up. Then they sign up for Basic Ministry Training (BMT).

These two stations will take around six months to a year. Subsequently, they will choose to be deployed to serve in a ministry. Over 80% of youths are serving. Some in a major way, others in a smaller way, but they are involved.

We have created over 60 ministries for youths to serve in. Honestly, there are some ministries that are created more for the benefit of the youths than the church. For example, we have a Décor ministry and a comedy production team. It started with Lia and me discovering that some kids were not interested in the usual church ministry options (Worship Team or leadership) but have other talents. We met this girl named Jessica and she's got a funny bone. I mean, she is just seriously hilarious... every story she tells has me ROFL. So we started a comedy production team and recruited a bunch of kids that are crazy like her. Now they produce short comedies as part of our Christmas and Easter productions. Today this young lady has over 220,000 followers across TikTok and Instagram. Her TikTok profile has 6.8 million likes. Jessica did not start out to be an influencer. Initially she did it in her free time so that she could reach out to more people. Through her social media she has led so many to Jesus and church. When she announced that she was going to share her testimony, 130 Instagram followers private-messaged her to ask where they could watch it. Within a year, she got more than 350 of her social media followers (who are total strangers) to watch our online services and YouTube sermons. Out of those, 47 gave or recommitted their lives to Jesus. They started out following her and ended up following Jesus. Now that deserves a huge *Like*!

So how to get youths involved?

Youths must know and feel that they have opportunities and abilities to make a difference.

The operative words here are *opportunities* and *abilities*.

> **Youths must know and feel that they have Opportunities and Abilities to make a difference.**

Every time I watch the news of some natural disaster like an earthquake or some humanitarian crisis like the refugee crisis or war in Syria, I am compelled to do something. The images of my fellow human beings in misery affect me deeply, especially children suffering.

But if you are like me, you probably end up doing nothing. It is not because I don't care or I don't want to help but because I don't know what I can do. I am this ordinary guy in Singapore, how do I help the kids in Syria or victims in Haiti?

I am not a doctor or politician or fireman. What can I do?

I don't even know anyone in Syria or Haiti. How do I even help?

There! That's the problem.

I feel like I don't have the *abilities* to help – I am not a doctor.

I feel like I don't have the *opportunity* to help – I don't know anyone. I don't have an inroad into the crisis.

So I end up lifting a prayer for the victims and maybe sending some money to the Red Cross, the "professionals" who know how to help them.

Sidebar – that is why most Christians end up just praying and giving money. Prayers and money are great but they could have done so much more if they knew they had the abilities and opportunities.

Now imagine this: If I have a Syrian friend. His family is still there. He comes to see me and tells me, "We need someone with your skill set – someone who can counsel and connect with youths. Anything else you don't know, we have a two-day course to train and prep you."

Then he continues, "I am travelling to the crisis zone next month. I am assembling a team. My family members are part of the local government and working with NGOs. Will you join me for two weeks?"

I will be booking my flights and packing my bags.

Or it could be as simple as, "Will you help me source for some medication to ship over?" I would be making calls.

What's the difference in this scenario?

I feel like I have the ability to help. I can counsel youths... I can do it.

I feel like I have the opportunity to help. I know a friend who is connected and has access. Now I know what medications are needed and I have a contact with an address I can ship it to. I can directly make a difference.

Basically, my Syrian friend just told me, "I need you. I want you. You can do it."

He invited me, included me, and involved me. So I will rise to the challenge.

And this is exactly what happens in youth ministries all over the world.

The young people feel like they don't have the abilities to serve God or build the church.

They feel like they don't have the opportunities too because only adults do the "important things" in church. *The vibe we send out is – church-building is for an inner circle of grown-ups who make sure the youths know it is a closed circle.*

Consequently and tragically, most young people leave it to the grown-ups and most church members leave it to the "professionals."

But what if leaders in church came to a kid, tapped him on the shoulder, and said, "Hey, you are really funny. I love your jokes. You can serve God with your humor."

"What!!! How do I serve God with jokes? You must be joking."

"No. You see, every Sunday, we have new friends coming. They may be guarded, feeling out of place, and awkward. With your personality, you can put them at ease, take care of them, and make them feel at home."

"That's it?"

"Yup. That's serving God. And no one is funny like you... so we really need you. We have a two-day training, BMT, and it will train you to take care of people. You will be all set."

"Done! Easy. I can do that. Where do I sign up for BMT and when do I start taking care of new friends?"

What just happened?

You have just involved a kid into ministry.

You just assured him that he has the abilities and will also train him. You just gave him an opportunity to do something because you believed in him.

You just communicated to this youth, "We need you. We want you. You can do it."

Now was that so difficult?

Do you need big budgets, big productions, or big names to recruit that youth?

A tap on the shoulder is more effective than all your recruitment videos and announcements on stage.

I have seen many kids start this way. Then rise up to lead 10 other youths. And mature into leaders of hundreds and become awesome preachers (with a sense of humor). It all started with a tap on the shoulder.

One of those kids is Jeanie.

Lia 🔘

Jeanie. Don't let her diminutive build fool you. She came to church when she was 13 years old. She became a Jesus follower.

Jeanie came to church at 13.

One day in church, Pastor How heard a loud and strong voice. He discovered Jeanie praying, tucked away in some corner. He was thrilled to see such powerful, strong prayers coming out of a small-built girl.

"Jeanie, you are only 13 but you pray with such faith and authority. You can be a leader for God!" he told her. She felt so believed in. Little did Pastor How know that God had just given her a dream to be a full-time staff in church.

Pastor How's tap on the shoulder that day catapulted Jeanie into her destiny. She started leading five people, and then in just a few months, this group grew to ten.

At 14, she sat in my preaching class. We went through her sermon line by line, and improved on it.

"Jeanie, you will be a great preacher!" were the last words she heard as she left the last session.

She started preaching in connect groups. Over the next few years, her connect group grew 8 times to 80 people. Faithfulness begets more trust. She started to lead another new group comprising 12–14-year-olds. She taught them how to preach. She told them they would be great preachers for God. She told them they could be leaders for God. Her first dream came to pass. She became a full-time church staff, leading 250 young people!

Let the 11-year-old serve!

Let the 16-year-old lead – now!

When Jeanie was 21, we sent her for an exposure trip to the US. It was where five of our young senior leaders were studying their Master of Divinity in Oral Roberts University. It was there she caught her second dream – to pursue her Master of Divinity one day!

She mused, *Ah, maybe about 20 years later when I am 40, I will do that!*

God must have heard her thoughts. Soon after, How and I called Jeanie into our room. We shared that we were sending another group of full-time staff to study for their Master of Divinity. And she was one of them!

Jeanie now preaches and trains 12–14-year-olds to preach in connect groups. She is en route to getting her MDiv.

'Shocked' was hardly the word to describe Jeanie's response. I believe it was more 'shell-shocked' – in a good sense.

We had bombarded her with opportunity after opportunity, belief after belief.

We had peppered her with strong words of encouragement.

We had tapped her on the shoulder.

So at 23, she started studying for her Master of Divinity! In our room that day, she could not quite articulate her thoughts except, "I thought I would do that when I am 40!"

See?

*Even youths themselves need to see that they are leaders **today**, not just tomorrow!*

Let the young people lead!

Let the 11-year-old serve!

Let the 16-year-old lead!

The singular image of a successful church leader being a man or woman with grey hair has been too entrenched. We need to put in another reference visual for leaders in your church landscape. It is time to show the youths that church is not about a closed circle of adults serving.

Even Jeanie herself had subconsciously imbibed that youths are leaders tomorrow, when she thought she could get her MDiv only later in her 40s! Show the young people that we need them and we want them!

I thank God that Pastor How spotted greatness in a Jeanie who was praying in the church corner. I thank God I had the privilege to hone her communicating abilities.

If Jeanie were not invited, included and involved at 13, she would have likely grown up to become a regular Christian. She probably wouldn't be leading 250 youths and be on track to getting her MDiv by 28 years old. Of course, God in His sovereignty and omnipotence, can miraculously ensure Jeanie walks into her destiny without us, but still, HOGC would have lost out on a great young leader like her.

And Jeanie is just one of many such stories in our church!

It is possible to make adults *and* youths alike see that – youths are leaders *today*!

If you are a young person reading this book – we need you. We want you.

You can do it. YOUth can do it.

Our best-kept secrets revealed:

Favourite ideas by youths, for youths, to reach youths.

All content creators are 13–18 years old!

The Woke & Awakened Generation - Idealistic, Activistic and Epic

If you don't captivate youths now for Christ,
something else will come in to carry them captive!

The HOGC Vision: "Raise up GenerationS of people who will
give God the best years of their lives, and God will use these
GenerationS to impact all levels of society and all walks of life."

How ✈

The best way to make your dreams come true is to wake up.

That is why this generation of youths has been called the *woke* generation.

They woke up because they are now captivated by visions to change the world. And they are willing to pay a price to make it happen. Whether you agree with them or not, one thing is for sure, they want to make a difference.

Youths are idealistic.

Youths are activistic.

Youths like epic.

Just watch the news, the fight for change is mostly powered by young people. The youths are leading the charge for climate change. Greta Thunberg was only 15 when she started sitting outside the

Swedish parliament calling for stronger action on climate change. She was the spark that youths around the world were waiting for and soon armies of youths joined the cause.

In Hong Kong, the protests were characterized by young people leading young people. These leaderless protesters were catalyzed by Joshua Wong, who has since been nominated for Time's Person of the Year and the Nobel Peace Prize... and also imprisoned. He started his activism when he was 15.

In the late '60s, the Vietnam anti-war protests in America were also driven by university students. As I am writing now, the #BlackLivesMatter movement is also birthing a new generation of civil rights activists.

I am not debating the politics, positions, or methods of these movements but I just want to point out that youths are idealistic and activistic. They want to fight for a cause. They want to live for something bigger than themselves. The rock band Coldplay captured it succinctly with these lyrics: "I'm gonna buy a gun and start a war if you can tell me something worth fighting for." There is nothing more worthy to fight for than the cause of Christ. What if the church can give young people a godly, spiritual vision? What if the church can captivate their hearts and minds to live for Christ?

Lia

Right now we have a young lady named Valerie heading the music arm of our church. She comes from a family that has always been very prominent in the music scene. Her father was an influential figure. He worked with international jazz singer Laura Fygi and superstars in the Mandarin world.

So the music scene was Valerie's entire world. When she was 14, various management agencies offered her a chance to become a performing artiste. She was all set to study music at Berklee – the iconic college of all things musical.

When she was 19, the local newspaper featured her as one of the 25 youths under 25 to look out for in our nation. They interviewed her as one of the top 25 young achievers in Singapore with great potential! Her future looked promising and secure. She did not need to search out opportunities, an entire machinery was waiting to make her successful and famous. Her stars were aligned. But a star was not what she was looking to become.

"I could choose to have a degree from Berklee. I could have a great music career and I could even start a business because my family was so well-connected. But inside of me, I was looking for a greater purpose in life. It went beyond a successful career or being rich or having a glamorous life," she shared.

"I was looking for not just success but significance," Valerie concluded. Being friends with church people rubbed off on her. She caught a vision of living for *Others*. It turns out that she finds it fulfilling to build other young hopeful musicians from church. What she was looking for was not to build a music career but to build young people! Her music lessons with our church youths go beyond music theory. She mentors them, counsels them and coaches them in all areas.

Music is her connection with her dad. In our church, we have always believed in using the church to build people and not making use of people to build the church. So to make her dreams come true, we initiated the idea of letting father and daughter perform as a duet so that they could make memories together.

What originated as a fun idea became a divine and timely event, in hindsight. Shortly after that performance, her dad was diagnosed with cancer. He passed away.

Her father was a man of many chords but few words. He didn't say much after the event. But he displayed a huge framed-up photo of him and his daughter in the middle of his studio so that he could see it every day.

Recalling the event with fondness, Valerie said, "I knew that the church did not need another performance. But it was a great opportunity created just for me to play music and create memories together with my dad. I am so thankful for that. He loved that framed-up photo gift from church very much! It took centre stage in his beloved studio.

"I have found significance in making others' dreams come to pass like how the church made mine become a reality. I am convinced that my skills and talents are not meant to make myself successful. But they are to be used to change the lives of people," she concluded.

Today Valerie runs our music arm and our Communications department. She is also the Head of Global Partnerships.

Thank God that she is captivated by significance and not just success. That is why we need to fan the flames of idealism in young people right now.

If not, it will either be doused by the realities of life or hijacked by other causes. That is why we must encourage them to lead now... today. Don't wait till tomorrow.

If we had waited, the world would have captivated Jeanie, Wei Ze and Valerie with another vision. Remember, these are talented and driven young people. School coaches will mesmerise them with the glory of winning sports championships. YouTube will enchant them to become influencers. Business people will take them under their wings to mentor them so that they can build their companies. These young people will find another purpose to live for. Valerie might be an entrepreneur in the music industry, living just for herself instead of Others.

If we had waited, Jeanie might be serving a humanistic cause and Wei Ze might be running the corporate rat race. Again, nothing wrong with these career choices, but they would not be building HOGC and the Kingdom of God. There is already an abundance of young people running after a myriad of causes and careers but there are few building the House of God. If you don't captivate them now for Christ, something else will come in to carry them captive!

If you don't captivate youths now for Christ, something else will come in to carry them captive!

How

I have also seen so many potential young people lulled into spiritual mediocrity by the realities of life. Life has a way of sucking out idealism and activism – jobs, bills to pay, buying their first car, loans to repay, and just the busyness of life. Marriage, kids, house, mortgage, and before you can take stock of your life, you are 50 years old.

The HOGC Vision:
"Raise up GenerationS of people who will give God the best years of their lives, and God will use these GenerationS to impact all levels of society and all walks of life."

That is why Heart of God Church's vision is "Raise up GenerationS of people who will give God the best years of their lives, and God will use these GenerationS to impact all levels of society and all walks of life."

Let's give God the best years of our lives, not the leftover years of our lives!

When Lia and I were in our early 20s, this was before we started the church, one story that gripped us was of Jim Elliot and his four friends. They were young men, the best and brightest with potential to be of enormous success in the world, but they chose to be missionaries to the unreached tribes of Ecuador. All five were martyred. One of them, Peter Fleming, wrote in his diary that his favorite hymn was *Lord, in the Fulness of My Might,* and these are the lyrics.

> I would not give the world my heart,
> And then profess Thy love;
> I would not feel my strength depart,
> And then Thy service prove.
>
> I would not with swift-winged zeal
> On the world's errands go;
> And labour up the heavenly hill
> With weary feet and slow.
>
> O not for Thee my weak desires,
> My poorer baser part!
> O not for Thee my fading fires,
> The ashes of my heart.
>
> O choose me in my golden time;
> In my clear joys have part!
> For Thee the glory of my prime,
> The fulness of my heart.

These words captivated my heart and Lia's heart. They became our prayers and passion.

> "Oh Lord, I would not with swift-winged zeal on the world's errands go, and labor up the heavenly hill with weary feet and slow."

> "Jesus, not for You my fading fires... not the ashes of my heart."

> "God take me in my golden time, in the glory of my prime... I give you the fullness of my heart."

If you are a young person reading this and it resonates with you, join the cause of Christ. Give the best years of your life to build His Kingdom. Pastor Lia and I prayed this prayer when we were in our 20s. As we write this now, we are 50 years old. We have given the best years of our lives to build HOGC.

Now it's your time. Now it's your turn.

THE POWER OF VISION

Young people are drawn to vision because they are idealistic and activistic.

We hear many pastors lamenting. They are struggling to get their young people to spend less time on YouTube, lessen their obsession with gaming or for the more serious cases, give up vices they have picked up.

Our hearts go out to the pastors because it is not easy chasing youths around like naggy spiritual nannies. And that should be the last thing we become to young people!

Many parents have also asked Pastor How and me, "How do you get these kids to be disciplined, exercise self-control, sacrifice, come early to church, pray at home and the whole gamut?"

Parents bring their kids and tell us all the problems and bad habits of the kids and want us to change them. Then after a few weeks they ask, "Are you counselling them about this and that? Why are you not addressing these issues specifically?" Well, we have found that most teenage issues drop off when they find a vision!

Think for a minute.

Let's say you have a dog which is biting your Air Jordans. It refuses to let go, no matter what you do. The more you pull, the harder it bites your prized footwear. It devolves into a tug of war.

So what do you do to prevent a tug of war or more importantly, to save your bespoke sneakers? The smarter thing to do is to brandish (no, not a knife) a piece of meat on a bone. I guarantee you, the dog will immediately let go of your classy footwear and go for the bone!

It is the same with young people. No, I am not calling them dogs. I am saying, instead of nagging, threatening and cajoling young people to let go of their unhealthy pursuits, all you need to do is to brandish a vision in front of them. They will naturally let go of the bad food and go for the meat of a godly vision!

That's good news. We do not have to get into a tug of war with youths over their gaming, sleeping habits, alcohol, girls and guys or TikTok obsession. No more 'Give this up, give that up. Oh, that is not good for you.' Remember, the more you tell them don't, they will. The more you ask them to do, they won't. Youths are numbed by pain of threats and lulled to sleep by nags.

Instead, cast a godly vision for them. Brandish that bone. Live out that cause of Christ for them to emulate. Once they are awakened by Christ, they will be woke to the cause of Christ. Once they are woke, they can make a difference!

Once youths are awakened by Christ, they will be 'woke' to the cause of Christ.

One 13-year-old boy was failing in school but excelled at one thing – gaming. For four years, he trained for the game *Wolf Team*. He played for 16 hours every day, neglecting to brush his teeth for one week and took three minutes to shower each time. (Maybe that was how he killed his opponents.) He was every parent's nightmare but everyone's dream gamer, becoming the No. 1 local player and highly ranked in the world. His YouTube instructional videos garnered over 17,000 views! Then he broke up with his eighth girlfriend and was so sad that he drank his father's vodka till he fell asleep. But God met him when he came to a Heart of God Church service. Pastor Charleston preached about how God wanted them to wait for the right time to be in a serious relationship. This boy was so shocked by the timely sermon. He gave his heart to Jesus and started being serious about everything in his life. He lost interest in gaming. His school grades improved. Once he was awakened by Christ, he became woke to the cause of Christ! He caught a vision and saw the power of influence of the Video Production ministry. Right now, he is a crucial player in our post-production team!

How A HEAVENLY VISION

In Acts 26, Paul shares his testimony of salvation to King Agrippa. In the same encounter with Christ, Paul not only received his salvation but also his calling. Jesus said to him:

> Acts 26:16-18
> … I have appeared to you for this *purpose,* to make you a minister and a witness… *I now send you,* to open their eyes, in order to turn them from darkness to light, and from the power of Satan to God, that they may receive forgiveness of sins and an inheritance…

Paul received the purpose and mission for his life. He had a heavenly vision now. So in verse 19, Paul declared that he was not disobedient to the heavenly vision.

Most of the time, we focus on Paul's obedience, which is impeccable and indisputable. But let's focus on the "heavenly vision" part of this verse. Could it be possible that it's the other way around? Perhaps it's because Paul caught sight of a heavenly vision, and it so gripped him that it helped him to be obedient. The Message version paraphrased the verse this way:

Acts 26:19 (MSG)

What could I do, King Agrippa? I couldn't just walk away from a vision like that! *I became* an *obedient* believer on the spot.

Paul had been searching for his purpose all his life. He fought for the pharisaical traditions, he fought against the Christians, he fought for the wrong cause against the wrong people. Now that he found the one true God and his life vision, he wasn't gonna let go. Paul was going to live and die for Christ and His cause.

In the same way, the young people have spent their whole lives groping in darkness, wallowing in insecurities and meaninglessness. They dabbled in drugs and alcohol, cut themselves, looked for love in the wrong places, gave up everything for relationships that were supposed to be for life, were misled to fight the wrong war and manipulated to fight the wrong people. And *now...* they have found the one true God and their life purpose. They are not gonna let go. They are going to live and die for Christ and His cause.

So how did Lia and I raise up GenerationS of young people who would give God the best years of their lives? On every level, from church to connect groups to a personal level, we simply help young men and women catch sight of the heavenly vision. It will turn a generation of Sauls into an army of Pauls.

That is why *vision eats discipline for breakfast.*

Vision eats disobedience for lunch.

Proverbs 29:18 teaches that "without vision, the people cast off restraint." When we do not have a vision, we lose discipline and slip into disobedience. Dr. A.R. Bernard teaches so insightfully that "People who lose their vision for the future will go back to their past." Lia and I have witnessed this with so many people. The moment they lose their vision, they go back to their past – past sins, past habits, past friends, and past life.

If the youths don't have a heavenly vision, the world will lull them into spiritual mediocrity. The youths are gaming because they want a challenge, a sense of achievement, and purpose. So the world entices them to channel their energy into the virtual world. It is a decoy, so that they don't use their energy in the spiritual world.

The youths are so capable of loving and being loved. But the world lures them into wrong company, bad relationships, sex, same-sex experimentation, and popularity competitions. It is a distraction, so that they don't use the innocence of their friendships and purity of their affections to win their generation for Jesus.

There was a 14-year-old boy who came to HOGC. His initials are YYY, so we affectionately call him Y³. Y³ was born in Malaysia. His dad always came home drunk, picked fights, and trashed the house. Whenever it happened, he ran into the arms of his mom for refuge. One night when he was eight, the fighting was the worst ever and later he found out that his mom was seeing another man. She was leaving the family and moving to Singapore to be with him. Just like that, the boy's world fell apart. Two years passed, and dad remarried too and left the house. Y³ and his younger brother were left behind to be cared for by his grandparents.

In Y³'s own words,

"I felt abandoned... passed around like rubbish... nobody cared, nobody wanted me. Once, in school, the teacher asked the class to draw their families. I stared at the blank paper and didn't know what to do. Eventually I drew a fake father and a fake mother and pretended that I had a perfect family. I also added in a fake car, a fake house and a fake dog.

"I really missed my mum. I spent nights convincing my grandparents to let me study in Singapore so that I could stay with my mum. When they finally agreed, I was so happy. When I was

nine years old, I moved to Singapore. My mum was remarrying and preparing for her wedding. She was excited to start her new life, so I guess me showing up wasn't part of her plan. So she got her parents to take me in. At least my mum could visit me. Whenever she did, I must have looked like the happiest puppy in the world. However, once she remarried, the visits lessened and finally, they stopped completely. To be rejected once, I tried to convince myself that maybe she had no choice. But to be rejected twice... now I know for sure that I am unwanted. I just didn't know why I was so dislikable or what I had done wrong? My mum was my refuge but now I felt like a refugee in a foreign country, pushed from grandparent to grandparent.

"My life had no meaning. Then, my cousin introduced me to the computer game, League of Legends. Gaming soon became my escape from reality. At one point, I stayed in the gaming cafe for almost 48 hours. To buy more game credits, I skipped meals and even lied to my grandparents that I needed money for school. At first, I spent $10 a week. Then, it became $30, $50 and then $100. During my 2-year League of Legends 'career', I spent a total of $5,680! I achieved the Diamond 4 rank and was in the top 0.13% of all 81 million players. You could say that I was indeed a legend. As expected, my grades crashed, but I didn't care. Gaming was the one thing that made me feel good.

"Soon, I started secondary school and met Xin Yi! He used to be a naughty kid. Then suddenly, he changed so much. He even gave me a box of chocolates with a handwritten note to encourage me. I thought, that's quite nice of him. So, when he invited me to Heart of God Church, I agreed! During service, when praise and worship started, love and peace filled my heart. I felt as if all my fears faded away. Curious about what I felt, I kept coming back! Every week, the same love and peace flooded my heart. I knew it was God. So a few weeks later, I decided to become a Christian!

"As I came back to church, God showed me the depths of His love for me. Once, the verse in Isaiah 49:16 stood out to me. It says, 'See, I have written your name on the palms of my hands...' I realised that even though my earthly parents didn't want me, my name was written on God's palms. He is always thinking about me! God is my Heavenly Father and He was mending my broken heart. This verse became my strength every time I felt down.

"Heart of God Church also became the home I always dreamt of. Once, my connect group surprised me with a cake and a card. At first, I wondered why. Then they told me it was for my birthday. Throughout my life, no one had ever celebrated my birthday. I was special and important to them... Also, the hardest day for me to get through was always Mother's Day. I used to feel so down on that day, but here, Mother's Day is different! One Mother's Day, Pastor Lia passed me a gift and a card. She knew how hard Mother's Day was for me and wanted to tell me she remembered me. I remember just staring at the gift and tears just flowed.

"Another time, Pastors included me in a dinner. During the dinner, they were so happy to put food on my plate and happily asked me about my life and dreams. That day, I caught a glimpse of what a complete family felt like. After that, Pastors gave me a personalised notebook with an engraved verse. I was shocked when I saw the verse. It was Isaiah 49:16, the verse I held so close to heart. Pastor Lia told me that when she was praying, she felt prompted by God to give me this verse. I was amazed because I never told anyone about this verse before. God's love for me was so real.

When Pastor Lia and Pastor How gave him a personalised notebook, Y³ was shocked because it had the exact verse God had spoken to him, which he had never shared with anyone.

"When Building Fund 2017 came around, I heard stories of how Pastors and generations of people in HOGC first sacrificed to build the church. They did it so that youths like me can find a spiritual home and come to know God. I wanted to give back to this place that first loved me. So I prayed and asked God for an amount to give. I calculated that after setting aside $10 for tithes and offerings, $10 for food and $5 to bless others, I could save up $160 over 4 months. It wasn't much. But in one service, an amount to give kept coming to my mind. $600. As I was praying and thinking about how to give this amount, God prompted me with an amazing idea! To sell my League of Legends gaming account. But I thought, 'Really God?' I was still addicted to playing League of Legends. It held the only good memories of my childhood. But then, I realised that gaming had made me a selfish person. I had no room to think about the people around me, or my studies. So there and then, I decided that I no longer wanted to be confined within the walls of the virtual world. With God, I now had the courage to get my life in order. So, right after service, I placed my account on Carousell (an app for selling pre-loved items)! One week later, someone offered to buy my account for $550!

I was so excited! When I received the money, I added $50 of my savings to it and fulfilled my Building Fund pledge of $600! I felt such a joy knowing that my money was going to be used for a greater purpose – to build God's home.

"I've also grown to be more generous. I saw that my younger brother was hurting too. I saved up for weeks to buy him a jacket just to love him. It was the first time I did anything for him! Seeing his genuine smile brought a warmth to my heart. I want my brother to experience the love of God too. I also brought three of my friends to church, where they encountered God! 'Legend' used to be what they called me, but now, I pray that spreading God's love will always be what I'm known for. My dream is to get my brother saved so that he can experience a life transformation like I did."

How

Today, Y³ serves as a crew in our Motion Graphics and Effects ministries. He is also part of the Social Media team.

"Now as I think back about my life, I know that it would be so different if not for God and church. From feeling so unwanted, my life is now filled with love and purpose."

Y³ is just one of many stories in HOGC. They gave up bad meat because they have found a greater purpose. They don't want to go back to their old lives because they now have a heavenly vision.

THE POWER OF HOPE
FROM YOUR GENERATION ONWARDS, IT WILL BE DIFFERENT

Besides a heavenly vision, kids like Y³, who come from a broken family, need *hope*. They need hope for their personal lives, family, and future. They need to know that with Christ, their history is not going to repeat itself. They need to know that they are going to have a godly and good marriage and their kids will not go through what they have gone through.

Jeremiah 29:11 may be a cliché verse to seasoned Christians but when Y³ reads "For I know the thoughts that I think toward you, says the Lord, thoughts of peace and not of evil, to give you a future and a hope," it is a lifeline.

"Nobody thinks of me... nobody cares... but God thinks of me."

Wow!

"My family is broken, I am a loser, and my future marriage is doomed to fail too... but now God promised me that He will give me a future and a hope!"

So don't ever dilute your message to youths. They need the unadulterated gospel even more. That is why we preach Christ, the blessed hope and Christ in you, the hope of glory. Three phrases that I repeat to them religiously are: "With Christ...

- ... from you and your generation onwards, it will be different."
- ... your future is amazing."
- ... you may be poor now, but you will not be poor the rest of your life."

This is the hope that got Klennan through tough times. He came to church when he was 16 years old. Klennan's story is iconic in our church. We need you to hear it directly from his lips and straight from his heart. Here's what he shared to over 6,500 pastors and leaders at a conference in Taiwan:

"Hi everyone, I'm Klennan. I did not have a happy childhood. But today, because of God and church, I'm excited for my future!

"My mum was an alcoholic and my father was a drug addict.

As a child, I often saw my mum coming home drunk and screaming at everyone. My father spent all his money and borrowed money from loan sharks to buy drugs.

"When I was eight, one night, my mum told me she wasn't coming home anymore. I cried and begged her to stay. Still, she left the house. I ran around looking for her, but I couldn't find her. I felt so lost.

"That same year, my parents separated and my father moved out. Later on, I found out he was actually sent to prison for drug abuse. My mum always said, 'Don't visit your father. Everything is his fault.' My mum hated my dad, and soon, I started to hate him too. My parents had a failed marriage, and my grandparents did too. So, the thought of growing up scared me. What if I became like them?

"To forget my problems. I drove my teachers crazy by breaking stuff and damaging property! At 12, I got into a fight. I found myself in the principal's office, and later in the police station. I was still young, so I was let off with a warning.

"When my mum met me, she scolded me for troubling her. She didn't seem to care that my life was in a mess. When I was 13, I started stealing as well. I was notorious in school. I knew what I was doing was wrong. But bad attention was better than no attention at all.

"When I was 16, things became worse. I broke up with my girlfriend and my friends went against me. I felt so hurt. At the lowest point of my life, my only true friend Claire invited me to HOGC!

"When I came, so many people welcomed me with the biggest smiles! Then during service, I felt a strong peace in my heart. I thought, 'Maybe God and church are what I need. Maybe, this is where I can find something to live for.' So, I made the best decision ever – I gave my life to Jesus.

"Church became the home I never had. In the past, Father's Day meant nothing. But on my first Father's Day in church, Pastor How gave me a keychain and a letter. I felt the love of a father for the first time. In the letter, Pastor How wrote: 'Your past does not determine your future. Leave the past. Let it go. You can't embrace the future holding on to the past.' My perspective towards my past changed. I needed to let go of the bitterness I felt towards my parents.

"A few months later, my mum came home very drunk and screaming. My neighbours called the police. Six officers came and took my mum away in handcuffs. In the past, I would have been crying, lost and angry. But that night, no matter how sad I felt, I knew God was still greater than my situation. I knelt on the floor of my mum's room, lifted my hands and prayed, 'God, I lift my family up to You.'

"The next day, my mum came back home and everything was okay! Slowly, I started talking to her more. I even brought her out to celebrate her birthday and Mother's Day!

"Now, she does not drink as often. My mum also shared that whenever I played worship songs at home, she felt a peace in her heart. Then, she told me to create a playlist of Christian songs for her! God is moving in her heart!

"As for my father, I found out he was released from prison. I thought it was good news. But it turned out that he had stage 4 nose cancer and they only released him for treatment. He was so weak and he only weighed 45 kilograms. Honestly, I wanted to pretend I didn't know anything. But there was a service coming where Pastor Lia was going to pray for the sick. So I plucked up all my courage and texted my father to invite him for service. After a few minutes, he replied, 'OK'!

"That day in service, I kept praying for God to move. Then, Pastor Lia asked those who needed healing to come up to be *prayed for. My father stood up and went forward! As I followed him to the front, I struggled on the inside. I still couldn't forgive him. But as Pastor Lia prayed for him, I laid my hands on him and prayed too. In that moment, somehow, every grudge I ever had against him was gone. And that day, as Pastor Lia prayed for him, I forgave my father.*

"A few months later, my father's condition improved and he returned to prison. I wrote a letter to him for Christmas. For the first time, I called him 'Dad'. I wrote:

Hi Dad,

This Christmas, I'm writing to let you know that you are forgiven. I know that things have not been easy for everyone and especially you over the past 10 years or more. As you read this, know that you do not need to feel sorry or guilty about the past anymore. I no longer blame you for my life.

Today, my life has been changed ever since I knew God and I believe you could too. I am a testimony of how God has enabled me to forgive, so you shall also forgive yourself.

Leave your past, and your past will leave you.

God is very much still in control over our lives and I know that He will always be there with you each and every step of the way.

Live a life for God, start afresh in life again.

谢谢你多年来对我的关心、出狱后要好好做人。

20 December 2016

Love,
Klennan

Klennan's letter to his father – the first time he calls him 'Dad'.

Hi Dad,

This Christmas, I'm writing to let you know that you are forgiven. I know that things have not been easy for everyone and especially you over the past 10 years or more. As you read this, know that you do not need to feel sorry or guilty about the past anymore. I no longer blame you for my life.

Today, my life has been changed ever since I knew God and I believe you could too. I am a testimony of how God has enabled me to forgive, so you shall also forgive yourself.

Leave your past, and your past will leave you. God is very much still in control of our lives and I know that He will always be there with you each and every step of the way.

Live a life for God, start afresh in life again.

谢谢你多年来对我的关心, 出狱后要好好做人。*(Translation: Thank you for all the care you've shown me through the years, be a good person once you've come out of prison.)*

Love, Klennan
20 December 2016

"But God was not done yet! One afternoon, my aunt told me that there was a letter for me. It was from my dad. He wrote to me from prison:

Dearest Klennan

Hope that everything is OK with you. I'm so surprise to receive your card and more even so you have forgiven me as a lousy father. "Thanks God."

Glad that you have found peace in God, trust Him completely and follow His lifestyle, for sure this is the right path.

As for your studies, I would encourage and support throughout. this I can promise. Also remember this, the only way to improve the quality of life is through education.

For myself, my health has getting better and now my weight is around 70kg. I have just completed my Christian Intensive Religious Counseling Programme (CIRCP) for the past eight months. And also attending bible study every Tuesday and chapel service on Sunday afternoon, my guitar has improve a lot, I even play during praise and worship.

Please do care more for your sister, she is the only sibling to you so treasure her, if possible bring her to know Christ. Show her this letter cos what I've told you is also what I'm going to tell her either. Would it be nice to have a card from her also? Do take care of yourself and continuous to walk on God's way.

"GOD BLESS"

Love, faithfully Dad.
22 Jan 2017.

Klennan's dad replies from prison.
This is their longest and deepest
conversation since he was a child.

"I couldn't stop crying. These letters were the longest and deepest conversations we ever had. I have always been praying for my family's salvation. But I never expected that my dad would be the first to accept Jesus! I was also so amazed to hear that my dad is healthy! Now, he is both physically and spiritually healed!

"From a drug addict to a church guitarist bringing down the presence of God... Truly, God is a God of redemption! My mum has also stepped into Heart of God Church for service before! This is just the start of God moving in my family. I believe that my whole family will be saved one day!

"Today, I'm a leader in church. I was also given the opportunity to be a guitarist on the children's church worship team. All this is only possible because of God. As Pastor Lia preached before, my pain has become a platform of proclamation of God's goodness in my life.

"I want to thank God for finding me, redeeming my past and giving me hope for my future. I also want to thank Pastors for being my spiritual parents.

"Pastor How, when I first shared my testimony, you told me that one day you would bring me to change the world with you. You really brought me to Taiwan to share my story! I am really changing the world with you. It was also my very first time taking a plane! Thank you Pastor. It's really a dream come true.

"Because of God and HOGC, I can have a future and a hope! From my generation onwards, it will be different!"

Klennan's first time on a plane to Taiwan to share his testimony to over 6,500 pastors and leaders at a conference in 2018. (Bottom Left) A proud Pastor How cheering Klennan on from the side. (Bottom Right) Having a meal with Pastor Lia and Pastor How after Strong Church Hong Kong Conference 2019.

How

Amen, Klennan!!

Truly he has risen above his background. Klennan was commissioned as an officer in the Singapore Air Force. It's a position bestowed upon young men who exhibit the character of a gentleman and the qualities of a leader. After a stint in the army, he is now in university. And at the time of this writing, he has just been awarded a full-year scholarship from our Scholarship and Opportunity Fund. In church, Klennan serves in the Visuals Production ministry. He is also leading a group of youths from similar backgrounds. Having tasted the Lord and knowing that He is good,

Klennan commissioned as an officer in the Singapore Air Force.

Klennan's greatest passion is to share the love of God. He has brought at least 50 people to church to date.

Those of you in HOGC may wonder why I always tell youths that from their generation onwards, it will be different. Well, because a long time ago, it was what God told me.

My grandfather was a temple medium. (For my Western friends, he is like a shaman, practicing voodoo, going into a trance, and summoning demonic spirits for money.)

My father was a good father to me but a bad husband. He was a womanizer with a bad temper. He physically abused my mom... almost weekly. When I was a kid, I would hide whenever they fought. My modus operandi was to pretend to be asleep. When I grew older and bigger in size, my mom would drag me into their fights as her protector. So now I graduated to refereeing and breaking up fights. As expected, my mom was depressed, addicted to sleeping pills, and suicidal. So by my secondary school years, I was promoted to a new role – First Responder – literally saving my mom from overdosing on pills. My childhood memories were a blur of fights, blood, frantic searches for mom, talking her off buildings, hospital visits, and repeat.

When I gave my heart to Jesus, He was my *hope*. He gave me a purpose. Jesus gave me meaning in life. Now you know why I have never backslid from Jesus a single day, because He is my lifeline. I will never forget how Jesus saved me. One day, after their usual fights... after cleaning up the broken glass... after settling my mom, I went on my knees. That's when I heard the voice of my Father in my spirit: *"From you and your generation onwards, it will be different."*

From your generation onwards, it will be different.

So when I tell Y³, Klennan, and the hundreds of kids in church "From your generation onwards, it will be different," guess who I am talking about?

Yes... I am talking about... me.

A long time ago... when I was a young man, *Jesus* gave me hope.

Now I bring the same words of hope to other young men and women.

What made Pastor How write letters to fatherless youths every Father's Day? Find out in this preview of *GenerationS Volume 2.*

Mindset Shift #2
GENERATIONS - Reinforcements Not Replacements

Isaiah 58:12
"... You shall raise up the foundations of many *GenerationS...*"

GenerationS is having layers and layers of leaders at the same time.

GenerationS enables us to build a Deep Bench
and have an endless pipeline of leaders.

Lia 🪀

Slash. Poison. Burn. Three aggressive words for three treatment protocols so necessary to fight for life.

In 2012, I went through a whole year of surgeries (slash), chemotherapy (poison) and radiation (burn) to overcome stage 3 breast cancer. My cancer had spread to my lymph nodes, thus requiring dose-dense schedule chemotherapy. It essentially meant that there was shorter recovery time between treatment cycles. The usual rest cycle is three weeks in between chemotherapy sessions. But mine was two weeks. That could make chemotherapy more effective for a relatively young person like me with stage 3 breast cancer but it also increased the risk of more side effects. In light of that, you can imagine the feeling I had when all my treatments ended in November that year.

Slash! Dose-dense poison! Burn! Let me add a last word: *Phew!*

2012 was a significant year in another way. I received an insurance payout because of my cancer. Together with profits from our personal family business (yes, we also have a business. If you want to read more about it, Pastor How wrote a series on PastorHow.com) and all our insurance money, we gave $1 million to the church Building Fund! To the rational mind, it does not make sense. What if cancer comes back? We will need money for a rainy day.

But in sports, they say the best defence is offence. In the year that the devil set us back, the best defence we could put up was an attack. Both How and I were determined to move forward and gain ground even when we were down in the valley. My insurance is in God and because we love the House of God, we gave it all to church! I need insurance but I put my faith in God.

People asked me after my treatments were over how I would live life differently. Many cancer survivors say, "My life has changed so much after cancer." Some say, "I want to retire and spend more time with my family." Some people, after cancer, change to a job they love. Well, all these things are good. But not everyone is the same.

For me, after cancer, I asked myself, should I change anything?

The answer is — no. I wouldn't change anything.

So my life has *not* changed after cancer.

I have dedicated my life to young people. I am going to continue to devote my life to young people. I will continue to work with youth, lead them, pastor them, believe in them, disciple them and build GenerationS in Heart of God Church!

My Life Verse: Isaiah 58:12
"... You shall raise up the foundations
of many *GenerationS*..."

Many years ago, God spoke to me in this verse. It is my life verse.

Isaiah 58:12
... You shall raise up the foundations of many generations...

More than 20 years later, by the grace of God, we now have 6 GenerationS of leaders. Each generation is three to five years apart. The 1st Generation of leaders includes homegrown pastors in their 30s, while the newest generation rose up to be leaders when they were as young as 14 years old!

GenerationS is a key word in Heart of God Church. You hear every leader, every department, every member using this word. It has been a buzzing, operative word for 20 years. Yet we waited 20 years to write this book because we are still busy doing it!

Let me explain to you exactly what GenerationS means. The word *GenerationS* means different things to different people.

When we say GenerationS, people think of succession. People think of the older person dying and a younger person taking over. Well, that is succession. GenerationS is not succession. GenerationS is having layers and layers of leaders *at the same time* serving God together. It is not a 40-year gap between generations but only a 3–5-year gap.

So when I say GenerationS, I do not mean succession. Because succession is all about replacement. *GenerationS are Not Replacements. GenerationS are Reinforcements.*

GenerationS are Not Replacements.
GenerationS are Reinforcements.

Nobody is replaced! It is the younger people rising up, serving and leading alongside the older generations, *not replacing* them. It is having layers and layers of leaders serving God *at the same time*. Nobody is being replaced.

That is one of the reasons Heart of God Church is a Strong Church. We are not into replacing leaders. Neither are we into phasing out older youths. But these older youths are *reinforced* as the younger leaders rise to serve alongside them.

Every story has its origin. Our genesis of GenerationS started with a group of 9 teenagers. I named them the 9 Stones. In 1999, I started a youth group for these 9 youths because they looked listless in children's church and lost in adult services. Too old for children's church, too young for older services. This generation got on fire for Jesus. They grew up.

When they started growing up, I went back down to the next generation to start another group. But this time, I brought some of the 1st Generation leaders with me.

So we launched Zone F in 2006 with 20 people. It consisted of 13–14-year-olds (again, yes!). This group grew up as well.

In 2013, we launched another youth group to reach the 13–14-year-olds. Zone M started with 114 people. Again in 2016, we created another group called Zone Z. The average age of that zone was 12.9! We launched it with 100 people.

Then in 2021, during one youth service, we launched yet another youth group – Zone A (Gen Alpha)! They were 200 people, with an average age of 13.4!

Every generation of young people in our church, they Grow Up and Grow Old together in their generation. In HOGC, every few years, we start a new youth group. We keep going back down to reach the young ones. Just imagine yourself running down an upward escalator!

Young people grow up so quickly. Today they are 13, and in the blink of an eye, they are 18! We keep going back down for another generation, another generation, another generation. We do that intentionally. We build the GenerationS deliberately. We want to keep reaching the 13-year-old, the 14-year-old.

Remember: ***GenerationS are Not Replacements. GenerationS are Reinforcements.***

1999 - Pastor Lia launched the first
youth group – the 9 Stones

2006 - Zone F launch

2013 - Zone M launch

2016 - Zone Z launch

2021 - Zone A launch

We know the church is reinforced and steeled with great strength when there are layers and layers of leaders. We keep running down that moving escalator to build young leaders. Many churches have one or two layers of leaders, ministry volunteers and staff. But in HOGC, we want more than one or two layers. We want *many* layers of leaders serving God *at the same time*! GenerationS enables us to have an *endless pipeline of leaders.*

DEEP BENCH

Now, if you whisper the word *GenerationS* with a strong emphasis on the 'S' to any leader in our church, their eyes will immediately light up with respect for you. Let me tell you a secret. In our church, there is another buzzword: *Deep Bench.* If you also throw in the word *Deep Bench* in your whisper, that could earn you a standing ovation. If not, those two words should get you a backstage pass to see how each church department is built during our all-access intensive training course, HOGC Xperience!

Deep Bench is a sports term. It means that when one team is playing on the court, there are many substitutes sitting on the bench. They can be called on to play anytime. They are not inferior players. They are equally skilled! So the standard does not drop when the crew from the deep bench is called upon. That is what a quality deep bench means. In NBA basketball lore, the Golden State Warriors won championships because of the starting players on court *and* its quality deep bench of players such as Andre Iguodala. He was called the Sixth Man.

The sixth man in basketball is a player who is not a starter. However, he is the first player to be substituted in. They activate the sixth man off the bench more often than the other reserves. When you have a sixth man, it usually means that your team has incredible depth because the sixth man is usually so talented that he can easily be the starter for most other teams!

In HOGC, we believe in the Deep Bench. We believe in having many sixth men on the bench in every department in our church! That is why we are always training up many reinforcements to serve God in all the departments. I believe strongly that the House of God shall have no lack of people serving Him!

THERE ARE MANY BENEFITS TO HAVING A DEEP BENCH

On Fire but Don't Burn

A Deep Bench in our church helps ensure our faithful people keep being on fire but don't burn out. The perennial problem with most churches is that once they build one good team they use them every weekend till Jesus Christ comes back! As a Christian in my teenage years, I can almost swear that I saw cobwebs forming under the arm of the *only* organist our church had! Deep Bench ensures that you don't have to tap on the same team. Another team can serve as the first team rests and the quality does not drop. (I hear burnt-out leaders heave a sigh of relief here!)

Another HOGC buzzword? *Sustainable* – which means *able to keep at a good pace.* We want our crew to serve at a sustainable pace so that nobody burns out. In HOGC, we are volunteer-reliant. So we want to take care of our volunteers. A crew in our church only serves a maximum of twice a month. With the Deep Bench in church, everybody dares to be on fire for Jesus and nobody needs to burn out!

Expand but Don't Weaken

We don't want to be a church that is a mile wide but an inch deep. Expansion is good but don't weaken your church. With a Deep Bench, if the church expands into new grounds (e.g., global, missions) the local church which is home base will always be strong.

The ideal goal HOGC strives for is to have three different teams in every department. One team will be serving at home base, the second team will either be sent out for missions or training new crew and the third team will be doing the most important – resting!

Having a Deep Bench has enabled us to do missions the way we do. In 2018 and 2019, we brought 143 and 212 ministry crew respectively to run the Strong Church Hong Kong Conference. It was like exporting a full conference. Our crew did everything from the ground up. They ran everything from the worship team, sound, operations and media to ushering, security, hosts, décor and even building maintenance! Even the crew who served in Hong Kong were rostered and did not have to serve every session. Both years, we still ran services at home without compromising quality! Expand but don't weaken!

And back in 2018, we also brought 85 members to Chiang Mai, Thailand, when HOGC had the wonderful opportunity to partner John and Lisa Bevere in running a conference. Again, services at home still ran as per normal while 85 first-team, experienced ministry members were engaged in missions overseas!

I say this not to brag but to stress how important it is to build the Deep Bench in your church, because ultimately it is about people, people, people, which leads me to the next point.

Rest to Recreate

Rest is the next best-loved four-letter word after *love*. If you can rest your ministry volunteers on a regular basis, I assure you, they will come back refreshed, recharged and will recreate some fresh moves in their department. Take care of your volunteers!

Serve With No Expiry Date

Even as our youths grow up and enter into a new phase of life, they may not be able to serve as much as they want to. Work commitments or parenthood may reduce their ministry scope. But with Deep Bench, there will always be reinforcements. This ensures that the church will always have volunteers serving at a high capacity. More importantly, this also liberates and enables people at different stages of life to serve at a level best suited to them, even if it means serving at a lower capacity. Everyone in HOGC enters into each new demanding 'grown up' phase of life with confidence because they know they can continue to serve in church with no expiry date. Deep Bench is about people, people, people.

WHY AREN'T DEEP BENCHES MORE COMMONLY SEEN IN CHURCHES?

The toughest hurdle in people development in church is when those with ministry experience view the new, younger crew as a threat to themselves. From the usher ministry to platform ministry – any ministry you name – you see the veterans holding tight to their post, refusing even an inch of space for the younger people. Why is this so? That is because the older generation fears being replaced! The younger generation is viewed as pests who are so competitive that they would even arm wrestle their grandmothers for a glass of water! Replacement fear is so commonplace that it has become part of the cultural wallpaper in most churches. It is time for churches to have an epochal advance in ministry by having a seismic shift in mindset! GenerationS are *Not Replacements* but *Reinforcements*!

If you can assure the veterans that the younger generation is *not there to replace them* but to *reinforce them,* you can start building the Deep Bench.

I am constantly telling the experienced generation of older youths:

"You are not threatened. You are secure in who you are."

Then I turn to the fresh-faced, wide-eyed younger generation and teach them:

"You are not arrogant. You are grateful for what you have."

To the young crew, we tell them that the seasoned trainers do not have to give time to train them. But they *choose to*. So they ought to be grateful and not act entitled.

We then tell the older generation that the young guys are *not here to replace* you but *reinforce* you. They are not waiting for you to slip up or die (whichever comes first) so that they can take your place! The young generation is *not here to push you out* but to *push you up*!

> ## The young generation is not here to push you OUT but to push you UP!

I keep assuring both the older and younger generations. Assurance is not just talk but you must follow it up with action.

HOGC's philosophy of Deep Bench is fleshed out in the life of a young bassist. He came to Heart of God Church when he was just five years old. He is now in his mid-20s and is a key bassist and worship team leader in church.

In his own words, he describes himself as the quietest person and the most passive about almost everything. But he loves music and joined our School of Worship at 12. By 13, he made his debut as a bassist in front of 700 people in our main services. I must applaud our SOW instructors! SOW and the first generation of trainers made his dream come true. He also became an SOW instructor himself.

Years later, we asked him again what his dream was. He said it was to be a worship team leader. The worship team leader plans the rehearsals, musical arrangements and pulls the entire team together for the weekend services.

Seeing his dream and how he was all in, we decided to empower him by subsidising a brand new bass guitar for him. And knowing that his roles required communication abilities, I personally trained him in speaking and communicating. I knew words were not his strong suit but in HOGC, we love to make your dreams come true. I met him every weekend for six consecutive weeks to train him how to think in structured thoughts, how to communicate precisely in point form and how to be bold. Why six weeks? Because it takes time to form a permanent habit. I am so happy to say that when I see him conduct debriefs for the worship team after services now, I can hear his structured thoughts and clear communication! It takes a village in HOGC to make someone successful!

Our commitment to carving out a Deep Bench has made this young bassist flourish. With his success at a higher level, the landscape of the entire worship team in church improved too. This young bassist used to play bass on most weekends but now, you only see him on some weeks. Why? Because there are other young bassists that he has trained in SOW who have risen up, not to replace him but *reinforce* him in the bass section! The younger bassists have not pushed him out but in reality, they freed him up for more weeks of rest. In actual fact, the younger generation has pushed him *up* instead because he has developed another set of skills as a worship team leader! Now he is skilled in two things. He plays bass and also serves as a worship team leader! How cool is that? He is being reinforced, not replaced! He has been pushed *up,* not pushed out!

As pastor of Heart of God Church, you don't know how gratifying it is to see each generation reinforcing the previous. And then see at the other end of the spectrum, the experienced veterans selflessly training, imparting and discipling the younger generations.

I never tire of seeing how, during worship team soundcheck, a trainer would run home to get a piece of equipment for a younger generation musician just so that the new guy can play better. Older generations who are richer in skills and finances, often accompany their younger charges to buy their first instrument.

During COVID-19, the lockdown put a dampener on the progress of a very young bassist on our team. He had nothing to practise with at home. Upon hearing it, our veteran bassist Ming Rong personally and promptly delivered his own bass guitar to the youth's house! He said he remembered that when he was 15 and he dreamt of playing on the worship team, his SOW instructor Peck Lian lent him a bass for practice.

16 years later, he is doing the same for a youth.

Such acts displaying the Deep Bench spirit are not just in the worship teams. HOGC's IT Ministry was recruiting intensely during the pandemic. They even took in youths who did not have prior background in IT.

Veteran bassists, Peck Lian and Ming Rong.

Trainers Hendro and Henry patiently imparted skills to them, mainly over Zoom. They came up with a training syllabus and ensured there were homework assignments for the youths. After one month of training, two youths were fluent enough in IT to revamp the homepage of our church website! By the way, one of them was also our front of house engineer whose ministry was put in cold storage when church services were decentralised. They coded and styled the buttons, text and pictures for our church website. The enhancements helped direct new visitors on our church website seamlessly to our online services. Two selfless trainers raised two new youths with no IT literacy from the next generation! The pipeline of leaders and crew is healthy!

Today, these events are still taking place in HOGC in every department because the mandate to build GenerationS still runs deep after more than 20 years.

I implore you. Don't let your church grow old. There are GenerationS waiting to be birthed in your church. Grow your church younger, not just bigger. It is possible to build GenerationS, and out of that a Deep Bench in every single department of your church. I am cheering for you!

I am right now in my 9th year of being cancer-free. What am I looking forward to? Heart of God Church will always be a *home* and *training ground* for youths. Within my dream window are the 8th Generation, 9th Generation, 10th Generation...

Tip of the cap and bow to the past for the last 20 years. But we must continue to vibe future GenerationS waiting to be discovered and built in the next 20!

GROWING YOUR OWN PASTORS

GenerationS has made Heart of God Church unique. One of Heart of God Church's hallmarks is that all three of our currently ordained pastors are homegrown. Actively building a GenerationS church has helped us unlock an age-old stranglehold on the practice of just hiring pastors from outside of the church. Your own spiritual sons and daughters carry your spiritual DNA. They are naturals at catching and imparting the vision of the church.

In HOGC, when we are passionate about reaching young people, we open ourselves to countless opportunities to shape those with a pastor's calling over their lives – from as young as 13 years old! We have a chance to encourage them *before* they become pastors! Shape them, mould them, equip them into becoming capable and godly shepherds.

Pastor Lynette is one of our three homegrown pastors. She broke the age curve because she came in as an eight-year-old. At that age, her leadership leanings were already evident. She fit into a crowd five years older than her, hence, among the 9 Stones she was the youngest. Before being part of HOGC, this little dynamite of a go-getter had hatched a plan. She wanted to wean herself off adult-provided transport and was planning to never go back to her church once she was able to travel on her own. She disliked church that much. Kids schemed to run away from home but this kid planned to run away from church! Thank God, He intervened even if the formidable plans were thought up by a resolute eight-year-old. Pastor Lynette then came to our church and like they said, the rest was history. Even her history-making herculean feats are legendary.

At 14, she was already in charge of our Vacation Bible School programme for the whole youth department. Right now at 32, she and her husband Pastor Charleston are the pastoral oversights of the church. She is overseeing 3,000 people. During the 2020 pandemic, this extrovert was suffering tremendously during the lockdown. Personality aside – as a mother of a 7.5-month-old, lockdown was made even more stressful. But she pulled steel out of her will and together with Pastor Charleston, grew the church from 4,000 to 5,200 from their living room via Zoom and many out-of-the-box training sessions with the pastoral leaders. She now wears another leadership title: Pastor Pandemic-Proof.

That is the kind of woman leader she is. We often quip that in HOGC, the women leaders will give birth standing up if they need to! 😄 As a woman leader, I stand at the wings and smile, watching this young, spunky, feisty girl become a godly icon. Whatever HOGC has sown into her life, it is now being replicated in the thousands she leads.

Let's hear it directly from her:

Eight-year-old Lynette with Pastor Lia after children's church.

"I came to church at eight years old. I am honoured to be in the very first generation of youth in Heart of God Church. I have been in HOGC for 24 years.

"When I was 12, I told Pastor Lia I liked to sing! Before I knew it, she auditioned me, and she said, 'You have a good voice. I like your voice.' And soon, I was on the worship team! That was the first time I felt affirmed that I could sing.

"Pastor Lia also personally paid for my vocal lessons for two whole years. She invested in me. As a 14-year-old, Pastors empowered me to plan an important event in church – Vacation

Bible School. Planning that event grew my confidence as a leader. In that same year, Pastor Lia asked me if I had a dream to worship lead! I said yes! And she asked, 'When?' I said, 'Um... When I am 18?' Then she said, 'Lynette, how about now? You will worship lead. And I will train you.' I was shocked! She then trained me to worship lead not in children's church but in the main service!

"After my debut, Pastors gave me a book on worship. In it was a note: 'Dear Lynette, always before the Audience of One. Love you much always. Pastor Lia & Pastor How. 2003, Worship Leading Debut.' It meant a lot to me.

"Once, Pastor Lia laid hands and prayed for all of us leaders. Our church had fewer than 200 people then. She asked us to see with our eyes of faith how God would use us. That day, we saw visions of ourselves on stage leading thousands of people! Back then, we already saw the Heart of God Church of today! It was so powerful! We were so captivated. We had such a sense of destiny. We knew that one day HOGC was going to change the world.

"Pastor Lia also gave me the greatest privilege to preach in services. Once, before I preached, she sent me this text: 'Jeremiah 1:7-10. "But the Lord said to me:... 'For you shall go to all to whom I send you, and whatever I command you, you shall speak. Do not be afraid of their faces, for I am with you to deliver you,' says the Lord." Lynette, three words for you – Lead, Preach & Sing.'

"I read the message right before service started.

"As I stood on stage to preach, not only did I feel faith in my spirit, I felt so empowered by my pastors.

"When I was 23, Pastors told five of us that they wanted to send us to take our Master of Divinity! They wanted to give us young leaders the opportunity that they didn't have. My family was not rich and I could never afford to go overseas to take my Masters.

"For our graduation, Pastors flew more than 30 hours to be there. They were just sitting there smiling and clapping for us. And I kept *thinking to myself, my pastors could have sent themselves to take their Masters but instead they sent us. I never thought I could take my Masters but I did. This is only possible because my pastors selflessly created many opportunities for me.*

"Right now, I am doing the same for the next generation. In 2016, we started the youngest zone at the time – Zone Z! Many of them were 12 and 13 years old. I saw so much of my younger self in all of them! And just five years later in 2021, we reached down and launched a brand new zone of 13-year-olds, Zone A! As I had been believed in, I am now doing the same for these 6th Gen and 7th Gen young leaders.

"Out of the 1st Generation of leaders, we now have three ordained pastors in Heart of God Church. Thank God, He intervened in my life! He dismantled my escape-from-church plot and started assembling a plan to call and equip me to become a pastor. I am forever grateful to Him and HOGC!"

Lynette, homegrown pastor: From an eight-year-old girl to an anointed preacher and worship leader. She oversees 3,000 people together with her husband, Pastor Charleston.

Lia ⚾

The first 9 Stones were distinct characters. On kinder days, I thought they were colourful. On bad days, I thought God had sent them to humble me. Even Australia has a wonderful tourist site called The Twelve Apostles. And me? I had 9 inexpressive Stones. Maybe I needed more punishment.

Pastor Lynette had learnt to say 'no' before she even knew the word 'yes' existed. But strong-willed kids turn out to be strong leaders when they are harnessed by God. They just have to be taught what to say 'no' to. Pastor Lynette learnt to flex her steel will against the pandemic. Turns out she said 'no' to COVID-19 setbacks and 'yes' to church growth!

Daniel was always in a corner, self-meditating, ruminating and at one point in his youth, I swear, he was levitating. You just never, never ever come between Daniel and his daily guitar practice. He is till today our most anointed, Bible-loving, skillful musician with a heart for God. You never want to come between him and Bible truth because he didn't just get his Master of Theological Studies to look good.

Dominic – you never go on holiday with Dominic. If the roller coaster ever malfunctioned, it meant Dom was on it. (True story. Happened in Australia.) He was the originator of many radical but fun activities that almost always got the 9 Stones into trouble. He is well-loved by his peers. His sense of adventure translated into a faith attitude in ministry!

Pastor Charleston was everyone's friend. There was no guile about Charleston. He was always available, so was his house. So the boys always hung out there, courtesy of Charleston's ever-welcoming generous parents. He is a legend. When Pastor How and I were cleaning our small church venue together with the 9 Stones, Charleston was the one who always presented the shiniest toilet bowl at the end! This boy is conscientious. We knew if he could be trusted with a toilet bowl, he could be trusted with pastoring the church. Pastor Charleston, when you are reading this, I would like to tell you that Pastor How and I have privately ordained you Master of the Mundane. Deep respect for you!

Pastor Garrett Lee was slightly older than everyone. He learnt to say 'yes' before he even knew 'no' was a word. Pleasant boy. While everyone talked at Charleston like a buddy, everyone liked to throw questions at Garrett. Over time, his smartness was evident. Everyone ordained him – Wiki-Lee.

Until today, Pastor Garrett is legendary in church for being brilliant. Like Wikipedia, you can ask him anything. He can tell you how to cook a sous vide egg to why the blood moon exists to deciphering complicated numbers on the balance sheet. If he had tried, I believe he could have also delivered his two babies by himself at home too.

Yet under all that smartness lies a heart that is so soft and quick to change when corrected with the truth of God. A true disciple of Christ.

Garrett came to church when he was 13. He played the guitar on the worship team and ran our overhead projectors for transparencies (yes ancient machines that flashed lyrics). He preached and led connect groups. At 16, he emailed us and said that he wanted to be a pastor. Our hearts leapt.

Pastor How took him under his wing to run events. Garrett was and still is an integral Events Director in our church. An all-rounded, capable young man! As a university student, he lifted the bar when he gave $10,000 to the Building Fund in a crucial year when we were moving into our third worship venue.

Then at 25, Pastor How told him, "I believe you can now be the head of the Finance and Accounts Department."

As our Finance Director handling millions of dollars, he ran into obstacles with the auditors. Nobody could believe that someone as young as him could be in charge of the Finance Department. They kept wanting to meet his boss in Finance. But he kept saying, "I am the head. I am in charge." All the auditors would ask the accounts staff incredulously, "How old is your boss? So young!" One auditor had so much trouble wrapping her mind around Garrett's age that she became difficult to work with. She probably thought the board game Monopoly was more right up Garrett's alley. Thank God, she didn't stay long in her job. This really young man on the other hand, excelled as Finance Director and went on to become a pastor and our church CEO!

Garrett, homegrown pastor: From a 12-year-old boy to preacher, Finance Director, CEO of HOGC and he is also the first of the 9 Stones to become a father.

There you have it — Pastor Garrett, Pastor Lynette and Pastor Charleston. Our very first three homegrown pastors. And the rest are all key heads of ministries in Heart of God Church. Have you ever looked at your youth group and done a facepalm? I did. Many times, way before the facepalm emoji was ever a thing. So I am qualified to tell you — dare to dream! They can become your key leaders and homegrown pastors too!

Seven of our staff have completed their Master of Divinity from Oral Roberts University and Regent University in the USA. And in the pipeline we have five more currently studying for their Masters as well and four of them are below 30 years old. Who knows how many more homegrown pastors will come through this pipeline?

Do you dare to dream GenerationS?

Do you dare to dream GenerationS of homegrown pastors?

FINAL THOUGHTS

Some people ask incredulously: "Can *my church* still be relevant to youths when I am in my 30s, 40s and 50s?" Yes it can – if you keep building GenerationS and never let up. Every generation will have a slightly older generation to lead them. In that sense, the youths you have built earlier will be your hands, feet, ears and heart on the ground, now leading the younger youths. They embody your heart, vision and values to the next generation. Now, our three homegrown pastors from the 1st Generation of youths carry our heart and vision down through the pipeline. It is so crucial to have each generation just a few years apart, not 40 years!

Then, the even more incredulous question: "Can *I* still be relevant to youths when I am in my 30s, 40s, 50s?" Yes you can. Until today (I just turned 50 in the year I am writing this book!), I am still ministering in youth services. I am still writing some of my sermons purely just for young people. I am still meeting youths to disciple them on a regular basis. I am still going crazy with them at the baseball batting cage. I am still relevant. You know why? I have never related to them just based on trends and cool looks. But I can still relate to them because spiritual principles are timeless. Love, belief and passion for young people can never be eroded by time. Vision and values are never the victims of passing epochs.

I have been doing the same thing for 20 years. I am still doing it. Yes, I am boring that way. But hey, like I always say, there are Miracles in the Mundane, Beauty in the Banal and Riches in the Routine!

There are Miracles in the Mundane, Beauty in the Banal and Riches in the Routine!

See Deep Bench implemented operationally in departments and GenerationS applied practically across ministries.

Lia

In this next part, we want to give the space to our homegrown pastors. They are from the original 9 Stones. They came in their teens, today they are ordained pastors in Heart of God Church. As we write our first book about GenerationS and empowering young people, we share our platform with them and give them a voice.

Pastor Charleston, Pastor Lynette, Pastor Garrett

Homegrown pastors, Heart of God Church

Introduction

Garrett: Charleston, Lynette and I came to Heart of God Church as teenagers, and over the next 20 years we grew in God and as leaders. In 2018, Lynette, Charleston and I were ordained as pastors at the age of 29, 30, 34 respectively.

When we were given the opportunity to take our Master of Divinity at Oral Roberts University in 2014, we learnt interesting subjects, such as Church History and Systematic Theology. Through the years, we have also read many leadership books where we learnt a lot of principles. However there are some lessons that can only be learnt when you are up close and personal with your pastors, and I guess that's what discipleship is all about. Some things are caught, not just taught. We learnt so many lessons just from observing Pastor How and Pastor Lia that maybe one day we have to write a book ourselves.

As the first three homegrown pastors, we believe there will be many more HOGC pastors to come through the GenerationS. For us, it is a sacred calling, and we have a responsibility to be good role models for future pastors. So, we would like to share with you seven lessons we learnt from our senior pastors.

7 Lessons We Learnt From Our Pastors

Lesson 1 - Keep the Office of the Pastor sacred.

Garrett: In recent times, we see many pastors and churches in financial or moral scandals. The Office of the Pastor was once sacred and respected, but is now unfortunately tarnished on the news and social media.

To Pastor How and Pastor Lia, this reproach breaks God's heart and is detrimental to the preaching of the gospel. That is why, one of their crusades in life is to redeem the Office of the Pastor.

In Singapore, one of the greatest mistrusts towards pastors is in the area of finances. That is why Pastor How and Pastor Lia are especially adamant in redeeming the Office of the Pastor in this area. In HOGC, they are the most generous givers. They were the first to give $1 million to our church from their family business. Beyond giving, they would even go to the extent of personally paying for all the renovations and furniture in their own office and the church's guest room. They have given more to the church than they have received.

On several occasions, I have personally observed how my pastors upheld the integrity of the Office of the Pastor.

Once, a businessman who started attending our church passed a gift to Pastor How and Pastor Lia. It was a cheque for $5,000. I was happy to see my pastors blessed, but what Pastor How and Pastor Lia did next was totally unexpected – they politely returned the cheque.

At first, I was puzzled because it is good to honour and bless pastors. In fact, it is an edifying and biblical culture. But for this person, Pastors knew that it would not be healthy for him. I saw Pastors' wisdom and heart in how they responded. They acknowledged his generosity and in a card to him, they wrote, "... We do not want to start our relationship like this... Let HOGC be an oasis for you and your family... a place where you can simply worship, grow, get connected..."

I learnt how Pastor How and Pastor Lia made decisions out of the integrity of their hearts and never let money cloud their judgment.

Another time, there was a church member who was struggling with a huge credit card debt. It was not due to bad spending habits, but because his previous senior pastor took advantage of him. His ex-pastor misled him to use his credit card to pay for church rental and never paid him back despite multiple reminders. Because of this, he was rolling over credit card debt.

When Pastor How and Pastor Lia heard about this, they called him to their office. They passed him an envelope, and in it was $5,000.

Pastor How said, "On behalf of the Office of the Pastor, I want to apologise to you. This is not how a pastor should conduct himself. Here, take this money to clear your debt."

As I witnessed what happened, I was so moved. Why would Pastor How and Pastor Lia even apologise and take responsibility for the mistake of another pastor?

They simply wanted to redeem the Office of the Pastor. I will never forget what they said to me. *"If the Office of the Pastor is degraded, then no one would dream to be a pastor anymore. We would lose generations of potential pastors."*

I learnt that the Office of the Pastor is sacred, and not to be taken lightly or cheaply.

Lesson 2 - Live simply. Be contented.

Lynette: Many people would not think twice before getting a cup of bubble tea or Starbucks. But when HOGC first started, these were luxuries that both Pastors could not afford. Yet, I recall seeing Pastor Lia's contented smile drinking her 80-cent Teh-C (local milk tea) back in the day. Even up till today, a common sight we see in the office: Pastor How having his $3 Khong Guan biscuits between meetings or Pastor Lia giving out her favourite cheap local fare called sardine puffs to everyone.

For over 20 years, they have been living way up north (our church is in the east!). Pastors were receiving no pay or little pay during the pioneering years so they could only afford to stay in Woodlands – one of the cheapest estates in Singapore. Once, our staff had to deliver some files to Pastors' house from church. It was more than an hour's journey! He joked, "Pastors live closer to Malaysia than to church!" In those years, I never heard them complain. Instead they would say that they could use the time in the car to pray or catch up with each other.

Contentment has nothing to do with one's financial status. It is not about having little or much. Twenty years on, even with more, they are content with living simply. I suppose this is the secret Paul learnt:

Philippians 4:12 (NIV)

… I have learned the secret of *being content* in any and every situation…

Lesson 3 - Never touch God's glory.

Charleston: Over the past 20 years, Pastors never allowed us to celebrate their birthdays during the service. Not even a simple cake or birthday song. Every personal celebration was held outside of the church service. To them, the service is holy and solely reserved for Jesus.

The glory always belongs to Jesus. I remember whenever Pastor Lia preaches for Miracles & Breakthroughs Services, we would see healings, miracles and the power of God being released. One thing that has always struck me is what happens at the end of every M&B Service. As the crowds leave, Pastor Lia always does one thing first: she goes behind closed doors, gets down on both knees and gives thanks to God.

Pastor How and Pastor Lia's hearts echo that of John's: "He must increase, but I must decrease." As pastors, we are not celebrities or divas but servants of God. We never touch God's glory.

Garrett: Pastoring is more than a vocation or duty. Pastor How and Pastor Lia have shown us that the Office of the Pastor is sacred. As pastors, let's uphold this office with utmost character and reverence. When we were ordained, we took this oath before God:

The Heart of God Church Pastor's Oath
I am committed to live worthy of the sacred calling of God on my life, to uphold a life of integrity and dignity befitting of the time-honoured office of a pastor and to be faithful to the eternal truth of the Bible.

May we continue to live this out for the rest of our lives.

Lesson 4 - Do the important, not the impressive.

Charleston: I remember in the mid-2000s, our church was at a size where people started telling us we should write songs and produce an album. Having an HOGC album sounded impressive and exciting. But Pastor Lia had a different idea. She gathered the leadership team and said, "Recording an album should not be our focus now. We should invest our time to build a pipeline of musicians and singers. If not, our veterans will burn out."

Out of that, she started the School of Music and School of Worship – the La Masia of the HOGC Worship Team. Instead of going into the spotlight with an album, we put our hands back to the plough to build other musicians. Our team didn't write songs but wrote syllabi, training materials and invested into the next generation of musicians. Building the Deep Bench was the more important and strategic choice to Pastor Lia.

Years later... we decided we were ready to release our first album. By then, there were more than 200 people in the Worship Team and Sound Ministry. We also had a well-oiled system of recruiting and training new musicians. Today, whenever guests visit our church, many of them are intrigued by the size of our homegrown worship team. They usually wonder, *What's the secret?*

Well, that's because years ago, Pastor Lia chose to focus on the important, not the impressive.

And this is the origin of HOGC's mantra in the mid-2000s – ***Do the Important, Not the Impressive.***

Lesson 5 - Use every opportunity for discipleship.

Charleston: One question most overseas pastors ask is: "What programme and syllabus do you use to disciple your members? They are so trained and well-discipled." While we have some teaching materials, the real discipleship happens outside the classroom. That's the Jesus-way of discipleship.

One of my most impactful discipleship moments happened during... Pastor Lia's cancer. In fact, it happened right in the middle of her chemotherapy treatment! Who would have thought that even chemo could be used for discipleship?

Pastor Lia invited some of us to join her chemotherapy session. To most, it's probably a painful and private affair to go for cancer treatment. However, Pastor Lia saw an opportunity for discipleship. She said we would usually not get a chance to see what cancer patients go through. This opportunity would help us better empathise with people who are sick.

I was only 24 years old then. I didn't know anything about sickness and it was my first time in a cancer treatment facility. Everything was foreign, cold and clinical. Yet there was a warmth when Pastor Lia smiled and asked the nurse how her day was. Pastor Lia sat down on the treatment chair and rolled up her sleeves. I noticed Pastor Lia's arm had swelled from the constant pricking of needles. The nurse could not hit a vein, and she repeatedly jabbed Pastor Lia's arm with the needle. The nurse was apologising profusely, but Pastor Lia simply smiled back at the nurse, and told her assuringly, "It is okay, you can try again." As I saw the thick needle prick through the arms of Pastor Lia, I couldn't believe she had to go through such pain every session. I saw the courage and resilience of Pastor Lia that day.

Seeing all the cancer patients at the treatment centre, for the first time, their challenges and pain became real to me. That day, I learnt empathy. Now when I hear someone is sick, I have a reference point of what it could possibly mean. When I pray for the sick, there is a deeper compassion for them.

Leaders, just like Pastor Lia, you can use your pain for a purpose. It could be the most powerful discipleship lesson.

Garrett: Discipleship is also leading by example. In our church, members are rostered to help clean the church premises and toilets, because this is our home. For the first 10 years of the church, Pastor How and Pastor Lia put themselves on the cleaning roster. Armed with a mop and pail, they would tackle every dirt and stain in the toilets. (We often joke that in HOGC, leadership starts from cleaning toilets.) I realised that no role in the church was beneath them. Pastor How and Pastor Lia showed us that as leaders we should never expect people to do something we are not first willing to do ourselves. Our pastors not only taught but lived out this principle: **If serving is beneath you, then leading is beyond you.**

Leaders, let's use every opportunity for discipleship.

Lesson 6 - Being a parent and pastor – not 'either-or' but 'both-and'!

Lynette: 'Finding success in both the church front and the home front'.

This could possibly be one of the biggest challenges for every pastor. As Pastor Lia's niece, I saw them in their private lives. Many know them as spiritual parents, but I also saw them as Rinnah's parents. Here are some home front lessons that I have observed.

Both pastors were equally available for Rinnah, no matter how busy the church was. When they got off stage, Rinnah was at their centre stage. Swimming dates or essay writing 'dates' (or lessons) with Mama were some of her favourite activities. Mama was the best storyteller! Rinnah had her personal Hi-5 show right in the bedroom! I guess that's one of the benefits of having a preacher as your mum. When I would go over to their place, Rinnah would tell me with pride, "Today, Dad Dad is making mac 'n' cheese for me. He makes the BEST mac 'n' cheese in the whole world. Do you want?" And before I could reply anything, she would exclaim, "Dad Dad, Net Net says that she is VERY HUNGRY. She wants mac 'n' cheese too." Of course, I got to see the disciplining moments too. But I shall not embarrass Rinnah! (Don't I love you, Nana?)

While taking long flights with Pastors, I have also learnt a few travel hacks from them. It's as easy as 1-2-3:

1. Station yourself in front of your laptop.
2. For a family of three, pre-book the entire centre row of seats (usually four seats) by leaving one of the middle

seats empty. The idea is that lone travellers will not choose seats sandwiched in the middle and will avoid booking that seat. (Parents, you can thank me later!)

3. Cross your fingers and pray that it is not a full flight.

I remember when passengers were boarding and walking down the aisle, we would all be praying. Finally when the aircraft door closed, we would all exhale in relief haha. We got the full row to ourselves!!! Little but 'long' Rinnah could now stretch out between mum and dad. Pastor Lia prides herself on being able to create the best nest for her! It is amazing how Rinnah would sleep comfortably through every single red eye flight. Rinnah is so 'sleep-trained' now, even at 16, she can sleep through every turbulence or uncomfortable seat.

But there was once this hack failed. Maybe we did not pray enough, or perhaps it was simply a lonely man looking for some company? But on that particular red eye flight to Sydney, one guy chose to be sandwiched in the middle of the Tan family. That night, young Rinnah was half hugging, half lying on Pastor Lia throughout the flight. Pastor Lia was sitting in an awkward position as part-sofa-part-teddy-bear. Imagine being a body contortionist for eight hours. When we landed in Sydney, Pastor Lia's back muscles went into massive spasms. She was in so much pain that she was in bed for the following few days. Even walking to the toilet was next to impossible. In the end, she was unable to attend the conference that she flew eight hours for. Eventually, the doctor had to pump her with strong painkillers and she had to upgrade to business class for the return flight so that she could lie flat.

From these, I saw how Pastor Lia gave her best not just to church but to Rinnah. They are not just 24/7 pastors, but also 24/7 parents.

It was clear to Rinnah that she never had to compete with the church for her parents. She knew that they would always come home to her. Both of them were fully present at every milestone in her life. Now, Rinnah has grown up to love the church with the same fervency as her parents. To all the pastors and leaders who are starting a family in ministry,

I would like to encourage you that it is possible to have success in both the church front and the home front.

Lesson 7 - Real men respect women.

Charleston: As a male leader, one of the most powerful things I observe about Pastor How is how he values, respects and elevates women. On our staff team, we have a very special HR arrangement for working mothers. This stemmed from Pastor How's concern for working parents' childcare arrangements. So that is why right in our church office, there is a dedicated playroom for our working mothers to bring their children to. Lynette and I are able to leave our daughter in the playroom before we start work. While many career mums have to find alternative arrangements for childcare, Lynette is able to fully focus on both motherhood and ministry. Pastor How's heart is for all full-time staff to continue living their calling at all stages of their life, even when they become parents.

Just as Pastor How values and respects women, I feel challenged to empower women leaders around me. Men, let's allow the women to rise up and serve alongside us. If not, it will be a great disadvantage to the Kingdom of God. As Pastor Lia always shares: "Women carry 50% of God's plan on their shoulders."

Real men value and respect women. As I observe and learn from Pastor How, I am not just a better pastor, but a better husband, better father, better man.

Closing Words

Lynette: On our first trip to Tulsa to attend our Master of Divinity classes, we noticed that we were the youngest. Many of our classmates were much older. Many were in their 40s, 50s and some 60s. Initially, I thought it was just an interesting observation.

When we spoke to our dean, we suddenly realised the significance. Dr Thomson Mathew told us that in all of his 20 over years at the ORU

College of Theology and Ministry, he had never seen any senior pastor send their second guys to be more 'educated' than them. Especially if the 'Number Twos' were much younger than the senior pastors. Why? Because of the natural fear of being replaced and overtaken by someone more qualified.

Then he lowered his voice and said, *"Do not ever take Pastor How and Pastor Lia for granted. There's really no one like them in this world."*

The weight of that line sank into my heart. When Pastor How and Pastor Lia were in their 20s, they were young pastors who followed the call of God on their lives to pioneer HOGC. There was no scholarship available for them then. So our scholarship for our MDiv does not just reflect the generosity of my pastors' hearts, it also shows their selfless belief for the next generation in its purest form.

We are their Deep Bench. Their Reinforcements, not their replacements.

Homegrown Pastors Charleston, Lynette, Garrett.

Bonus! Hear Pastor Charleston, Pastor Lynette and Pastor Garrett preach.

Mindset Shift #3
Church Is Our Home, Not Just a House

The House of God must be a Home for Youths.
Home is not 'WHERE' but 'WHO'.
Church is not 'WHERE' but 'WHO'.

Traditionally: Believe ➜ Become ➜ Belong
This Generation: Belong ➜ Believe ➜ Become

Lia 🐝

During COVID-19, when church services were not allowed for months, our youths missed church so much that they built a virtual replica of Imaginarium in the Minecraft world.

Although we had online services and they could meet their friends, the youths still missed being in the physical building. They still missed attending in-person services. This is pretty mind-blowing. Youths will miss their friends, or handphone or pizza but they usually don't miss church.

How did this happen?

HOGC is built like a home.

If you want a Strong GenerationS Church, you need to build it like a home.

THE HOUSE OF GOD MUST BE A HOME FOR YOUTHS

A house is built by hand but a home is built by the heart. That is why we are the Heart of God Church. *The hand of God will build this House and the heart of God will build this Home.*

The church is the House of God and also the Home of Christians. It is the dwelling place of God and the spiritual residence of His children. All pastors know how to build the House of God but we often neglect the Home aspects.

A house is just a building. But when I am talking about a home, I am thinking of 'who'. Often we ask – 'where' is your house? But we inquire, 'who' is at home?

House has to do with 'where' while home has to do with 'who'. Home is where family and friends are. A home has warmth and love. It is about relationships. Home is not 'where' but 'who'.

Home is not 'WHERE' but 'WHO'.

Sometimes people ask you, "Where is your house?" And sometimes people ask you, "Where is your home?"

When you get those two questions, you usually answer, "My house? Well, I live in New York but home is Singapore because home is where my family is, where my friends are. It is where I grew up. Home is where I will go back to retire and die!" So *home* is all about relationships! It is *not about where* but about *who*.

Heaven is similar. Many people ask, "Where is heaven?" But the right question should be, "Who is in heaven?" God is in heaven. Heaven is His home! The great, big, benevolent God is in heaven. That is why we want to go to heaven – because of the Who!

Same for church – it is not so much 'where' is church as much as it is 'who' is in church. Our church must be a *home*. Church is *not 'where'* but *'who'.*

Where is your church? Well for us, HOGC is at Paya Lebar, a place in Singapore. For some of you, your church could be in a city in Australia or Indonesia or in a locality in South America.

Where is your church? It is at a place.

Who is in your church? My friends and family are in church!

Church is not a house, it is a *home*. Church is not a place but it is about *people and relationships*!

That is why even with COVID-19 bringing most of the world into a lockdown, church still goes on! We cannot gather in a building but that is alright because church is not about a place but about its *people*. Church is about *who*!

So wherever you gather with a small group of friends and family – that is church! You are the *who*.

Church is not 'where' but 'who'. Church is not about the place but the people. Church is our home. Church is about the people and relationships.

Church is not 'Where' but 'Who'.
Church is not about the Place but the People.
Church is our HOME.
Church is about the People & Relationships.

Everybody needs to hear the story of siblings Elliot and Eliora who live across the border from Singapore in Malaysia. These two youths usher in a new level of Christian commitment towards church.

Every weekend both of them will cross the border from Malaysia, stamp their passports and come to Heart of God Church in Singapore. It takes them at least 2.5 hours to come to church. There are four parts to their weekly journey.

1st part: A 15-minute bus ride from their home to the Malaysian immigration.

2nd part: Another bus ride across the border to the Singapore immigration and after clearing immigration, another bus ride to a Singapore train station.

For the 3rd and 4th parts, they take another train over 14 stations to get to our church! Sometimes when there are crowds at the immigration points, they will take up to four hours to come to our church. So they have to leave their home in Malaysia very, very early just to come over to attend church! But they never stopped coming. Missing church services was not an option for both. They are so on fire for Jesus that they have become leaders in our church.

Both siblings have proven that church is not about 'where' (four hours away, no sweat!), they came because of the 'who'. Jesus and deep godly friendships were enough reasons for them to make that regular, arduous journey.

Eliora explained, "I will always remember how my close church friends came all the way to my doorstep in Malaysia just to celebrate my birthday!" *That* is a real deep connection.

How and I have deliberately built HOGC as a *home*. When you step into our church services, before you even detect the scent from the diffuser in our church lobby, you will see *deep relationships* and a sense of *belonging* permeating our church atmosphere. That is the real aroma of a *home*!

That is how God has related to us.

That is how the Church should engage people.

> Psalm 100:3 (NIrV)
> I want you to realize that the Lord is God. He made us, and we *belong* to him. We are his people. We are the sheep *belonging* to his flock.

How

Here's the third mindset shift needed if you want to reach this generation. Traditionally, for a person to join a church, he or she goes through this sequence:

Believe → Become → Belong

He must first Believe, then Become a Christian. Let me add another "B" word, Behave. We expect the youth to Behave to our standards and expectations. And when we are satisfied, then we extend our fellowship and offer him church membership. It's almost like he is on probation until finally approved. Only then do we open our circle for him to Belong.

How many times do we see Christian parents warning their pristine children not to hang out with that smoking, gangster-looking kid? Or the pious Christian kids giving the eye to new kids who don't look the part or speak Christianese.

"Oh... but we are only trying to protect our saintly church youths from worldly corruption."

"Or worse... people might mistake them for our members, and it will bring a reproach to our church name."

And that is why this kind of church has about five kids left in the youth group.

This is not going to work for the young generation.

The youths want to know and feel that they Belong first, then they decide if they want to Believe and Become a Christian. This should be the sequence:

Belong → Believe → Become

In HOGC, after the youths feel like they Belong, they tend to take the next step to Believe. In case you haven't noticed, kids are not really into theology. They don't really care if your church teaches pre-tribulation rapture or can recite the Nicene Creed backwards. When they Belong, they find it easier to Believe in Christ.

Christianity is not just believing but also belonging. Jesus died for us not just so that we believe but that we belong. We are now part of

God's family. He is now our Father. We now belong to a spiritual home (the church) and eventually belong to an eternal home.

Traditionally: Believe → Become → Belong
This Generation: Belong → Believe → Become

Here's what we found in HOGC. When the youths Belong and Believe, they will almost naturally Become and Behave. Then we usually don't have to tell them to do this and stop doing that.

Wait... does it sound familiar in the Bible?

How did Matthew the tax collector "become" Matthew the disciple?

In Matthew 9, Jesus made him feel that he *belonged*... invited him to follow... went to his house, and hung out with him and his disreputable friends. In Matthew 10, the Bible announced the list of disciples and guess who was on that legendary list? Notice the sequence? *Belonging* first, then *behaving* like a Christian, and *becoming* a disciple.

Jesus made Zacchaeus feel he *belonged* by going to visit his house, then Zac decided to give away half his wealth to the poor and repay fourfold those he ripped off. If that is not *behaving*, I don't know what that is. And Jesus declared salvation has come to this house. They *became* a Christian household.

Jesus made the woman at the well, the woman with multiple partners, feel she *belonged*, and she stopped sinning and *behaved*.

I could go on and on. I think you get it.

Don't get me wrong. *Believing* and *behaving* and *becoming* are all very important. But perhaps we got the sequence wrong. When the sequence is out of order, people feel judged. When we send people the vibe that only if you behave then you can belong, they feel discriminated against. But when the sequence is right, Matthew becomes a great disciple, Zacchaeus becomes a generous giver and that woman at the well becomes a great evangelist.

So we have youths coming to church regularly for a whole year before believing and becoming Christians. It's a strange sight. Youths with cigarette breaths, boys spewing vulgarities, and girls spewing cleavages coming to HOGC regularly. (That's why we keep our air conditioning super cold, hopefully the girls will put on more layers. 😄)

We also have completely introverted and disengaged youths and you would think they are not interested, yet they come back week after week.

Geek, goth, gangster, hypebeast, hipster – they all come because they feel like they belong. It reminds me of David's motley crew. All who were down on their luck came around – losers and vagrants and misfits of all sorts. David became their leader (1 Samuel 22:2, MSG).

Then it begins to happen. Weeks and months later they start giving their hearts and lives to Jesus. When you visit HOGC, you will see 40–50 hands lifted up, responding to the altar call each service. Don't be mistaken. Most of these people are not first or second-time visitors. Many have been attending our services for months and on that day, they are finally ready to take that next significant step.

For all the pastors, preachers, and leaders reading this – this mindset shift is a game changer. It relieves us of the pressure to "get them saved" on their first visit. You are no longer on a 40-minute countdown to "close the deal" immediately. Now your initial goal is just to make the youths feel that they belong so that they will keep coming back.

"THIS IS OUR HOME"

It's 11:00pm on a Saturday night. Many youths are still hanging out in church. No sign of leaving. So I go to them and ask, "Shouldn't you be going home?"

They give me a cheeky reply, "Pastor, this is our home."

What is unique about HOGC is not just the two-hour service, but before and after. It is not the weekends but the weekdays. After school, the students hang out in church, especially on Fridays. On Saturday and Sunday, they are in church from 10-ish, preparing, having rehearsals and

Bible studies. After service, they hang out till 10-ish at night. And that is when and where the magic happens. New friends (we call Integrations) make friends with the HOGC people and develop real relationships. We emphasize to our people, *"Don't just be friendly. Be friends."*

It's not just about having friendly ushers and door greeters. We actually have to be real friends. "Welcome Home" is not just a tagline or a slogan on the wall.

Nobody wants to leave! HOGC young people hanging out in church, long after weekend services have ended. Our church is open even on weekdays for them to hang out and study together (Top: SingPost, Bottom: Imaginarium).

Lia 🔵

Cheryl grew up with abusive parents. Her parents would punish her by banging her head against the wall or making her kneel on the floor overnight till she could not walk properly the next morning. After school, she did not want to go home. So she wandered aimlessly around shopping malls till late. When she did go home, she hid in the toilet to get away from her family. Food was just rice or canned food.

At 13, Cheryl started work at McDonalds and Pizza Hut to survive. Many times her parents would take away the money she earned. That is why she learnt to hide her money in books and cupboards. Her grand plan was to save enough money and run away from home the day she turned 16. But that year, just before her birthday, a friend brought her to HOGC. During worship, love and comfort flooded her heart. She gave her heart to Jesus!

Then she started hanging out in church. She found a spiritual family. For the first time, she opened up about her life to someone. Her connect group even surprised her with a guitar in the exact colour and design that she wanted. We also put her on the church Scholarship and Opportunity Fund, which gave her an allowance every month. We did not want her to worry about her daily expenses and wanted her to have savings. She shared that she felt so loved for the first time in her life and was smiling a lot more than she ever did in her whole life. The greatest miracle? She even started to care for others! Everyone in school thought they met a new Cheryl!

When Building Fund came along, she said, "I am going to give back to my spiritual home!" So she pledged $3,000. She was only 17 years old then. Our leaders spoke to her, "Please cut down your pledge." But she insisted.

Every day after school, she worked and saved every cent. Finally she saved up enough. Just before she brought her cash to church, her mum found the money in her room and just took it. And that was the end of it. After crying a few nights, she said, "She can take away my money but she cannot take away my heart, my time and my energy. If I cannot give money, I will give my time." And she started serving in two ministries and leading a connect group.

Next year, Building Fund came again. She pledged again. She worked again and to save more money, she took the earliest bus at 5:00am because it was free. For weeks, she bought a pack of pasta and a bottle of spaghetti sauce for $5 and she ate that for dinner. She said, "When I gave my BF, I never felt such joy in my entire life!" When she entered Imaginarium for the first time, she cried and cried. She is just one of many. So many young people cried when they walked into Imaginarium for the inaugural service. Because for these youths, this is their *home*. No wonder Jesus said – where your treasure is, there your heart will be also.

As she matured in her faith, she knew she had to forgive her parents. So on Mother's Day and Father's Day, she wrote a letter to her parents. She wrote 'I love you' to them. It was her way of saying, 'I forgive you'. That moment, the weight of all the hurts from the past was released. She also invited her mum and sister to church and they have visited once before!

Cheryl is a young lady now but her home situation has not changed. So our church gathered a few of these young women from broken homes and helped them to rent a house together. They are paying a monthly church-subsidised rental and the taste of having their own peace is priceless. The broken can now bond together in a real physical home.

When she moved into her new apartment with her church friends, Cheryl happily texted me pictures of her new home. She had packed all her stuff and settled in. I thought to myself, *That was fast?*

She said, "Packing was quick and easy! All my belongings are just in one box!" Then it hit me. This 24-year-old girl, living in a first-world nation, has only one box of belongings.

Cheryl, who owned only one box of belongings, finally had her own closet in the rented house that church subsidised.

People say, financially, it's impossible to build a youth church. Youths don't have money. True, but they have a heart of sacrifice. HOGC is not built by millionaires, but by ordinary people — like Cheryl. That is why when you walk into our church, you can sense that it is more than an auditorium. It is an altar.

Unfortunately, Cheryl is just one of many broken youths who came into our church with a thirst for a caring home. Little surprise then that they collectively became a connect group or rather a support group because their CG was as much about supporting each other as it was about connecting. Some who came in earlier and matured as Christians started to mentor those who came in the same condition as them. They know they are not alone because someone else in the CG understands. The list of stories in this CG reads like a Korean drama:

A girl from a complicated background felt like an accident because her dad refused to put his name on her birth certificate. She found love, joy and a purpose in church and is now a full-time staff and one of our sound engineers!

One boy lived miserably at home. He loved a local dish, chicken rice. But poor as they were, the mum who is mentally unsound, made poverty even more painful when she would only let him eat the rice while she ate all the chicken herself! But this neglected boy went from gang leader to connect group leader, from failing in school to scoring a perfect GPA and from being told that he would 'never make it in life' to sharing his story and impacting thousands in a Christian conference in Taiwan! The redemption of God and a spiritual home!

Another girl had a mum with a huge gambling addiction that left the family with no money for food. But after coming to church and experiencing God and a spiritual home, God gave the girl the strength to forgive her mum, who had cancer...

How

For all these young people, church is the only place they have stability and warmth. They have no love at home. They get moved from house to house.

Their stepfathers change more frequently than their school teachers.

So they have learned how to smile without their eyes and relate without their hearts.

That is why we try to keep the same youth pastor or leader for them. Week after week, they build relationships with the same few leaders. These leaders look out for every aspect of their lives. Sometimes they flag up situations so that we can give financial assistance through the church's Scholarship and Opportunity Fund. The youth may backslide, leave, and return... they may go up and down, but their leaders will always be here.

A word to youth pastors and leaders: Youth pastoring is not a stepping stone to another more prominent ministry. Don't church hop or ministry hop. The youths have already been traumatized at home, abandoned, and left behind with empty promises, so the last thing they need is to experience the same in church.

Families may leave, friends may move on, classmates graduate, but in HOGC, we "Grow Up and Grow Old" together. It always warms my heart to see photos of youths serving together in their teens, years later getting married, and becoming parents, and they are all still together, friends since forever till forever.

One of our favorite quotes is from C.S. Lewis:

> Friendship is unnecessary, like philosophy, like art...
> It has no survival value; rather it is one of those things
> which give value to survival.

Some people are friends because they have a common past, purpose, work, or interests. In other words, it is necessary. But for us, it is beyond that – we are friends for no reason except that we actually like each other and enjoy hanging out with each other. Therefore we are "unnecessary friends." So if you come to HOGC, and we call you an "unnecessary friend," it is not an insult, it is a welcome and promotion into our circle.

We also say that *HOGC is the place where friends become family and family become friends.*

I have seen in our church so many people who have found friends who stick closer than a brother (Proverbs 18:24).

HOGC is the place where friends become family and family become friends.

Conversely, just because someone is your brother or sister doesn't automatically mean you are close. Then these siblings come to HOGC and they learn to put aside petty differences, pray together at home, reach out to their parents together, and they become friends too. I have seen this happen in HOGC over and over again. And it still warms my heart every time.

Watch: The victories and valleys. The moments and milestones. The HOGC story. Prepare your tissues. Catch this video and many more here.

This Is Our Home

Moving from "I belong to HOGC" to "HOGC belongs to me"

From *membership* to *ownership*
From *fellowship* to *stewardship*

 How

When church members feel strongly that they belong, then something beautiful happens...

A shift happens.

These young people mature from *membership* to *ownership*... from *fellowship* to *stewardship*.

They move from a mentality of *"I belong to HOGC"* to *"HOGC belongs to me."*

I guess when you've never had a warm, loving home and never had true, uplifting friendships, then when you find it, you will protect it with all your might.

When the church becomes their home, they will build it, defend it, and fight for it.

Moving from "I belong to HOGC" to "HOGC belongs to me"

As you know by now, I am a WWII military buff. War is evil and suffering for all. There is no glory in war, but there is a flickering light in all that darkness. I am inspired by the courageous, selfless sacrifice soldiers make for each other. I have observed that in the heat of the battle, when bullets are flying and men are bleeding, the soldiers are not fighting for ideologies or politics or even a religious cause. They are fighting for their brothers beside them. They make sacrifices to save their band of brothers. It is about their trench buddies.

In the same way, when a church becomes a *home* and when church attendees become a band of brothers and soul sisters, they will fight and sacrifice for their *home* and their spiritual family. Young people are not standing up for deep theology or fighting for an organization. However, they will give time, energy, money, everything they've got for their band of brothers and sisters and for a cause. Lia and I have so much respect for youths because they have consistently displayed camaraderie, solidarity, loyalty, and sacrifice for each other and our church.

I will never forget the time when we moved into the SingPost building (our third worship venue). We were scraping the barrel to pay rent. The youths paid their tithes, gave offering, gave to the Building Fund.

Some of the youths packed food from home to save lunch money to give to BF.

Some woke up at 5:00am, so that they could walk to school to save on bus fare to give.

Another one woke up at 4:30am to deliver newspapers before school to give to BF.

(This is what I call a "woke" generation.)

Many took jobs during school holidays so that they could give their earnings. They worked as waiters, in Starbucks, in boba tea shops, etc.

Some sold away their old stuff to raise money.

One boy got a free iPhone when he subscribed to a two-year plan from the telephone company. He decided to sell his brand new iPhone and continue using his old one.

Many also got entrepreneurial and started little businesses – selling cookies, cupcakes, etc.

And when I ask them why they give... their reply – "This is our home."

In fact, they are so passionate that we take extra precaution to help them navigate that passion with wisdom. For example, during the Building Fund pledging season, we teach practical and easy-to-remember wisdom such as *"Be radical but not reckless."* You can sell away stuff you don't need but don't let your dad come home to find the living room TV missing and your mom to discover her handbag in a second-hand store. And most definitely don't put your baby brother on eBay. The last brother who was sold away in the Bible, became the number two to Pharaoh. Another wisdom we teach is *"Sacrifice luxury not living,"* meaning drink water, cut the Coke, boba tea, Starbucks, and ice cream. HOGC parents have come to love BF season because their teenagers are the healthiest in those months.

**Be radical but not reckless.
Sacrifice luxury not living.**

We had to roll out policies to limit their giving and get their parents' consent if they want to give beyond a certain amount. It is also part of our process to review their pledges and advise them to reduce their pledge amounts.

This reminds me of

> Exodus 36:6 (NIV)
> Then Moses gave an order and they sent this word throughout the camp: "No man or woman is to make anything else as an offering for the sanctuary." And so the people were *restrained* from bringing more,

We had to restrain the young people from giving more. I secretly derived a lot of pleasure telling people to stop giving. We are very proud of them.

Even the young adults and family zones in our church sacrificed. They cut back on honeymoons and holidays, house renovations, delayed purchases of cars, sold cars, bought simpler houses just to give a significant sum. The spiritually significant and symbolic act that always brings Lia and me to tears is when an HOGC young adult receives their first salary from their first real job. They will come down to church, even on a weeknight to tithe. They could have given when they come on Sundays or electronically, but to those young men and women who grew up in HOGC, this first tithe is a coming of age moment. Their refrain – "I have received so much from church since I was a youth. Now I can finally give back. I have been waiting for this day all my life."

"I was a kid and now I am an adult in church. I want my first tithe from my first real income to be a declaration that my love for the God of my youth will always remain the same." This rite of passage has become an HOGC culture.

Lia

Jessel is a boy who has this conviction tattooed on his heart: 'I belong to HOGC. HOGC belongs to me.'

He was one of those who missed church Home during the 2020 pandemic. Locked down in his own physical home, many nights, he lay on the sofa and scrolled through his Instagram photos of church. He replayed old praise and worship videos from past services again and again.

Jessel sleeps on the sofa in the living room. He does not have his own room. His living conditions are not the best. And that's an understatement. Not only is his house broken, his home is broken too. When he was three, his father passed away. His mum became the sole breadwinner. She started working as a waitress from morning till night, and still could not afford enough beds. At night, Jessel slept on the floor. So the sofa is an upgrade. His wallet only had $2 for emergencies.

Whenever his friends talked about buying new sneakers, he pretended he did not like them. But deep inside, he always wondered if his family would run out of money one day.

To compensate for feeling scared and helpless, Jessel started to act cool by fighting with people and behaving like a gangster. "Yet deep down," he said, "I didn't like it at all. Honestly, I felt like I was wasting my life away."

But God intervened through his mum's friend, Aunt Deborah. She brought Jessel to Heart of God Church when he was 12. He loved the worship. Peace entered his heart as he sang and he felt like Someone loved him very, very much. He burst out crying. Then he heard a still small voice in his heart, "Jessel, I was there through your struggles and your hurts and I'm here with you." He knew it was God and so he gave his life to Jesus that day! As he kept coming back to church, he grew in his relationship with God. He felt a sense of belonging in church.

Jessel shared, "Church became the home I never thought I could have. After school, I didn't hang around basketball courts or go back to an empty house. Instead I went to church! The safest and happiest place I knew. I did not have to eat dinner alone or play computer games by myself anymore. I had my connect group! They are my best friends and we do life together every day. My favourite moments with them are the long, deep talks. We share our lives, our dreams and our encounters with God. They always inspire me to have faith and joy in my life! Also, I never thought I could do anything significant. But here in church, Pastors always tell us, youths can do great things for Jesus. That gave me faith and confidence to serve God in the Visuals Production ministry! That's where I get to control the big screens in service. I love playing a part to impact lives for Jesus! Here in church, I'm not only loved, but also trained and believed in."

So you can understand now why during the COVID-19 lockdown, Jessel lies on his sofa in the living room and scrolls through pictures and videos of church.

Ever since we heard about his background when he first came to HOGC, we placed him on the church's Scholarship and Opportunity Fund (SOF). Every month, he received an allowance from church. For the first time in his life, he had money to save. He felt more secure. The phone that he used to sustain himself during the pandemic – that was also given by a church member. He had always used second-hand and very old model phones. "That was the first time I unboxed a phone! Now I have more than enough memory space to finally listen to music and store photos!" he exclaimed. #TeenageSpeak

His church leaders also assigned a tutor to help with his anaemic grades. He commented, "No one cared for me so much before. I was so grateful." #HomeSpeak

Never underestimate a young life that has felt God's goodness. When Building Fund came along, Jessel was fighting to give. He explained, "Even though I tithe and give to the BF, it is so little compared to the financial help I have received from church. I have a conviction to build the place that first built me. And I was very shocked when I discovered how much it cost to rent our church premises! I felt so burdened to take responsibility for my *home*."

During the pandemic, Jessel's mum earned very little. As their stress increased, church increased Jessel's SOF allowance by a huge amount. He cried. When he passed his mum the money, she teared.

Then came the real tear-jerker for Jessel. The government relaxed the COVID-19 lockdown rules a little and we were allowed to open the church for private worship for just five people. He recalled, "Pastors wanted ME to be one of the first people who got to do so! I was so happy. I missed church so much. When I went back to church, I felt like a fish back in water! I could pray as long as I wanted and read the Bible with no distractions. I worshipped with my arms wide open! I was finally *home*!"

And do you know what was the first thing he did when he stepped into church? He paid his tithes. Oh yes, I forgot to tell you Jessel had

been tithing to God out of his SOF allowance that church had been giving him all along. He had not one but five separate envelopes when he came to church that day. He had meticulously saved and prepared his tithes and offerings for those lockdown months and back paid them. We all have much to learn from this young man about faithfulness and resilience. Yup. HOGC belongs to him.

A recipient of the HOGC Scholarship and Opportunity Fund,
Jessel gave his tithes the moment he stepped into church post-lockdown.

I'm happy to tell you that this is not the end of the story. When Pastor How shared Jessel's story and convictions to the church, it moved them. Some gave money, others bought a brand new MacBook Pro for Jessel to use in school and ministry. Through Heart Community Services, church also gave his home a makeover. Our church staff accompanied him to IKEA, helped him clean and renovate his house. (Go to the Digital Companion to check out his full testimony and see his home's transformation. Don't miss this video.)

How

This is why for us, it is not just a Sunday service.

It is not just a stage performance and hype.

For us, church is a *home*.

During the COVID-19 crisis, we did not gather as a church for many months. Three months into the crisis, I had a meeting with Pastor Garrett our CEO, and the accounts department. They showed me some very interesting financial figures. Our income went up significantly while the number of tithers went down slightly. That's puzzling. Usually income and tithers are correlated. Yes, we lost some tithers because some lost their jobs, while a small number could have lost their momentum or commitment. But how did income go up while givers went down?

As we asked around... mystery solved.

Stories after stories came back from hundreds of HOGC people:

"We figured that church income could be affected, so we stepped up and gave more to compensate. We gave 15%, 20% of our income."

"Even though there are no church services, but rent and salaries still have to be paid. We didn't want the church staff, who are our friends, to be affected."

Lia and I had to hold back our tears.

That day I learned something: *"Just keep carrying the people in your hearts and one day they will carry you on their backs."*

If you are a pastor or leader reading this, just keep carrying the vision and one day the vision will carry you in return.

> ## Just keep carrying the people in your hearts and one day they will carry you on their backs.

During the crisis, our church showed up and stood up. I did not breathe a word about the church's financial situation nor run any campaign, but the individuals were empathetic. Now that's personal ownership. And without talking with each other, as if by telepathy (but we know it is the Holy Spirit), they started giving more. When individuals can be empathetic towards their church, then the collective impact is emphatic. Their generosity enabled us to go beyond sustaining our church. During the first year of COVID-19, we were able to give $700,000 to 235 HOGC members and their families who were affected by the pandemic and an additional $200,000 in scholarships.

HOGC is not built by a few rich people but by the multitudes of sacrificial people. Modern-day widows with two mites and boys and girls with five loaves and two fish are among us as we worship. One Australian worship leader, in an anointed moment said, "As I walked into your auditorium, I sensed that the whole place is an altar. I tread with holy fear because I feel like I am walking on the sacrifices of people."

Pastors are astounded by how a youth church can raise millions. They are amazed how HOGC can be financially self-sufficient, without a dependency on multimillionaire backers or external support. While the money given is the fruit, it is really the ownership and responsibility of HOGC givers that is the root. The miracle of HOGC is not the money but the invaluable sense of ownership of those who call HOGC their home.

We talked a lot about giving but ownership is definitely much deeper than money.

Our church is cleaned and maintained by our members. Now that is a lot of cleaning. We have a combined area of 90,000 square feet. That is the floor space of nearly 20 basketball courts combined. We have more than 20 restrooms and over 100 cubicles. Even though we have hired professional cleaning services, every week, hundreds of members from different connect groups and zones are still rostered to come down to clean. When you watch our members clean the church, you would think that they were coming for a party. They are exuberant and enthusiastic. I see 14-year-olds cleaning toilet bowls like they were polishing their white sneakers. Parents tell me with a mixture of satisfaction and resignation that their teenagers won't even clean the toilet at home but would do it in church. This culture of ownership is reinforced by the family zones cleaning as well. They model for the young people that no one is too old or too successful to clean toilets. One person is Djonny. He is a successful Indonesian businessman whose company is listed on the stock exchange. He is based in Indonesia but his two girls are in HOGC. He will regularly fly back to Singapore to attend church services two to three times a month. He volunteered himself to serve in church. Our leaders wanted to deploy him to the Building Committee or Investment Committee. It is appropriate for his expertise, experience, and also schedule.

His reply was, "Not Building Committee but Building Maintenance team. I want to wash toilets and change light bulbs."

What!!!!

I said, "Djonny, you are from Indonesia – domestic helpers are a norm. You can send ten of your domestic helpers to clean the church. You don't have to do it yourself."

His reply, "Yes, but HOGC is my church not my workers' church. My church, my responsibility."

Wow.

What he said is true. HOGC could easily afford to outsource and pay professional cleaning companies to do the job. It will probably be more efficient and less work for our staff, but cleaning the church is not just about cost savings. It goes deeper than money. It is about ownership and responsibility. It is like parents expecting their children to clean their own room.

So every month, Djonny will fly to Singapore, drive his Mercedes to church, pick up the mop, and clean the toilet.

Ownership: Djonny, whose company is listed on the stock exchange, serving on the Building Maintenance team.

Here's the best part – he broke the curve. He is a role model for the youths and a benchmark for the adults. If this successful businessman can clean the church, no one has an excuse not to. As he broke the curve, he also broke the curse of consumerism and complacency in church. With every stroke of the mop and every bead of sweat, he is shouting out "HOGC belongs to me."

Ownership is expressed in different ways.

There are some youths who wanted to give to the Building Fund but could not because their parents are not Christians and objected. For us, we always counsel the youths to obey their parents (which is one of the Commandments). Yet, nothing can stop them from taking responsibility in other ways. Many of them said, "If I can't give money, then I will give time and energy." So there are people in our church serving in three, four, even five ministries.

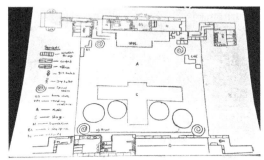

Ownership: 14-year-old Rena drew a floor plan of the church on her own accord so that she could systematically clean every area.

Others express their ownership by protecting the church. The earliest sign that young people will rise and protect the church was from Jian Ming. He was 16 at the time. Our church had a couple of hundred youths. There was a new kid who just started coming but he turned out to be a troublemaker. Jian Ming found out that this guy was harassing girls with text messages filled with sexual innuendos. Like a big brother, he confronted that guy and told him to stop it. But this kid was from a super rich and prominent family. So he went home and whined to dad, and dad complied by threatening us with police investigations and lawsuits.

I will remember this scene for the rest of my life. Jian Ming – then a plump kid, looking deflated and resolute at the same time – came up to Lia and me. He said, "Let me take the blame for everything. I will tell the police that it's my fault and it has nothing to do with the church." He still added, "I was a mischievous student in school, always in the principal's office, so it will be believable." He volunteered to take a bullet for his church. Of course, we didn't throw him under the bus. The whole episode fizzled off but that day, Jian Ming showed me that young people will fight for their church. It is not surprising that Jian Ming is now the head of our Guest Experience department (which includes the Security ministry, so don't mess with him. 😄)

As with any big church, we also attract more than our fair share of internet critics. Some are bloggers who don't even know us, but use us as clickbait, to stir up controversy in order to increase their viewership. Some years ago, there was an absurd post about me that went like this: "Pastor How runs a church and a temple *miào* (廟) at the same time." The image of me pastoring by day and moonlighting as a shaman by night is comical. Yup, I would have laughed too except that it was so sensational that it went viral. (Ok... How did that happen? It was from a sermon where I was sharing my personal testimony about how my grandfather was a temple medium (for the Western readers, think voodoo and black magic) and how God can turn a generational sin into a generational blessing. It was such a beautiful testimony of how God could turn things around. Who would have thought that a sorcerer's grandkid would become a pastor? My grandfather and even my father have passed away, so the dilapidated temple, which my uncle is occupying, is still in the family's estate. And that was how the internet haters connected two unrelated facts and turned a powerful testimony into fake news.) I guess my "defection" from the kingdom of darkness is such a kick in the devil's butt that he had to retaliate with a smear campaign.

There are also the usual preposterous false accusations of HOGC scamming youths, which is as bizarre and ridiculous as the "temple" allegations. I won't even dignify those internet attacks with a defense except that HOGC is meticulously audited by a top five audit firm and rigorously monitored by the Singapore Commissioner of Charities.

What touches my heart is that we have members who read those fake news and lies, and they are so triggered that they vow to protect the church and the leadership. As you have read in Chapter 4, Russell wanted to be a scientist so that his credibility can vouch for the church. His dad, Yang, is in our Investment Committee. His mom, Linda, who has a Masters in Accountancy and is very experienced and successful in the financial field, also stepped up to protect the church. After her intense day job, she still volunteers her nights to ensure that our accounts are impeccable and can withstand any accusations and substantiate our integrity. Many nights, when Lia and I leave the office around 11-ish, we see the accounts staff and Linda, still hustling, we are so moved. Since the internet attacks, so many lawyers, auditors, accountants, communications specialists, and civil servants have risen up and volunteered to work on policies, procedures, and protocols to safeguard our church. We call them HOGC Sentinels. One girl who works as an auditor in Ernst & Young initially wanted to change careers but decided to continue so that she can have the skills and credibility to help her church. When church members rally together like this, it really lifts our spirits.

These Sentinels really touched Pastor Lia's and my heart deeply. It is one thing to align with the church in good times, but it is another to stand with us and rise up to protect the church when things are not so rosy. Ordinary church attendees would be indifferent or even distance themselves from the church but these Sentinels, they closed ranks. To all the HOGC Sentinels reading this: We will never forget how you stood with us.

TURN YOUR CHURCH INTO A SPIRITUAL HOME

In order to build your church like a home, you need to build real relationships. That is why a slick stage production is not enough. You need to build a culture of care, warmth, and fun. We call it – the Fireplace. And Pastor Lia is the mother, comedian, and M.C. of the Fireplace. Everyone around her can feel the warmth, life, and care. She is a Barnabas, speaking life-giving words. She brings the buzz, humor, and energy.

Don't just focus on the stage and Sundays. That's just the front door. The important part of the home is the living and dining room. That's the backstage and weeknights of the church. Build on those. Have a lot of meals together. Play together. Spend time together with your "unnecessary friends."

You also need the facilities. For us, church is not something that happens two hours every Sunday. Church is a hangout for the whole weekend, with meetings and gatherings on weeknights. So we can't simply rent a cinema or hotel ballroom for a couple of hours. We need to provide a place to hang out. Our auditorium does not have fixed chairs so that we can turn it around into a massive hangout area. We have *The Living Room, Loft, Chapel, Clubhouse,* and about 20 other smaller rooms for the young people to use. Even when we just started and money was tight, we rented a warehouse space and used it as our worship venue, office, hangout, playground, youth camp, training space... we did everything in that warehouse. For many years, Lia and I slept in that warehouse every Friday night till Sunday. I always advise pastors with start-up churches that rent a hall by the hour to also rent a small space nearby 24/7. You can use it as an office, storage, children's church, youth room, and for training after service. That little space where all the buzz happens is the true "home" of your church.

Let me end the chapter with this – a church built as a home is also a Strong Church. That is why it is one of the five pillars of a

Strong Church. When Planetshakers Church wanted to plant a campus in Singapore, they felt a lack of enthusiasm from some local pastors. And understandably so, after all, Planetshakers is a respected global brand.

I had lunch with their Senior Pastor, Russell Evans, to welcome them and give him the lay of the land... literally. Someone had recommended a possible location, which a local would immediately know is less than ideal. So out of concern, after lunch, I drove him to see it for himself. Pastor Garrett also walked the Planetshakers finance guy through the accounting regulations of Singapore. In their opening service, we sent our guys to show our support. You know, Planetshakers is so brilliant and capable, they can successfully plant a campus in Singapore with or without my support. My point is that if churches are built like a home for their members, they can be more Kingdom-minded and less territorial. The church world can do with more unity and collaborations.

Imagine with me – if your new neighbor moved in next door into their newly renovated house. The house has a swimming pool, a dedicated games room with the latest Xbox, and a home cinema. (Think Tony Stark's house.) The dude has a Ferrari and a Ducati and invites your sons over to check out his ride. The mom serves A3 grade wagyu burgers, truffle fries, and free flow air-flown gelato from Italy for lunch. He has two cute beagle puppies and invites your daughters to come play with them.

So your children go over and have the greatest time of their lives. They are raving about everything and you are already plotting how to scratch his car and poison his dogs. And that's only phase one of your plan.

Wait... Before you sin...

If you have given your heart to build a home of warmth, love, and fun...

If you have given your time to build a family who cares for each other and fights for each other...

If you have given your energy to build a home where there is purpose and significance...

When night comes, guess where your kids will go?

Yes, *home.*

When they are sick, who do they look for?

Mom and dad.

When the novelty and thrill is over, they will come back to the family, play board games beside the fireplace, and eat mac 'n' cheese.

I have learned that happy kids in happy homes don't run away so easily. But if your church is just a show, then when the next, more happening show comes to town, they will be drawn away. *Disneyland may be the happiest place on earth but nobody lives there.* Disneyland is not a home. When the show is over, everyone goes home.

Heart of God Church is not a show. It is a home.

So even if Hillsong or Bethel or Elevation Church move in next door, I will roll out the red carpet and help them move in. I believe that if I devote myself to building my church like a home then I can stop worrying that my sheep will be stolen. A wise pastor once said to me, "If your sheep can be so easily stolen, you must not be a very good shepherd."

For years, this youth didn't even have a bed to sleep on. Watch how HOGC members rose up to help in his house makeover.

AUTHORS' NOTE
How to maximise this book

How ✈

OK, we are almost at the end of Volume 1.

In this volume, Lia and I have covered three out of five mindset shifts.

- Mindset Shift #1 - Youth Are Leaders TODAY, Not Just Tomorrow
- Mindset Shift #2 - GenerationS - Reinforcements Not Replacements
- Mindset Shift #3 - Church Is Our Home, Not Just a House

Volume 2 will delve into the nuts and bolts of building a church by youths, for youths, to reach youths. There we will also introduce the HOGC Strong Church Model and cover the last two mindset shifts:

- Mindset Shift #4 - Encouragement Not Endorsement
- Mindset Shift #5 - On the Contrary... Youths Want to Be Discipled

Lia and I will also share our heart and heartbreaks behind raising GenerationS.

The first three mindset shifts in Volume 1 are enough homework and hard work to last you many years. At this point, we need to share how you can *maximize* all the principles shared in this book.

First, a little history on the Church landscape. In the 1990s and early 2000s, as far as I know, there wasn't any excitement or brouhaha about youth churches. I don't recall many pastors, ministries, conferences, or books devoted to youths or building Strong GenerationS Churches. When Lia received her revelation of GenerationS from Isaiah 58:12, we scoured around the world for resources and examples. We could only find a handful like Ron Luce, Jeanne Mayo, Doug Fields,

Willie George, YWAM, YFC, and Campus Crusade who were talking about youths. Thank God for these early pioneers. However, they were mostly parachurches, ministries, or conferences rather than a *youth church – a church truly and fully operated by youths, for youths, to reach youths.*

The word *generations* certainly wasn't trending then. In fact, in those times, the focus was on building megachurches. In that model, senior pastors would usually hire and delegate youth ministry to a rookie young pastor. And youth pastoring was seen as a stepping stone to higher positions in the church hierarchy. It is therefore not surprising that the turnover for youth pastors can be as quick as 1.5 years. So from that perspective, youth ministry had understandably become a ministry for rookies to cut their teeth and make mistakes in. Unfortunately, the youths unintentionally ended up as guinea pigs. To us, that's as ironic as it is tragic. The adolescent years are when they are most fragile, vulnerable, and influenceable, yet we let the bull run the china shop.

Furthermore, the mindset toward youth ministries was still about "babysitting," much like an "older" children's church. The unsaid ministry philosophy was "keep them occupied, entertained, and out of trouble." The goal was the adults, but in order to get these parents to attend, the church needed to make their kids happy. Therefore, the kids and youths were not an end in themselves. For smaller churches, the youth worker was also the worship leader, who doubled up as the guy who made the announcements, the stage manager, the service coordinator plus the IT guy, admin guy, and driver.

That's the landscape when Lia and I started out to build a Strong Youth Church. So as you can imagine, when we talked about building a youth church, there wasn't much resonance. When Lia introduced the concept of raising multiple GenerationS, there was really not a lot of traction. We felt like the lone voice crying out in the wilderness. But we kept grinding away because we didn't want to be the king who struck the ground only three times (2 Kings 13:18). Time flew and we have already been banging the drum for GenerationS for over 20 years – humbly but unflinchingly, from small pastors' gatherings, youth workshops, seminars, Bible schools, small churches to big churches, denomination conferences, and international conferences. Our endearing memory was of us feeling like a start-up entrepreneur. Every meeting was an elevator pitch or a 20-slide presentation to VCs or investors. (I guess that is why now our sermons have so many attractive slides – old habits!) After our pitch, we would be bombarded with questions of whether what we were doing was scriptural or viable.

Then around the middle of the 2010s onwards, something changed globally. By God's grace, there was a shift to greater emphasis on youths. Pastors began to talk about the need to reach the next generation. The wind of the Holy Spirit caught the sails and pastors began to be interested in it. The word *generations* became the buzzword. Now it is cool and trending. Then they started preaching about it – echoing, "Youth are leaders today" and "GenerationS." Wow. God was moving.

Lia and I quietly rejoiced when we witnessed this pivot. When we shared in the youth workshops of conferences, senior pastors started attending. Typically, senior pastors don't attend youth workshops but send their youth pastors instead. Then I knew it was a turning point when the World Evangelical Alliance (WEA) invited me to talk about GenerationS in their once-in-five-year general assembly. Topics about youth were always in the backyard of obscure workshops, never the keynote session. WEA's invite was a watershed that signalled a global change in attitude toward GenerationS and youth churches.

Today, more well-known preachers who have farther reach and influence than Lia and me have also joined this cause. Major church movements have also picked up on GenerationS. Praise the Lord. Because of the awareness and interest generated, it might be why you are reading this book in your hands. GenerationS has a life of its own now. Lia and I can already RIP haha. For us, we are thankful that we heard the Holy Spirit correctly 20+ years ago. We count it a privilege to be called to youths. If we didn't respond, I am sure God would have called someone else.

With Phase 1's (1996 to 2016) growing momentum, Lia and I are onto Phase 2. (Guess we can't RIP yet.)

Phase 1 was beating the drum and telling the world "What's possible" with youth.

Phase 2 is about "How to make it possible" which includes this series of books about GenerationS.

With this increased attention, leaders globally are asking for more details and in-depth teachings – essentially the how-tos. So we launched HoGcX in 2009. At the time of writing we have run HoGcX 31 times. And every installment is an improved iteration with better and more content. Subsequently, the feedback was that they still needed something more to take home to share with their teams. So that is why we concluded that we need to put everything comprehensively in a book.

Even though Lia was a journalist, we never saw ourselves writing a book. I grew up in a family speaking Chinese dialect. If you spoke to me when I was in secondary school, you would have thought I came out of a badly dubbed '70s kung fu movie. Me grammar are so bad that me need a lot of helps. ☺

I must thank our dear friend Dr. Robi Sonderegger for pushing us to take what is in HOGC and tell it to the world. He has been HOGC's greatest evangelist. John and Lisa Bevere had seen the strength of a GenerationS Church too and have been natural HOGC advocates. Then it was Bishop Dale Bronner who kept telling us that what God raised up in secret will not be kept under a basket for long. God will put it on a lampstand so that the world may see and glorify the Father.

So this *GenerationS* series is like a portable HoGcX. It contains many of the principles and concepts shared in HoGcX which Lia and I have taught pastors and church leaders from all over the world. We have shared it in countless pastors' conferences, seminars, and webinars globally. We have also shared it on our websites, podcasts, articles, and social media. We are truly humbled that many of these pastors have been influenced and have taken this content back to run their own conferences and preach in their spheres of influence. So I won't be surprised if it sounds familiar to you. I am sure you probably have heard it verbatim or in bits and pieces. Finding confirmation from Gamaliel's advice in Acts 5:38-39, we are glad that this concept of GenerationS is not of men for it will come to nothing, but it is of God, because it has gone viral. Lia and I have read books, listened to sermons, and watched conferences on the internet where these concepts and ideas were used by the pastors whom Pastor Lia and I had the privilege of sharing with. It is encouraging to know that our content is so well received that they enthusiastically passed it along and transferred it. I am personally surprised by how far and fast our concepts, principles, quotes, and ideas have been put in print, in sermons, in conferences, and on the internet even before we did! It can only be the work of the Holy Spirit.

OUR 20+ YEAR CRUSADE TO CHAMPION GENERATIONS AND YOUTHS

Someone said to us, "Wow, you took one year to write this book."

Our spontaneous reply – "No, we took 20 years to write this book."

We took so long because we wanted to test it, try it, and trial it before we wrote it. So we took 10 years before we ran our first HoGcX to share with other leaders and another 10 years of refinement before we put it in print. As I said before, we dare not claim to be a successful youth church until we have fruits that remain. Honestly, another reason we have waited 20 years to write this book is because we were too busy doing it and living it. It took a global pandemic for Lia and me to have time to finally put this book together so that you can hear from us directly.

Knowing the context of all of this will help you maximize the use of this book. This book will help link all the bits and pieces you have been hearing from everywhere else. If you implement GenerationS piecemeal, it might have some benefits but not the full potential it can have. When we talk to the pastors who have implemented it successfully, we observe a common denominator: They are *all in*.

They have skin in the game.

Their *Heart, Head, and Hands* are all in.

This means they caught the heart of being a spiritual father and mother to youths. There is a *Heart* transformation. It also means they have a total mindset shift in their *Heads.* Finally, they are prepared to roll up their sleeves and get their hands dirty. Their *Hands* were on the plow. They are ready to do the hard work and homework.

Some people understood GenerationS cognitively but didn't catch the heart, so it didn't work. Others caught the heart and were moved, but did not put in the hard work, so it didn't work as well. There are no quick fixes or shortcuts. This book is not one which you can read, get some ideas from, put down, and move on. If your only takeaways are some ideas here and a few new initiatives there, then you would have missed out on what is possible. For it to have impact, it takes *heart* work, *head* work and *hard* work. If preachers view this book and HoGcX as sermon materials, they will be shortchanged. (Yes, we preachers are always on the hunt for sermon materials. I get it. It's tough coming up with original content every week.) However, I believe that God wants to use you to raise up GenerationS and build Strong Churches. So don't be satisfied with just taking away quotable quotes and smart concepts for your sermons. Turn these contents that you have learned into substance and fruits. Go beyond a few clever ideas. If God can use two Asian pastors who are as ordinary as white rice, God can use you.

Maximum impact requires a complete overhaul. It is probably more troublesome than moving from the Apple ecosystem to the Android ecosystem or vice versa. We prefer to upgrade to a new phone and update our apps but nobody enjoys OS changes.

For the pastors who are willing to go all in, they begin to see fruits for the long term.

Our friends, Pastors Roy and Jessica Marcellus in Sydney started implementing the Strong Church Model after they attended HoGcX. Lia and I also gave them access into the inner workings of HOGC and showed them how we disciple our leaders. They saw how discipleship is modeled in real life and were moved to tears. Determined to build the same kind of Strong Church with layers and layers of leaders, they took the heart, passion of discipleship, and Deep Bench back to their church and grew from 30 to 65 connect groups. They did not just get a bigger crowd, but added more connected and committed people.

Pastor Kerry Li from Hong Kong went back after attending HoGcX and started 11 new ministries for the youths to serve in. Then he empowered the youths to run evangelistic events and 200 new friends came. That's never been done before in his church. The best part? The adults didn't even lift a hand except to clap.

Also in Hong Kong, Pastor Daniel Fung went back to release and unleash his youths into ministry. One of the youths had a dream to be an interpreter. This pastor made her dream come true. When our team visited, she made her debut on stage, interpreting between Cantonese and English. She was visibly stressed and elated simultaneously. This girl was 15 years old. Let the future begin!

Tope and Kemi Koleoso, who pastor a vibrant and growing church in London, brought their teams to Singapore, not once but twice. In the team was a 15-year-old. This young man went back and was given opportunities to lead. Last heard, he was leading the whole Live Camera team for their annual Courage Conference for thousands of people. Now that is what I call real courage.

I can go on and on… Russia, Scandinavia, Europe, Indonesia, Taiwan, China…

When we return a few years later, the seeds have grown. We see and hear young people released into leadership. Entire youth ministries transformed. In some cases, the whole church is renewed.

We have observed that the degree of impact depends on the degree of systemic change. If they are able to go back, get buy-in and support from:

- senior leadership, staff, HODs, volunteers
- other departments
- board and elders
- youth leaders and the youths themselves
- congregations, especially parents

Then they can get the resources, support, spots on the event calendar, and platform to implement GenerationS. As you can imagine, it takes a lot of wisdom and savvy to "sell," pitch, and win over all the stakeholders. After that, the execution will require even more hard work. When the whole church is all in, then they will witness the impact gradually but surely in years.

Lia and I want to give a standing ovation to all these pastors who implemented the GenerationS vision into their churches. It is far from easy, but now you are starting to see fruits and testimonies. Concepts and quotable quotes can easily be regurgitated, but fruits take years to grow and testimonies of young people take grace and grind to birth. Jesus said that it is by our fruits that we are known and it is the testimonies of the saints that will defeat the devil. We know that it is not stagecraft or camera work. The authenticity test of GenerationS is the youth testimonies. The acid test of a Strong Church is its fruit. We salute you.

So in order to catalyze systemic change and get buy-in from all the stakeholders, we were strongly encouraged by pastors to write this book. They went back to their cities inspired but found it difficult to share persuasively with the stakeholders. Subsequently, many of them invested a lot of time and money to send their teams and leaders to visit us. But not everyone can afford it, so this book is a piece of HOGC they can bring back with them. If that's you, I encourage you to read this book and go through chapter by chapter with your team.

As mentioned at the beginning of this book, Lia and I deeply believe that money should never be an obstacle. So if you and your church/ Bible school are struggling financially but want to use this book as a resource, do email us. We are happy to work something out. Lia and I did not write this book for money but it's our mission and mandate. In fact, all royalties and proceeds from this book will be used to advance the cause of GenerationS in HOGC and globally.

We were also nudged to write by many pastors because they wanted to hear from the source. They didn't want it diluted or polluted. They didn't want second or third-hand revelation. They didn't want the photocopy of the photocopy. Some pastors were also concerned that content that is simply regurgitated usually loses the heart and spirit behind it. They understood that GenerationS is not just a strategy or method, but it is about the heart. They were also apprehensive that if people preach GenerationS but are not actually actively building GenerationS, the DNA transfer might be mutated and thus might not bear fruits. Here in this book, you will not just learn the concepts but I included the fruits – stories and testimonies of young people – so that you can expect the same fruits in your ministry. This book will help you turn a third-party message transfer into a personal life transformation.

So maybe you have heard these concepts about GenerationS and Strong Church without knowing the *origin and source*, well now you do. And if you know a friend who heard about GenerationS from a friend who heard from a friend, now you can point them to the OG. Or you could help a bro or sis out by pointing them to this book. Then they can get the full impact. Finally, we strongly encourage you to fly to Singapore, come visit HOGC and attend HoGcX. Come hear the testimonies and meet the kids who built a world-class church before they all grow up. Come witness this phenomenon that God has done.

Be a Kingmaker, Not Just a King - Heart Transformation

Don't use people to build the church.
Use the church to build people.

Our next generation leaders should walk in our footsteps,
not in our shadow.

 How

We have come to the last chapter of this volume. Before we go out and grow our churches younger and stronger, something must happen in our own hearts. Before the hard work, we must begin with heart work. It begins with us.

You can't bring change until you are first changed.

If you want to make a difference, then you must be different.

God has called you to be transformational leaders.

Transformational leaders are first transformed leaders.

A butterfly is not a flying caterpillar.

It is not a caterpillar with wings.

No. It has to go through a metamorphosis – transformation.

> **Transformational leaders are first transformed leaders.**

A butterfly is not the same caterpillar that has grown wings. It has gone through a transformation process –

its DNA is changed. It is radically and totally transformed from the inside out.

> ## A butterfly is not a flying caterpillar.

For Lia and me, our hopes are that after you finish this book or experience HOGC, you will be transformed from the inside out. The goal of this book is not just to "grow wings" to your youth program, not add some cool ideas for youth, or a cosmetic change. This book is about personal transformation that will lead to ministry reformation.

After HoGcX, one pastor in his 60s told me that he was on his knees praying that God would give him another 20 good years. And that he would devote all his remaining years to youths.

Another delegate, a Deputy Senior Pastor of a huge denominational church of 10,000, was slated to take over as Senior Pastor. After HoGcX, God refreshed and reminded him of his first calling to impact young people. He knew that being promoted to Senior Pastor of a denominational church meant that he would be inundated with committee meetings and other management roles, limiting his role with youths. He went back and declined the Senior Pastor position so that he could build up the next generation. What a radical, selfless, and sacrificial decision.

That is our prayer for you. That this book will be a destiny-defining moment for you too.

BRIDGING GENERATIONS

God is a God of the generations. He declares Himself as the God of Abraham, Isaac, and Jacob. That's three generations right there. He is a generational God.

It is very interesting as you begin to think about these three generations and these three men.

Abraham is significant for being the father of faith and his exploits start from Genesis 12, right through to chapters 23 and 25. Thirteen chapters of Genesis are dedicated to Abraham.

If you think of Jacob, we will remember him as the father of the nation of Israel. In fact, his name was changed to Israel by God – meaning, prince of God.

Genesis chapters 28 to 35 are about him – eight chapters devoted to him.

But when it comes to Isaac?

What is Isaac famous for? Hmmm... you have to pause and think hard.

Being sacrificed on the altar? But that episode was more about Abraham's obedience than him.

There are only two to three chapters on Isaac.

Isaac was not great in himself.

He did not do anything significant. There were no great exploits, epic battles, or miracles attributed to him. Isaac found himself in a trivial position in Bible history.

Isaac was the son of a great father and the father of a great son.

But he himself was inconspicuous.

Yet Isaac is significant for being the bridge between two generations!

He was the bridge between Abraham and Jacob. Without Isaac, the bridge to the next generation would be severed.

**Isaac was the son of a great father
and the father of a great son.
He was inconspicuous yet he was
significant for *Bridging Generations*!**

It is certainly more formidable to be Abraham or Jacob, but are we willing to be Isaac?

Let's be Isaac and connect the two generations.

We have a great Father too... His name is Jehovah God.

And we will have great spiritual sons and daughters – the next generation-in-waiting.

Let's connect God the Father to the generation after us... to the Israel generation.

We can be the Isaac generation.

This is my ethos: *I don't want to be the king. I'd rather be the kingmaker.*

Be a Kingmaker, Not Just a King.

We don't need to be the greatest and take all the glory. I'd rather the next generation do greater works than me.

Isn't this the spirit of Jesus?

> John 14:12
> ... he who believes in Me, the works that I do he will do also; and *greater works* than these he will do, because I go to My Father.

Our next generation should be greater than us. They should stand on our shoulders and see further and dream bigger.

Lia and I went to Bible school, but never had the opportunity to get our Master of Divinity. When we were pioneering the infant church, there wasn't time nor money to further our theological studies. Personally, I would love to get my MDiv. I told Lia that if I were to study, I would study Church History. Lia said, "While you major in history, I just want to make history." And that was how my academic ambition died. ☺

OK, jokes aside, when the church became more established, this option was on the table. But instead of enrolling ourselves, we decided it was better for us to hold the fort so that the next generation of pastors could pursue their MDiv. Our pastors started their four-year course, while still carrying the full load of their responsibilities in church. They flew frequently to Oral Roberts University for classes and back, hitting the ground running. When they graduated, Lia and I attended their commencement ceremonies at ORU. We felt like proud parents. They were 28 to 33 years old and had already completed their theological studies. Subsequently, they were ordained as the next generation of pastors in HOGC.

Pastor Lia and Pastor How attend the commencement ceremonies of our first batch of MDiv graduates at Oral Roberts University (USA).

Pastor How and Pastor Lia flew to the US to celebrate the graduation of our inaugural batch of MDiv students.

*Our Senior Pastors ordaining our first three
homegrown pastors — and they won't be the last!*

When Lia and I were in our mid-20s we preached to a fledgling connect group of a few people. The first time I preached to over 2,000 people, I was already in my late 30s. And my legs were shaking (not from the anointing but anxiety). But when our next generation pastors first started preaching at around the same age, they were already preaching to hundreds. Today Pastors Garrett, Lynette, and Charleston are our main preachers, delivering world-class, life-changing sermons to thousands every week. They have also preached in Bible schools and conferences in Southeast Asia, Hong Kong, Taiwan, Australia, and Europe. The best part is that because they are still so young, they connect so well with Gen Z and Gen Alpha.

This reminds me of a quote by the founding father and 2nd President of the USA, John Adams:

> I must study politics and war, so that my sons will have the liberty to study mathematics and philosophy. My sons must study navigation, commerce and agriculture, so that their children will have the right to study painting, poetry and music.

Currently, we are sending another batch of next generation pastors to get their MDiv.

And just as we brought our first batch of homegrown pastors overseas when they were youths, they now bring teams of youths with them when they preach.

That leaves me hopeful that the next generations will stand on their shoulders as they have stood on ours.

The Pipeline: our 2nd batch of students taking their MDiv at Oral Roberts University.

Let's be the kingmakers.

Let's be playmakers.

When I was still playing soccer (about 100 years ago), I always preferred to be the playmaker than the goal scorer. The goal scorer gets all the glory, but it is the playmaker who creates and sets up the goal. One of my favorite players from FC Barcelona is Sergio Busquets. Unless you really follow soccer, you probably have never heard of him. He is not a goal scorer like Ronaldo or Messi, but he is the metronome of the team. His coach, Vicente del Bosque, who led Spain to win the 2010 World Cup, has this to say about Busquets, "If you watch the whole game, you won't see Busquets – but watch Busquets, and you will see the whole game."

Wow. What an accolade. To the casual spectator, Busquets will be overlooked. But to the discerning, he is the playmaker.

Are we willing to be the inconspicuous playmaker, overlooked by the crowds? But to God, we are the playmakers setting up the next generation to score goals and win championships.

Bishop Bronner said this: "Legacy is not what you have achieved but what you set in motion."

Legacy is not what you have achieved but what you set in motion.

- Bishop Dale Bronner

Some successful people think – *My accomplishments and achievements are my legacy.*

No.

If it dies with you, it is not legacy, it is history. Only if it continues beyond you, then it becomes legacy.

Legacy is not about the past but the future.

Some successful people might leave behind a great history but not a legacy.

Legacy is not about the past but the future.

Psalm 127:3-4 (MSG)
Don't you see that children are God's best gift?
     the fruit of the womb his generous *legacy*?
Like a warrior's fistful of arrows
     are the children of a vigorous youth.

This verse is crystal clear. Our legacy is in our children and spiritual children. Legacy is about who not what. Legacy is about the future not the past.

Our legacy is what we set in motion, after we hand over, retire, or die.

Legacy is about movement.

Leaving a legacy is not about your achievements but what you set in motion.

Legacy is about movement

From a worldly perspective, Jesus didn't achieve much when He ascended to heaven. There was no megachurch or global denomination. But He started a movement that cannot be stopped – one-third of the planet are His followers today.

Pastors and leaders, allow me to ask a soul-searching question.

If you were asked to choose the outcome of your ministry, which would you pick?

a. Retire with a church of 10,000 but in 10 years it dwindles to 1,000

b. Retire with a church of 1,000 but in 10 years it grows to 10,000

Your choice will be revealing.

Leaders, are we secure enough for our next generation, our successor to do better than us?

Or do we have a need to be needed. Do we have a restrained satisfaction inside, that without us, the church will decline?

When the people started to sing, "Saul has killed his thousands, but David his ten thousands," Saul was so insecure, he decided to kill his next generation. Sadly, I have seen many insecure pastors get rid, clamp down, stifle, and snuff out their next generation leaders too. These young men and women were godsent to preserve their legacy, yet they killed their own legacy because of insecurities.

For Lia and me, we want our next generation pastors to "do greater works" than us. And the generation after them to be even greater than them. Let us decrease, so that they can increase.

The height and pinnacle of HOGC should not be in our lifetime.

It should be in the next generation and the next generation.

The pinnacle of your churches and movements should not be in your generation... It should be in the next generation and beyond. That is why this book is called *GenerationS*.

Ideally, no leader should experience the peak or plateau on their watch.

Pastors, you do not have to see your vision achieved in your lifetime. God's vision is greater and extends far beyond our lifetime.

Moses did not enter the promised land.

David did not get to build the temple.

Jesus ascended to heaven with only 11 disciples and a ragtag bunch of followers.

Let's not be so self-absorbed to think that God's plans must be fulfilled in our lifetime, as though God revolves his timeline around our 80 or so years.

No. *The everlasting God has a timeless plan and we are just a speck in eternity, given the privilege of stewarding His purpose and passing the baton to the next generation.*

HEART OF A FATHER - THE HEART TRANSFORMATION

Much has been spoken about that verse in Malachi 4:5-6, when God will turn the hearts of the fathers to the children. It has become somewhat of a cliché, a phrase that brings cognitive understanding and rhetorical repetition without real heart transformation. The result is echoed by Paul as history repeats itself, and we find ourselves with ten thousand instructors, coaches, mentors, but very few real fathers (1 Corinthians 4:15).

How do we know that we are a real father (or mother)?

How do we know that we are not just a coach or an instructor appearing as a father?

Answer this question. Fill in the blank.

Fathers reproduce _____.

In Genesis, God created every creature to reproduce according to its own kind.

Animals will reproduce according to their own kind.

Birds will reproduce according to their own kind.

Humans will reproduce according to their own kind.

Many people say fathers reproduce sons. That is too short-sighted. No.

Fathers should reproduce *fathers* – according to their own kind.

Fathers don't just reproduce sons. Fathers reproduce fathers.

Mothers reproduce mothers, not just children.

Fathers reproducing sons is just two generations. In God's paradigm, He is thinking of at least three generations. He is the God of Abraham, Isaac, and Jacob.

Fathers don't just reproduce sons.
Fathers reproduce fathers.

I hear so many parents heave a sigh of relief: "My son graduated from university, so my job is done." Or "My daughter is happily married, so I have done my part. Now I can relax." But study Proverbs 13:22 carefully. It says, "A good man leaves an inheritance to his children's children..." Again, three generations. Business people think of estate planning and we pat ourselves on the back when we plan for our children. But God's definition of a good man is at least planning for grandchildren – to the third generation.

When we understand that our responsibility does not end with raising up good sons and daughters, but extends to grandchildren, then we also renew our mindset that we need our sons to mature into fathers in their own right.

This is the game changer. Our goal is not just to raise up sons and daughters but fathers and mothers. With this change of mindset and heart, inherently, we will empower and release our sons to become fathers in their own right.

Unfortunately, what I have been observing in the church world is the opposite. What is common is the all-powerful patriarch, with two to three generations following him. He has established himself as the special anointed man of God. He could be in his 60s or 70s, but still holds all the influence and authority. His spiritual sons are already in their 40s or 50s but still relating to him exclusively as sons and disciples. They are never released to become fathers discipling sons. Subsequently, the patriarch collects more spiritual sons in their 20s and 30s, directly coaching them, when he should have stepped back and allowed his sons to father the next generation. They do not know how to let their "sons" and "daughters" grow up to be spiritual fathers and mothers in their own right.

It is a church leadership conundrum – pastors of successful ministries or megachurches tend to be the alpha male type. They are the all-conquering heroes who naturally see themselves to be Abraham (father of faith) or Israel (father of a nation). They would be insulted to be seen as an Isaac. Isaac is like a lameduck lying down sheepishly waiting to be sacrificed. Their force-of-nature personality, drive, and talents are a double-edged sword. It is what makes them successful but it is also what will eclipse and suffocate their next generation. Our next generation leaders should walk in our footsteps, not in our shadow.

Our next generation leaders should walk in our footsteps, not in our shadow.

I have also seen too many "great men of God" who think and act like they are the center of the universe. They attract idealistic young people who orbit around this person. It is fine and biblical if it is a couple of years (even 10–15 years) of apprenticeship, but they never release these young people into their destiny. Time flies and these "young" people are no longer young, but they are still "laying down their dreams" to make the patriarch's vision come to pass. These patriarchs are not fathers. They are just using these young people to build their own ministry. Great fathers don't make us chase their dreams, they help us chase ours.

I had a text conversation with a younger pastor with immense potential. He texted me to wish me Happy 50th Birthday. This is how it went:

Great fathers don't make us chase their dreams, they help us chase ours.

Me: Thank you. When you are 50, you will accomplish more than me.

Younger Pastor: hahaha, I would be grateful if I accomplished half what you accomplished in my lifetime.

Me: Then I would have failed.

Success without successors is failure.

For Lia and me, our ethos is, *"Don't use people to build the church, but use the church to build people."*

Our greatness comes from making others great, especially the next generation.

Don't use people to build the church.
Use the church to build people.
- Pastor How & Pastor Lia

I have observed that the relationship dynamic between alpha male patriarchs and their spiritual children or disciples is static. They do not allow their sons and daughters to grow up. Their relationship dynamic is locked down and fixed, never fluid. It is typically frozen in a time when it is a top-down pattern. In other words, how they lead and manage a 20-year-old apprentice is the same 20 years later when he is now 40.

For Lia and me, our working relationship with our spiritual sons and daughters constantly evolves. When they were in their youths, it was more top-down instructional and correctional cushioned with huge amounts of encouragement. But as they mature, they get more authority. Now they are in their 30s, I value their opinions and give equal weightage to their decisions. They honor me while I respect them. Lia and I are now like first among equals. But there will come a day, when they will lead us both. They will be the fathers and mothers of the church. Lia and I will humbly submit and follow their vision. And when asked, we will always be there to offer our advice and counsel, but mostly our role is to encourage, support, pray for them, and celebrate their victories.

A great leader must dare to do three things:

- Dare to dream
- Dare to do
- Dare to die

Successful leaders usually have no problems with the first two dares. They dare to dream big and dare to do great things, but they don't dare to die. Yet John 12:24 teaches us that unless a kernel of wheat falls to the ground and dies, it remains only a single seed. But if it dies, it produces many seeds.

A godly father must know when to exit the stage. He knows when to die, so that his sons can rise up to be fathers.

Jesus knew when to die. Jesus didn't die when He was 80 years old. He handed over the key to Peter and the disciples when He was 33.

The greatest test of a father is when his sons become fathers.

The greatest test of a leader is if he can cede power voluntarily.

A great leader knows when to leave the stage.

A great leader knows how to give the stage and mic over to the next generation.

So what differentiates a father from a coach or an instructor?

What does it mean to really turn the heart of a father to the children?

A true father's leadership is self-sacrificing and self-depreciating.

He is not insecure. He is not competing with his sons and daughters.

He releases them into their destiny.

He rejoices when David slays 10,000.

He celebrates his sons' and daughters' victories.

He is happy when his spiritual children outshine him, like when Elisha had double Elijah's anointing.

His ultimate goal is the greater success of his sons and daughters because he knows his success hinges on their success. There can never be great success without great successors.

Here comes the mind-blowing part: Now imagine if every generation of pastors and leaders has this mindset and heart. *Every generation wants to make the next generations more successful. The Kingdom of God will go from glory to glory.*

So we have come to the altar call moment.

Are you willing to have a heart transformation?

Are you willing to lay down your dreams for the next GenerationS?

Are you willing to be a kingmaker, playmaker?

Are you willing to be an Isaac?

If yes, say a prayer now. Make a covenant with God.

Write a note to yourself on this page and sign it now.

Fold the corner of this page.

Bookmark or screenshot this page.

Just do something symbolic as a commitment and reminder that from now on, you will have the heart of a father or mother.

MY COMMITMENT

Join the **GenerationS Movement!**

How

The highest high, the greatest reward and blessing is that our own daughter, Rinnah, is all in, full on, and on fire for Jesus. She is bringing revival to her generation and the GenerationS that she is leading. Actually, she is the 15-year-old leading 130 youths mentioned in the very first story of this book (Chapter 2). Our one and only arrow who is on track and on target... And to round off with an apt conclusion to this book, we will end with words from her.

Rinnah Tan

I'm a pastor's kid. PK – as people would call it. Pastor How and Pastor Lia are my parents. As far as I can remember, Heart of God Church has been a part of my life since I was born.

I brought my best friend to church when I was 8 years old. I didn't know why but I just knew I had to bring him. There was an urgency in my heart for him to know God. I want people to know God, to love Him and to revere Him. You can say that is why I wanted to become a leader in church.

I don't want to be a Christian who waits around just to receive a 'get out of hell' free pass when I die. God is so much more than just someone who gives out free passes. That is why I have to bring people to know Him.

I want to be a different kind of leader. I want to be real. Looking perfect is not something I desire. I want to be a leader who can show both her strengths and weaknesses to others. That, to me, is being real.

Perhaps I caught that from my parents because they are very real. Whether on stage, at home, or even when overseas, they are the same. What I see at home is exactly how they are like in church! What you see is what you get, and you never have to second-guess my parents.

Most people would say I'm biased because I'm the pastors' daughter and that I will always support them. However, I think I'm the most reliable and unbiased person who can tell you about who they truly are. I know everything and I see everything on stage, offstage, at home, behind the scenes. I see every flaw and every crack and I'm here to say that the church is good and my parents, they walk the talk.

The church is not perfect but the church leadership team has good hearts and good intentions. They genuinely want to build a great church. A lot of pastors are hurting because their kids are not following Jesus. My heart goes out to them and I, for one, understand how sensitive pastors' kids are to their Christian surroundings. For me to be here in church, on fire for God, that must prove a lot about the environment I grew up in.

I remember one day my parents came home from a long day of work. They were exceptionally overjoyed and happy. I thought maybe the church had an unusual breakthrough but no, it was because they had just given away a lot of money from their business to the staff in church. That's who my parents are – always giving. More than just being generous pastors, to me they are the most perfect parents in the world. (Dad, please raise my allowance after this... 😄😄) They have always parented and pastored me since I was young. Even though they weren't earning a lot when I was growing up, I felt like I had everything I wanted in the world. They had not allowed me to suffer lack, whether it be money, time or spiritual input.

Aside from my parents, one other reason why I am on fire for God is because Heart of God Church is a youth church that supports youths. The church empowers and emboldens youths like me to rise up and do something for the Kingdom of God. I held responsibilities I couldn't fully fathom at 11, yet despite not having any experience, I was given opportunities again and again to love God and serve Him. It's not just me, but there's a whole generation of young people like me in HOGC, wanting to live for God and become full-time staff or pastors!

Let me tell you what I have seen while growing up as my parents' child. (No, I'm not held hostage while writing this. :))

MY MUM

1. My mother loves without fear of hurt. Not that she's stupid or ignorant or oblivious. She knows. She knows you'll hurt her, yet she still loves. And she doesn't just love you. She loves you with her heart, her hands, with everything she has and more. I've always grown up with that unconditional love, that affection, that joy of knowing no matter what you do someone will still love you.

2. More than just being a loving mother, she is a strong woman leader. She is my dad's equal. She didn't just watch from the sidelines, no, she ploughed the ground and built the church from scratch together with my dad.

My mum is a fighter. I saw her fight cancer. I am the way I am today because I saw her fight. That fight is also in me.

My mum is a discipler. People have said that my dad and mum are great disciplers. I think I deserve at least half the credit because they've been practising on me at home.

Whenever I hit a snag while leading our members in church, I would go to my mother. Yes, she counsels me, loves me and encourages me but more than that, she trains me to be a better leader with her wise leadership advice.

3. My mother is a powerful preacher and communicator. She trained me to preach in my connect groups. There was once I had to prepare for a homiletics training where I had to preach in front of my leaders when I was 14. My mother took 4 hours out of her day off to teach me how to write a good sermon. She taught me sermon structure, the art of delivery and even the intangibles like the anointing of God. Afterwards, she let me write the sermon myself. She edited one part of the sermon carefully and taught me how to improve on it. She then let me edit the rest of the sermon myself so I could apply what I learned. This was how she trained me, led me and loved me.

4. Another thing you may observe or in fact hear when you live with her is that she prays really passionately. Like – really, really passionately loud. Sometimes a little too loud (especially in the morning when I'm sleeping $_zz^z$). On her 50th birthday, I awoke in the wee hours of the morning to her praying and worshipping God. I came out of my room to find her dedicating the next 50 years of her life to God all over again. That is who my mother is.

MY DAD

1. On the surface, my dad is strong, wise and serious. His plans for the church on the macro and micro levels always amaze me. I mean brains and brawn – he's great on the outside – but on the inside, I would say he's secretly a softie (oops). He is not the too mushy, sweet-tongued guy whose words are not backed by actions. His love is practical. He's the guy who ensures that you are properly covered by insurance, the guy who makes sure the car is cold enough on a hot day before you step in, the guy who cooks for you without you telling him you're hungry. The little things. I guess you could say my mum got a good one. :)

2. There are many good men in the world but I guess you could say my dad is an exceptionally good one. He is humble, never has any ill intentions and he's honest. To me, he is the most honourable man I've ever met. Some people love to showcase acts of kindness in public but he is the complete opposite – humble and blessing others in the background when no one is looking. He is always the same on stage and offstage, in church and at home. Everything he preaches on stage he lives it out.

3. His love for God and the church also inspires me every day. Once when I was talking to him, he was sharing his heart with me. He wants people to treat God with honour and to treat His church right. And that is why he wants to build a church that will bring honour to God's name. He just can't take it when people treat God and His church shabbily. He said the church is the Bride of Christ. How would you feel if people kept criticising your wife and dishonouring her? He wants to protect the Bride and build a church that will bring glory to God. And when he said that he teared.

I was so impacted by his pure motive for God and church. From that day, I also wanted to serve God with a pure heart and build a church that is worthy of Him.

4. Another time, during one of the services when my dad preached about the fear of the Lord, he preached with all his heart and strength.

I could see the passion and zeal for God in his eyes. During the altar call, I received a vision and word from God. God spoke to me that I would preach the fear of the Lord to the church like my father one day. Just as how my dad gave his all to build the church, I will build the best church for God. My dad has dedicated his life to the church and I want to do the same too.

Because of the way my parents live, I know that God is good and that He is real. I want to live for Him too. Now while I'm growing as a leader in church, I am experiencing a little of the same heartbreaks and pain that my parents have gone through. Some of my peers have left church and their faith. You may think that would discourage me from being on fire in church but it doesn't. It makes me fear God even more and want to serve Him for the rest of my life, knowing that there is so much more I can do in the Church and His Kingdom. I want to give the best years of my life to build Heart of God Church.

The greatest reward: Rinnah, Pastor Lia and Pastor How serving together.

Rinnah's testimony: Growing up in a youth church!

Turn the page for a
VOLUME 2 EXCLUSIVE PREVIEW

With contributions from **Joakim Lundqvist**, **Bill Wilson** and **Dr Robi Sonderegger** as they share personal insights about **Heart of God Church Singapore.**

Heart & Heartbreaks Behind Raising

GENERATIONS

Volume 2

How to Build a Church by Youths, for Youths, to Reach Youths

@Pastor.How @Pastor.Lia

Heartbreaks

After heart work and hard work come the heartbreaks.

How ✈

Sex, affairs, adultery, abortion, porn, voyeurism, rebellion, politics, manipulation, deception, lies, etc.

Sounds like a Hollywood movie or drama series.

Unfortunately, this is not House of Cards but House of God.

Yes... all these happened in Heart of God Church, perpetrated by youths who grew up in-house.

All these sins and crimes were committed by some youths who grew up in HOGC and we had to deal with them. Well, I guess the House of God also had the sons of Eli.

> 1 Samuel 2:22 (MSG)
> By this time Eli was very old. He kept getting reports on how his sons were ripping off the people and sleeping with the women who helped out at the sanctuary.

1 Samuel 2:24-25 (MSG)

Oh, my sons, this is not right! These are terrible reports I'm getting, stories spreading right and left among GOD'S people! If you sin against another person, there's help—God's help. But if you sin against GOD, who is around to help?" But they were far gone in disobedience and refused to listen to a thing their father said.

Pastor Lia and I refuse to make the mistakes of Eli. Instead of putting his sons on the altar of God (like Abraham), Eli put God on the altar of his sons. Even though we loved them like our own children, we had to hold them accountable. Though it pained us, God's House was more precious than our love and sentimentality for our spiritual children. When God began to expose their sins to the leadership and we confronted them, instead of repentance and remorse, we got more lies to cover their sins. Gradually their lies turned into accusations and eventually hate and attack.

But hate won't stop us. Hurt won't stop us.

We need to do the right thing and the righteous thing.

It is tough for Lia and me to even write this chapter...

Whatever Jesus does, we want to follow His ultimate example. So for many years after all their attacks and accusations, Lia and I kept silent. Except for our Senior Leadership Team and those who needed to know in order to repair the damage of these wicked people, we didn't tell on them. I am sure many people in church wanted to hear from us. Some encouraged us to speak up, especially when the wicked group was relentlessly spreading lies to whomever would listen. However, Lia and I just didn't feel released by the Holy Spirit to speak. Trust me, it was tempting to tell the church how bad they were. And we had the mic too.

I cried for these people more than my own cancer.

One of the principles I have lived by is to always *preach out of testimony not therapy.* Never bring to the pulpit your unresolved issues – I would always tell our young preachers in training sessions. We do not want the pulpit to be mixed with our flesh and unhealed emotions.

Preach out of Testimony Not Therapy.

Listen, perhaps you are going through a terrible time now. You are not only in the valley but scraping the bottom of the airless pit. I know, it is a very bad experience. But *don't build theology out of bad experiences.* Don't make your bad experience the reference point out of which you will live out the rest of your life. It is but one chapter in your life. A chapter does not make a book. Wait for the Lord. Don't be in a haste to build theology out of your current bad experiences! When you do what is right, you will come out on the other side to preach out of testimony and not therapy!

Don't build theology out of bad experiences.

After How and I were healed and healthy, we felt ready. However, just because we were ready to speak, it didn't mean God was ready.

Then one day, we received a phone call from the police.

And we knew God was ready.

But If Not

Lia ⚾

The irony about breast cancer is this: *You feel well but are told you're sick. And that you have to get really sick to get well.* That basically sums up my journey that began with a sentence from a doctor, "You have cancer. You need chemotherapy."

In 2012, I was diagnosed with stage 3 breast cancer. I went through surgeries, chemotherapy and radiation treatments that year. The surgeries and radiation were hard. Chemotherapy was the toughest. They pumped a cocktail of poison into my veins every 2 weeks for 12 cycles, over 20 times. Yes, you do have to get really sick to get well. Chemotherapy ensures that. There were so many rounds that once you started feeling a little better, you had to go for the next round of treatment. All mothers will understand this when I say chemotherapy is like giving birth on Sunday and on Monday, you discover you are pregnant again!

At one point in the treatment protocol the nurses were especially vigilant when it came to injecting one particular toxic deep red liquid into my veins. They even have a medical nickname for it. For the first time, I met a 'Red Devil' which was more potent than any Manchester United player.

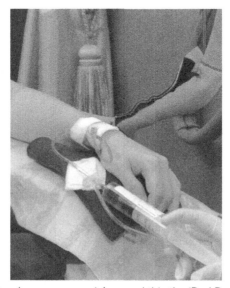

The chemo nurses nicknamed this the 'Red Devil'.

I lost all my hair. I was fat from chemotherapy and steroids. I was so fat that once I sat on my iPhone and it became an iPad. Once I even stepped on the weighing scale and it spoke to me, "One person at a time, please!"

At home, self-administered injections to boost my white blood count took place after each cycle of chemo treatment. My gallant husband, How, injected me for a total of 28 times. Many know him as Pastor How the Visionary but I wish everyone could see him as How the Husband. There is a quiet awe when you see a man who can commit to the 'in sickness' part of the wedding vow. If anxiety equates love, then he must be the most loving man on earth because when my surgery took longer than expected, his heart was going to leap out of his chest with nervousness outside the operating theatre. It took longer because the surgeon did not expect my cancer to have spread to my lymph nodes. After my surgeries, How helped me shower. He settled all my insurance. He would have gone for chemotherapy in my place if he could. He accompanied me for every single treatment that year. And till today, he goes with me to every doctor's appointment. (It's funny. I just realised that my oncologist has never once seen me alone in his clinic since I first saw him in 2012 till now!)

During the chemo days, How would give me my booster injections first before he went to work. His heart was heavy but his unflinching commitment would bring him to the church office. We had just expanded from three to four services before we found out we had a cancer crisis in hand. At that time, we were the only two pastors. The first generation of young potential pastors were still... young. So he was the only one left to handle everything in church from preaching to finances to acquiring our new worship venue Imaginarium, to endless, endless responsibilities. He loved his wife deeply but he treated the Bride of Christ equally well.

I tear as I write this because I have never seen this man back down from any stress. He simply does not know how to give his second best to people, to the church and to his family.

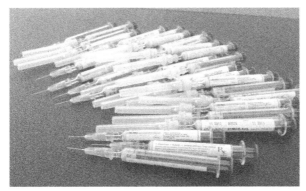

Pastor How injected me daily with booster shots before he went to work — a sharp reminder of his love.

After *slash* (surgery) and *poison* (chemotherapy) comes *burn* (radiation). Radiation was a daily commitment for 28 times as well. Yes, I counted. Cancer is a counting game. For every stage of treatment, you start an internal countdown clock. You know that better days are coming.

Many people asked me how I went through that hardship especially when my breast cancer was at stage 3. Cancer had invaded my regional lymph nodes. While many different studies give different sets of statistics, one common thread shows that at stage 3, the 5-year survival rate definitely drops. In one global study, 5-year survival rates of stage 1 and stage 2 are 86% and 69%, respectively. At stage 3, it drops to 51%. If it has spread to a distant part, the 5-year survival rate drops further to 32%.*

Based on these statistics, I have a 50-50 chance of living beyond five years. But I have already lived past five years! In Marvel lingo, that means I am the half that Thanos' Snap didn't kill off in The Blip! Wow.

I was sick with cancer. But I have always believed what Bishop Dale Bronner encouraged me in an email – **your CONDITION is NOT YOUR CONCLUSION.** I lost all my hair, but it grew back. God heals, He restores. Right now, I'm in my ninth year of being cancer-free. Way past the fifth year. Thank You, Jesus.

So how did I go through this valley of my life, many people asked.

First things first – when I had cancer, what helped was that I had put my faith in Christ. I was a Christian. I was already having a relationship with Jesus. So, I knew my end. Even if I did die from cancer, I was going to be in heaven. I was so assured of where I would be if I died. You can say that when I received my stage 3 diagnosis, I was actually processing my prognosis of eternity with Jesus and it looked promising!

---

* Khadije Maajani et al., "The Global and Regional Survival Rate of Women With Breast Cancer: A Systematic Review and Meta-analysis," *Clinical Breast Cancer* Vol. 19, No. 3 (2019): 165-177.

Jesus promised us and said, "In my Heavenly Father's House are many mansions." Heaven is not a crummy place. The Bible says God prepares for us mansions, not man caves. Thank God. I hear a lot of women breathing a sigh of relief there. It is also not a place filled with bare-bodied, winged angelic children who play the harp for eternity. God is in heaven. It is a place where there will be no more tears and no more pain. Once I am sure of the end, then I can deal with the in-between! C.S. Lewis said,

> Aim at heaven, and you will get earth thrown in.
> Aim at earth and you get neither.

When I had cancer, I was aiming at heaven. I had this conviction that Jesus had my end all nicely wrapped up. Because I had secured my eternity in Christ, I was able to work out how to walk through this valley in my life on earth. When you walk through the fire or see a life storm coming, ask yourself, "Have I secured my eternity in Jesus?" Knowing you have a secure end releases you to deal with the current.

Besides that, what got me through a crisis? *Faith and trust.* We need both in this Christian life that we live. There is a balance between *faith and trust.*

Trust is passive, faith is active.

I am not saying trust is no good. Let me explain it to you. The way *faith and trust* work together is that *trust* sees the end. But it is *faith* that carries us through the in-between. Trust is latent. *It sits there as a concealed power until it is activated.*

Trust is PASSIVE, Faith is ACTIVE.
Trust is LATENT POWER.

Both are important in our walk with God. There is a difference between *faith and trust. Faith is for the now.*

Hebrews 11:1

Now faith is the substance of things hoped for, the evidence of things not seen.

The Bible says that you can put your faith in God to perform great works for us *now* even though we can't see those works yet. Trust, on the other hand, is for the *future*. We need both.

Faith is for the Now.
Trust is for the Future.

TRUST, NO FAITH

However, some Christians have trust in God for the future but no faith in God for the now. Trust when it's not combined with faith becomes way too passive. On its own, trust simply says, "Que sera sera, whatever will be will be."

People with just trust don't do anything. They cross their fingers and hug their crosses and believe that everything will always turn out right someday. When not joined with faith, solo trust says:

"Relax, hard work is overrated. Someday I will pass my exams."

"Someday I will get out of this addiction..."

"Godly parenting is too tiring... Someday my children will turn out right..."

Trust without faith is like a lacklustre attitude that says, "Cross your fingers, hope for the best." When a person only has trust and no faith, they have nothing in them to fight their daily fights. They have no strength for the in-between. They have no spunk for the now.

They crumble when difficulties come. When they receive bad news, their world comes crashing down because they have no faith to fight for the *now*. People with just trust do not pray to God in faith for miracles. They don't seek God in active faith for a change in their circumstances and ominously believe their end is sealed!

We need to have faith to fight the daily fights. If not, we will be overwhelmed. We cannot simply have trust but no faith. We also need faith for the *now*.

FAITH, NO TRUST

On the other hand, some Christians are the complete opposite. They have faith but no trust. They have what we call 'hyper-faith'. Sometimes, this is the problem with us who are charismatic Christians. We are only big on faith confessions. It is almost like a denial wrapped up in faux strength. People with hyper-faith often say nervously, "Oh, I've already prayed. I have already confessed good things. I have been confessing and confessing positively. Everything will be alright... nothing bad will happen. Positive confession, only positive confession!"

So, when they receive a doctor's report that is negative, it completely shipwrecks their hyper-faith. Hyper-faith believers are set up for a crash and burn. When what they prayed for does not happen the way they expect, they crash because they only have faith for the now. They can't see beyond the now. They crash in the crisis and then they walk away from God.

This is the danger for many charismatic Christians who have faith but they don't have trust. When their hyper-faith bubble bursts, they can't see beyond the now to the end.

It is so important that we have *both* faith and trust. Faith is active. It carries us through the crisis but trust is also important. Trust sees the end. Trust is passive and must be activated like latent power. Trust rests in God. It believes that in every crisis, even if the reports continue to be bad, underneath are the everlasting arms of God (Deuteronomy 33:27).

In a crisis: Faith says, "I've got You God!" Trust says, "God, You've got me!"

> ## Faith says, "I've got You God!"
> ## Trust says, "God, You've got me!"

Have you ever seen the guy who walks the tightrope in a circus? Faith is what makes you dare to step off that platform to walk that tightrope. And trust is knowing that even if you fall, God's hands are there to pick you up like that safety net for the tightrope walker. Trust is like a safety net. It believes that God has got you!

There is a powerful story in the Bible that displays faith and trust. In Daniel 3, three young Jews – Shadrach, Meshach and Abed-Nego – were captured by their enemies and brought to Babylon.

Nebuchadnezzar, the king of Babylon at that time, built an image of gold and wanted everyone under his rulership to bow down and worship the image. Everyone bowed except the three young men. They refused to comply because they wanted to worship the one true God.

The incensed king confronted them. He threatened to throw them into the fiery furnace. An intense conversation arose. The king asked them, "And which god will deliver you from my hands?"

Shadrach, Meshach and Abed-Nego were caught in a crisis. They were literally facing a fire! But look at their response:

> Daniel 3:16-17
> Shadrach, Meshach, and Abed-Nego answered and said to
> the king, "O Nebuchadnezzar, we have no need to answer

you in this matter. If that is the case, our God whom we serve *is able to deliver us from the burning fiery furnace,* and He will deliver us from your hand, O king.

These three young Hebrew men had faith in the *now* to carry them through their crisis. "God is able to deliver us," they proclaimed. Their faith cried out loud and clear in their actions. With their defiant stance, they were saying, "We've got You God, in this crisis!" They had faith in God's power. But faith was not all they had. Look at what else they proclaimed:

> Daniel 3:18
> *But if not,* let it be known to you, O king, that we do not serve your gods, nor will we worship the gold image which you have set up."

They said, "Yes God can deliver us, we have faith. *But if not...*"

They were proclaiming, "We believe God has the power to deliver us. *But if not,* it is still alright because we trust in our God." Essentially, they were saying – not only have we got God, *but if not,* God has got us!

But if not – three crucial words. Sometimes hyper-faith Christians criticise these three words. They are horrified and accuse us, "Oh, how can you say 'but if not'? It shows that you are doubting God. You cannot be negative!"

Those in the hyper-faith camp will brand the three young men as doubters and as people who lack faith in God. But that is far from the truth. The three young men had something stronger than faith. They had faith *and* trust!

They are saying, I have faith for now. *But if not,* I have trust for the future. God can deliver us *but if not,* we will still worship Him and none other because He has got our end secured. God has got us in this crisis! They have *both* faith *and* trust!

Still, the king threw them into the furnace. However, God delivered them out of the fiery flames! Not a hair was burnt! The king witnessed the miracle.

> Daniel 3:28
>
> Nebuchadnezzar spoke, saying, "Blessed be the God of Shadrach, Meshach, and Abed-Nego, who sent His Angel and delivered His servants who *trusted* in Him, and they have frustrated the king's word, and yielded their bodies, that they should not serve nor worship any god except their own God!

What did the king see? He saw their trust! He heard their three words – ***but if not***!

BUT IF NOT...

Those three words got me through stage 3 breast cancer.

"God, I know You can deliver me from stage 3 breast cancer, *but if not*, I've secured my eternity with You."

"God, You know my life's work is GenerationS. After training and raising so many young leaders in our church, I will be alive when it is time to raise my own daughter to lead. *But if not*, she will still be trained by the leaders we have raised."

"God, I believe You can help ease up the surgeries, chemo and radiation. *But if not*, I will still praise You with my voice."

Some of you reading this, you need these three words to get you through a difficult time right now. You have got to start shifting your prayers to ones that have both faith *and* trust.

Don't just be stuck on the faith part for the 'now'. The Apostle Peter is the guy in the moment. He is the 'now' guy. So faith pushes him out of the boat onto the water. Faith empowers him to take those miraculous steps. However, when he started to look around and saw the problems, he started to sink as fast as his faith leaked. That's when Jesus came and taught him another lesson – *trust*. Peter was the 'faith' guy who needed to learn how to trust God when things go bad.

Some of you are like Peter seeing the waves of problems around you, you need to learn to trust God.

Some of you, however, need greater faith to push you out of the boat onto the water.

Faith says, "I can do all things through Christ who strengthens me."

Trust says, "*But if not.*"

We need both.

We must have *both* faith and trust – one last thought on this:

Faith moves the hands of God. Trust touches the heart of God.

> ## FAITH moves the Hands of God.
> ## TRUST touches the Heart of God.

Some of you can't understand why you are going through this difficult time in your life right now. I want to encourage you: ***If you can't see His hands, trust His heart.*** *(Inspired by Charles Spurgeon)* Trust His character.

In Volume 2, I wrote that we should not break but we can trust God and allow ourselves to be broken by the Holy Spirit on the inside. The Bible says:

Psalm 34:18

The Lord is near to those who have a broken heart...

Rarely have I heard people praising God for the state of brokenness they are in. But I have discovered that God can use our brokenness more than our gifts and talents.

After cancer, I started what we call Miracles & Breakthroughs Services. A new healing dimension in our church has been birthed. God has added a new dimension to my ministry. More and more people are encountering the power of God in our church and getting healed. More and more people are walking into their miracles and breakthroughs.

I minister not just with sympathy where we say, "I am sorry you are going through this." But because of the cancer valley I have walked right through to the mountaintop, I can minister with a brokenness that says, "I know exactly how you feel. And I have experienced His resurrection power. Come, let us have faith and trust in Him together." That is empathy. *Sympathy morphs strongly into empathy simply because of brokenness.*

Sympathy is good and empathy is even better but don't stop there. *Move from sympathy to empathy and then to authority!*

Move from Sympathy to Empathy and then to Authority!

Our *authority* is in Jesus. The Bread of Life who was broken on the cross has secured our healing for us!

Isaiah 53:5

But He was wounded for our transgressions,

He was bruised for our iniquities;

The chastisement for our peace was upon Him,

And by His stripes we are healed.

Our M&B Services work because of the *authority* we have in Him. Our brokenness gives us *empathy* while His brokenness on the cross gives us *authority*!

> ## Our brokenness gives us empathy.
> ## His brokenness on the cross gives us authority!

Coming back to the thought of brokenness, I realise that God feeds the multitudes with the brokenness of our lives. The bread had to be broken in the hands of Jesus before the people could be miraculously fed. The anointing only flows when the alabaster jar is broken. Blessings are found in the brokenness.

Determined to be a blessing, in my cancer year, I took my insurance payout and together with our savings and monies from our personal family business, Pastor How and I gave $1 million to our church Building Fund that year. The feeling of loving and honouring His House was indescribable!

Aside from M&B Services which have blessed so many people and the $1 million that feeds the multitudes, God has a way of putting the cherry on your cake when you are celebrating brokenness. Out of this message, Matt Redman co-wrote a song with us called *But If Not*!

Just watching Matt create in the studio was already a jaw-dropping event. He puts the 'W' in 'wordsmith' and 'M' in 'maestro' and 'H' in 'humility'. And so to have him co-write a song with us after he heard this message *But If Not* was something that I had never imagined would take place. This song collaboration with Matt ranks in the top five highlights of my life!

Friends, put your faith and trust in Him.

Let *But If Not* be the holy defiant attitude of your heart.

The blessing is found in the brokenness.

Know this — God is not breaking you. He is not killing you. He is blessing you!

How to Grow Your Church Younger and Stronger

A big church may not be strong,
but a Strong Church will always grow big.

How ✈

The question on most pastors' minds is "How do I grow my church bigger?" This is a good place to start but this is not the only question. In life as well as in ministry, it is more important to ask the right questions than to find the right answers. Another really important question to ask is "How do I grow my church stronger?" Because a big church may not necessarily be strong, but a Strong Church will eventually grow big. In life, anything healthy will grow. Parents don't set a target for their child to grow to a certain height or size but to ensure he is healthy. I have never heard of a father saying to his nine-year-old son, "Hey, the Lord spoke to me that the vision for the new year is for you to grow to 150cm. And you will grow faster than all your friends and cousins. Then I will have the tallest son in the neighborhood. So every day we are going to pray hard for 150. And every weekend, we are going to take measurements."

That's just ridiculous right?

But that is how we measure our churches. Attendance is not the be-all and end-all. There is a place and time for measuring attendance but the obsession with it obscures some other barometers. Growth is a byproduct of health. A healthy child will grow up naturally. While it is important and biblical to grow the church bigger, Lia and I have always been focused on growing the church *stronger*.

> ### A big church may not be strong, but a Strong Church will always grow big.

Measurements are important because what you measure becomes the standard of appraisal and the results you aim for. So if we measure only church attendance and finances, then that will be our narrow focus and we may not be getting the full picture. The Bible calls the Church the Body of Christ. And just as a body can be big but flabby, a church can also be big but flabby. We don't want to be a fat church. We want to be a fit and fighting spiritual army.

That is why the HOGC church model is what we have coined the *Strong Church Model.*

5 PILLARS OF A
STRONG CHURCH

**YOUTH &
YOUNG ADULT
REVIVAL**

MOBILIZATION

HOME

**CULTURE &
ATMOSPHERE**

CHARACTER

Sneak Peek:
Contents Page of Volume 2

Scan the QR code to View

END OF VOLUME 2 EXCLUSIVE PREVIEW

VOLUME 1
INSIDE STORIES

In this book, you've heard from global Christian leaders, HOGC's homegrown pastors, and even How and Lia's own daughter. To complete the 360° view, the last four 'inside stories' will be told by some of the people who work closest with them. Hopefully they will shed light on some FAQs people ask about Heart of God Church.

- Head of Global Partnerships, on what co-senior pastoring looks like
- Board member in his 60s, on what older people do in a youth church
- Director of Global Relations, a Westerner's perspective on an Asian church
- Chief of Staff, on what goes on inside the Senior Pastors' Office

Valerie Fifi
on what co-senior pastoring looks like
Head of Global Partnerships, Heart of God Church

It's often said, "Everything rises and falls on leadership." I am extremely blessed to be under the leadership of not just one, but TWO Senior Pastors! Pastor How and Pastor Lia's distinct yet complementary giftings are the undeniable reason HOGC has been able to grow in numbers and stature all this while.

As co-founders and co-senior pastors, they have both been at the frontlines of building HOGC together from day one. Besides preaching in the weekly services and Bible studies, both pastors oversaw their own scopes. Pastor How ran the weekly services and Events planning meetings while Pastor Lia was head of the Worship Team. Later on, as more leaders rose up to reinforce them, they were able to expand to other job scopes. Pastor How went on to work on the church system and structures while Pastor Lia oversaw the entire operations and every training aspect of the church.

Observing how they build the church side by side is akin to watching Bono-The Edge in a concert, Xavi-Iniesta in soccer or Bumgarner-Posey in baseball. They each have their own space to shine yet work seamlessly towards the same goal.

Up to this day, Pastor How and Pastor Lia sit through countless meetings *together*. As staff we see this as double the wisdom and blessing because they add equally important perspectives to all our discussions – from church vision and strategy meetings, to pastoral and operations meetings, board meetings and even those hard-to-navigate crisis management meetings. I guess they are the scriptural example of 'two are better than one'!

The secret of HOGC is having two senior pastors who preach powerfully and yet are distinct in their own anointing. That partnership is on full display during Revival Night Services. Everybody looks forward to those times when Pastor How and Pastor Lia would preach one night each. A left jab by Pastor How, a right hook by Pastor Lia, and the devil is KO and all heaven breaks loose! Two atoms coming together for a nuclear fusion and only HOGC has the privilege of experiencing that on a regular basis. This combination of TWO senior pastors' anointings builds every generation, every leader, every member in our church.

As Head of Global Partnerships, I have witnessed that taking place overseas too on a few rare occasions.

There was an overseas conference fortunate enough to experience this for themselves! Somehow, Pastor How and Pastor Lia's schedules aligned and they ended up preaching in a conference together! They took turns to preach a two-part series. They gave stirring altar calls where many leaders rose up and some responded to the full-time calling of God. Others found answers they had been seeking. One of them was a European senior pastor. He had spent the past few months seeking God for the next steps in his movement. That day, after hearing both parts of the series, God finally spoke to him through Pastor Lia's altar call. He not only received a personal revelation, but also a vision for his movement for the following year. He was so excited as he was sharing this with Pastors! But I quietly smiled to myself and had to resist bragging – you've just had a full 'HOGC Revival Night' experience!

Growing up in HOGC since I was 16, I have never experienced gender discrimination. But as I started travelling with Pastors I heard many stories which really shocked me!

There is a couple who are both Christian ministers. They were invited to preach on separate occasions at the same church. The husband was placed in a nice hotel while the wife, in a motel. That church, somehow, allocated a bigger budget for the male minister.

Another famous founder of a prominent Christian organisation shared that when she walks into a room with her husband, people would always engage her husband and ignore her. He always had to direct them to her and explain that she was the founder of the organisation.

I heard of another church which refused to ordain their female ministers for many years, even though the females and males were taking on the exact same responsibilities in church.

Hearing all these stories, I was appalled! In HOGC, I have never been shortchanged because of my gender. I have never once felt a male leader was more honoured than me. In fact, in all my years of training and selecting leaders, gender was *never* a criteria that crossed my mind! Little did I know, as my pastors continually build a 'gender-discrimination-free bubble world' in HOGC, they would experience such discrimination for themselves as they preached overseas.

I have seen how the same overseas church would invite Pastor How and Pastor Lia on different occasions but the treatment would be worlds apart. When they hosted Pastor How, the church rolled out the full red carpet experience but for Pastor Lia, it seemed like most things were done as an afterthought. I know Pastor Lia, she is not looking to be wined and dined. She is not a diva. She doesn't need posh hotels or need people to wait on her hand and foot. In fact, the introvert in her (yes, people think she is an extrovert) prefers to stay alone in the room and prepare for her preaching sessions. She's very simple. If she is hungry, she will just eat a banana. As long as she has her latte, she can survive even a nuclear fallout. She knows when to abase and abound. I am just pointing out the disparity I observed.

I struggled to understand why there would be such a disparity. Pastor Lia, however, seemed unfazed by these trivial matters. After all, she's been on mission trips to places like India where she would preach to throngs of youths by day, and lay on straw mats in dilapidated huts to sleep by night. My pastors have always taught us – relationship precedes ministry. They would often accept invites to places because of a personal friend or even return honorariums to smaller ministries to bless them back in return!

As I travel around the world to various churches and conferences, the difference between how the man and woman of God are treated is prevalent in many places.

WHAT CO-SENIOR PASTORING LOOKS LIKE

Even as people from overseas look to hear about God's work in HOGC, their first instinct is to look for the male voice. But they do not understand that HOGC is built by two voices – Pastor How's and Pastor Lia's. Today, I would like to tell all my global friends, don't miss out on the female voice we have in HOGC!

Pastor Lia is not the alternative to Pastor How when he is unavailable. Pastor Lia is more than just the supportive wife of Pastor How. She is not just married to a man with the vision. She has her own vision, her own calling, her own anointing! In fact, I believe if Pastor How had not been a pastor and chose to be a businessman, Pastor Lia would still be pastoring a Strong Youth Church today... except she might be very lonely without Pastor How!

Pastor Lia's mandate is not limited by gender. Over the past 20 years, she has raised both male and female leaders under her leadership. She values women and she considers it a privilege to speak to women because she herself is one. However, it is our loss to limit Pastor Lia to just women's topics when her calling is to pastors and church-building too. I feel sad for those who have not heard her best sermons addressing topics such as leadership, pioneering and church-building.

HOGC, thank God there is no discrimination here. This church has always been 50% men and 50% women serving together. The strength of HOGC is having both a male and a female voice. This is only possible because Pastor Lia constantly pushes the standard of what it means to be a co-senior pastor and an Asian female leader. I also believe Pastor How plays a huge part – I have seen how he empowers and gives equal space to Pastor Lia's voice both at home and on the global platform.

To all the men in HOGC, it will be your greatest gain if you receive from Pastor Lia too and continue to respect other women leaders. To all the women in HOGC, we are free to serve and lead as God calls. Let's keep building on what we have!

Jacob Tan
on what older people do in a youth church

Heart of God Church Board Member
Advisor to the Executive Leadership Team

I am in my 60s, a former aggressive fighter pilot, flying instructor, forward airborne controller, and squadron commander, leading a highly specialised unit and eventually becoming an ops/tech consultant. As Operations Manager dealing with various critical systems developments, I managed multimillion-dollar projects. Because of my technological contributions, I was awarded the Defence Technology Award in 2001. At the height of my flying days, I made history. There are only three fighter pilots in Singapore who clocked 2,000 flight hours in an F5 fighter jet. I am one of them. We, F5 fighter pilots, brought the Singapore Air Force into the supersonic age in 1979!

I was good at what I did. But I lacked empathy. I couldn't understand why I could accomplish tasks and others couldn't. To me, fear meant weakness and to trust in God meant a lack of ability. 'Above All' was my favourite motto.

I was also a third generation traditional Christian but I didn't know anything about character change, renewal of the mind and finding God's true purpose for me. But all that was about to change for me.

In 2004, after a break of four years away from God and church, I stepped into Heart of God Church on Christmas Eve. The atmosphere and the sermon took me completely by surprise. Pastor How was talking about sin and how it separates us from God. Frankly, the judgmental me was expecting some typical Christmas message. I decided to come back for the service. I came to check out HOGC because my daughter attended the church, but since then, I have never checked out.

I began my journey as a mere member then eventually became a board member. In fact, I am now working closely with the Executive Leadership Team as an advisor.

I'm known for being out of the box – a maverick! Fellow board member Teck Chuan (who is the other head of grey hair on the board) summarised it aptly. He said, "Jacob, every pastor wants you on their team but not everyone can 'handle' you. Our senior pastors are exceptional and rare."

I am right now trying to fulfil two roles: path finder and gap filler.

Path finder means leading and exploring new directions. My biggest value add is in strategic positioning which requires exploring new options or new paths. For example, dealing with government agencies, landlords and community organisations.

Gap filler is to plug any holes, deficiencies – to cover your back! I cover areas that are missed in the church or where there is lack of expertise such as crisis management and media requests, etc.

I am just one of many adults serving in the church. There are many more fulfilling other roles.

From member to board member to advisor for the Executive Leadership Team – how was the journey like for me?

Spiritual Encounters

In the early years during an overnight prayer meeting, a group of adults including myself were at the front where Pastor How and Pastor Lia were praying for people. I noticed that others were falling under the power of God. I had heard of it before but coming from a traditional church background, I seriously had my doubts. Besides, I was an accomplished fighter pilot who was used to handling 6 or 7Gs easily. I could handle upside-down manoeuvres without G LOC (loss of consciousness from G forces)! I told myself I would not be made to fall by the 'young pastors'. I decided to stand firm, lock my knees, just like a military sentry guard. *I WILL NOT FALL*, I told myself. Then Pastor Lia prayed for me and touched my palms gently. Immediately, I felt a warmth travelling from my hands, through my body and down to my knees. As soon as the warmth reached my knees, it broke the knee lock. God's presence washed over me and I fell, panting heavily as if I had just gone running. I heard a gentle voice near my ear, saying, "Jacob... don't fight me!" I was very conscious, all of my life I had resisted God because of my pride and God was challenging me to change. I knew then in my heart that I had to humble myself and submit to Him, the real Above All! As our pastors imitate Christ, I must imitate them and follow their teachings.

More Spiritual Encounters

There were more of such spiritual encounters. On another occasion, Pastors invited the adults who were new in HOGC to be prayed for. I was a bit proud and said to myself, *What can the young pastor do to me!* As I was closing my eyes and joining others in prayer, I suddenly felt a shockwave come from my left and it stopped at my body – it was the same supersonic wave I had encountered during a dogfight, whereby my wingman flew head on and missed my fighter jet by a few feet.

I was shocked and confused as to how I could have experienced that near-death shockwave in church! At that moment, I heard Pastor How praying for me on my immediate left. He said, "You will be calm in your future encounters; it is from God, not from your years of training and experiences." Immediately, I realised that the message was from the Holy Spirit through Pastor How.

God has a perfect plan for everyone, we just need to be humble and obey God to discover it. I began to get closer to Pastors and to ask questions. Once, I had issues regarding my work and Pastor How texted me to meet him near his house at Woodlands after my flight. When I picked him up I realised that he was on crutches hopping down the stairway; he didn't seem annoyed at all, and we talked from 11:00pm till 2:00am!

He was willing to hear, sincere to share and was very frank. I realised that his experiences and wisdom are not only because he is competent but there is this spirituality that is backing whatever he is doing.

I began to pay very close attention to Pastors' sermons. Their constant emphasis on the need for character change had influenced me greatly. I learnt to nail my old self and put on the armour of Christ, I began to empathise with others as I struggled to get rid of my aggressiveness, impatience, being judgmental and progressed level to level, trusting in God and not self. My staff whom I had worked with commented that – *Jacob wasn't like this before!*

Character Change - Humility

I have seen how people come to church and grow, and some do not. I realised that having an open mind is important, but more crucial is having a humble mind wanting to be corrected.

Once, Pastor How shared a book, *Man in the Mirror.* Basically, it is about finding someone to act as a mirror to spot dirt on your face. I know my strengths and weaknesses but there are blind spots that someone must be able to point out, this is someone whom you must be able to trust and who you know is really happy when you succeed.

Someone asked me, "How come you can humble yourself and work with young people and young pastors in HOGC?" I can simply say that I learned from them! It is not the external 'act of humility' but rather knowing that I'm strong and yet I'm weak! It is the confidence in my ability and the lack of it that makes me teachable. I realise that there are things that I don't see and don't understand.

I started to see youths in a completely new light. They can be messy but I see their enthusiasm, their idealism and their total commitment. I want to be like them! Be young again in my mind!

I have been in enough organisations to know that some organisations are good from far, but once up close, they are far from good. In HOGC, the more I journeyed from the outer sphere into the inner core of the church leadership, I realised it was the reverse. From afar, they are good. Once up close, they are even better. I am a hard man to win over, as my fellow board member Teck Chuan would say. But what I saw in the leadership of the church gave me the confidence to serve.

Pastor How and Pastor Lia

One word to describe the two senior pastors: OTHERS.

There are many examples about how they are always putting others above self. A simple example: they will adjust the aircon temperature when they notice someone fidgeting! Once, Pastor Lia quietly passed me a pillow for my back as the meeting was stretching longer and longer.

On one occasion, they taught us adult leaders that for funeral services, we must always remember to focus on and respect the person who passed on and the family. If not careful, people would use the occasion to highlight oneself or to put on a show for others to see. That is just one of many 'heart lessons' I have learnt.

I have had many opportunities to interact closely with them – they are genuine, real and personal. It is very comfortable to engage them. They are not the kind of people that you need to second-guess. I saw raw emotions, joy, laughter, etc.

One occasion forged a lasting memory for me. During a leaders' meeting to celebrate five leaders who had completed their Master of Divinity course in the USA, Pastor How said, "Pastor Lia and I didn't have the opportunity as we were focused on building the church. Now that these younger leaders are better equipped, they can stand on our shoulders to achieve greater heights, we are so happy that they can do better than us!" If you were there, you could catch his sincerity, just like a father talking proudly about his children who did well in their studies.

I also had a glimpse into what breaks their heart. There was once I was invited to provide a second opinion regarding a staff's disciplinary proceeding. This event may be painful for the senior pastors so I'll dwell only on the behind the scenes: Never had I seen Pastor Lia cry so many times and Pastor How mentally drained in managing this. I saw how much they have done for their staff and family. I saw the pains that they went through with the difficult but necessary processes to ensure highest qualities are maintained in the team serving others. They had to endure being misunderstood, bad-mouthed and attacked online. Yet until today, they are still all about others.

I can only speak of what I have seen and experienced. I may be in my 60s but these experiences have inspired me to serve in church with passion. I hope by describing my journey, it will help give some answers to those who always ask, "What do the adults in HOGC do?" Good question. I hope I have given you some good answers.

Christian Honegger

a Westerner's perspective on an Asian church

Director of Global Relations, Heart of God Church

CEO, TC Acoustic

Since 2005, Singapore and Heart of God Church have been my home. I grew up in Switzerland and became a Christian in my youth. I felt the call of God and so I enrolled in a Bible school in Europe. It was life-changing not just because I grew to know God more but I also got to know a Singaporean lady classmate who became my wife. She convinced me to join her church – Heart of God Church. Actually, I did not have much of a choice. 😊 She said that she was never going to leave her church, not even for a handsome Swiss guy. That's how I moved to Singapore.

Now, I am a part of the Executive Leadership Team in HOGC. I am also Director of Global Relations. With that, I come in contact with the West a lot. Also, I am the CEO of Pastors' business. We are the distributors of Sonos, Klipsch, Marshall across Singapore, Southeast Asia and Hong Kong. We have grown from a three-staff team when we took over in 2010 to 130 full-time and part-time employees in 2021.

Because of my background as a Westerner and my current roles, I am exposed to Western churches and business leaders. Having seen various organisations and leaders, I would like to share with you what is unique about HOGC and its founders Pastor How and Pastor Lia.

Charisma vs Character and Culture

The first thing I noticed about Pastor How and Pastor Lia is that people are very important to them. In 2002 I first met them in Sweden on a bus going to a conference. I was just a new Christian. They found out that I had a vision for youth ministry. As we chatted on the bus, they promised to send me a book about youth ministry. Two weeks later

I received it. True to their word, they sent it all the way from Singapore. I was surprised because most people just give a promise casually but these two Asian pastors kept their word. It didn't matter to them that at that point in time it looked like we would never meet again. Their commitment showed me that people and their dreams mattered. To them, people are very important.

I moved to Singapore and joined HOGC at 25, three years after meeting them on that bus. The very next thing that I learned is that character and culture are extremely important in church. In every ministry, there is a focus on discipleship and character. Ministry leaders also intentionally impart the church culture to the ministry members. I realised that in many modern churches the focus is more on charisma and abilities. Modern churches are often personality-driven or stage-driven, so they look for talents and abilities. But all these things are not what is first on the list in HOGC.

> 1 Samuel 16:7 (NLT)
> ... People judge by outward appearance, but the Lord looks at the heart."

Never had this verse been so true. In HOGC, truly, we don't look at outward appearances. When I joined HOGC, my wife and I were already entrepreneurs. At that time, almost all the leaders in church were teenagers. I came in older, graduated from Bible school and was a 'white guy' in an Asian church. I thought I would be put into a leadership position or at least given a role on stage immediately. Instead, Pastor How and Pastor Lia sent me to a unique ministry. It was the Building Maintenance Ministry, which included cleaning the toilets as one of its ministry scopes. Even in the very sophisticated science of toilet cleaning I was not made a leader but I had to start at the lowest level, as a crew member. I was made to clean toilets for the next 4–5 years. I am proud to say that I rose up the ranks and became the head janitor or shall I say, sanitation engineer.

Toilet cleaning was unglamorous and it had no glitz in it but it was effective character training. Through the ministry, my pastors could also observe my character and how I fit into the church culture.

In some modern churches and movements, because of their haste to grow, very often character and culture are an afterthought. As a leader, I have learned not to take shortcuts by focusing on charisma and abilities first.

On Stage vs Offstage

I have also seen that in some modern churches, they look for ready-made talents and abilities. Because the Western church thrives on onstage performance, naturally there is a need and a frenzied recruitment for onstage talents. Modern churches want it ready-made. The destination is on stage because that is considered by many to be the pinnacle of ministry success.

However in HOGC, the focus is the training process. Everyone is trained in-house. That brings to mind what Pastor Lia has always been saying: *Do the Important, Not the Impressive!*

In HOGC, the KPI is what happens offstage. Pastor Lia has made the concept of the Deep Bench a priority in our church. Ministries should not just have one team but each ministry must have a few teams so that volunteers don't burn out. The desire to train and release new people into serving God is important in this church.

I am part of the preaching team. When I first joined I wasn't impressive on stage. I wasn't born a preacher. English is not even my first language. If HOGC were looking for an impressive man, I would not have been here today. But thank God, they looked to do what was important. They trained and they nurtured me. It was here in HOGC that I learned how to craft and deliver a message. By the way, Pastor Lia is the one who trains all the preachers in HOGC.

After many training sessions and sending sermon drafts to and fro, it was finally the right time for me to preach my first message on a weekend in 2012. A few days before my debut on the preaching team, Pastor Lia met me and two others in her living room for a mock preaching session so that I could be successful on my debut. The really powerful thing is that Pastor Lia was going through chemotherapy for stage 3 breast cancer at that time. It would have been an easier choice to let me debut after her cancer treatment was over. But her conviction and determination are unmatched. She told me, "In the year that the devil silences my voice with cancer, I will raise up hundreds of other preachers."

The offstage and backstage focus is like a thread running throughout our church. Even our children are part of this. My older son Cohen was trained to serve God on the children's worship team and made his debut at the tender age of eight! (Unbiased review: He sounded amazing.) HOGC did it for his dad, now they are doing it for him. I can't remember what I was doing when I was eight years old back in my home country, certainly not ministering on the worship team.

You know sometimes when people find out that I am from Switzerland, they ask why I don't move back. I am thinking to myself, *Move back? Never!* I know Switzerland is a beautiful country. But if my son were in Switzerland, he would not be empowered, believed in and given the opportunity to serve God like he has been in HOGC.

This is why I will never leave HOGC: The revival is here in our church not just for now but for generations to come.

Brand / Ambition / Popularity vs Strategic Leadership

As a CEO I am so grateful to have my pastors as my mentors. I have worked with many CEOs and C-Suite members and I know that Pastor How and Pastor Lia are not just people of character and heart but they are also strategic thinkers.

Pastor How is the visionary and always sees 5 to 10 years ahead of all of us. He led us through HOGC 2.0, 3.0 and now 4.0. Pastor Lia saw the importance of going back to win young people. She strategically saw how the church could not become old and irrelevant. While we did not expand geographically, her strategy has been to expand generationally.

With Pastor How's business sense, it is so easy to commercialise the church, but he is the opposite. Do you know that in our church, the word 'merchandise' is banned by Pastor How? That is because my pastors have never seen the church as a *brand*. Pastor How reminds us constantly about Jesus taking out the whip in the temple and warns us to 'never monetise the church'.

Another strategic wisdom that Pastor How shared with me was, *"Successful businesses and organizations don't suffer because of starvation but indigestion."* What's important is to *"Be led by our identity, not opportunity."*

When you are successful, you will have endless opportunities, but problems start when you go after too many. That is so applicable in business and in church!

Often, Pastor How and Pastor Lia get many invites to preach but they accept the invites very selectively. What's their criteria? For them, it is about impact. When they know that their message of GenerationS and Strong Church will find open hearts, when they know that they will be received well, that is when they will go. They don't have worldly ambition and are not into empire-building. They are led by their identity and not by opportunity. They don't need popularity, they want maximum impact!

#StopAsianHate

I am sure I had you at the headline. Okay, I won't go as far as to call it hate. But please do hear me out. After all, I am from the West and I am as white as they come.

Sometimes I encounter funny incidents. Years ago, whenever I accompanied my pastors to conferences or preaching trips in the West, we would be invited to the green room. Other pastors would talk to me as though I was the senior pastor. I would have to redirect and explain to them that Pastor How is the senior pastor and I am his staff. Awkward moment for them... haha. I guess Western people are used to Green (White) Hornet and his sidekick Cato (Bruce Lee). There were times when Pastor How was bored and cheeky, so we played along. He would walk one step behind me and bow a little when I spoke to him. And sadly that's the world order white people are used to.

While traveling with Pastor How and Pastor Lia, I have seen that whenever they preach overseas they are well received by the Western people and the Western audience. A little bit like Bruce Lee, they are masters of their craft when it comes to building GenerationS, churches and business, and it has such an impact with the Christians everywhere. Unfortunately I am sad to observe it's usually the top leaders who are sometimes not so open to Asians, especially Asian women.

God wants to bring youth revival back to the churches worldwide. Young people must be saved and their hearts must be changed, no matter which part of the world they are in. Maybe we need to be receptive to an Asian church like HOGC, which is doing it so successfully. Maybe we need to change the way we approach doing church for young people.

An example: One pastor told me that European youth have a very short attention span. So the sermon that his pastor was going to preach in his church could only be 25 minutes, and that included interpretation. I notice that in some Western churches, it has become normal to pacify the audience and culture. This will never happen in HOGC. The moment Pastor How and Pastor Lia realise that our people have a short attention span, they will deliberately preach just a bit longer for a season so that they can train and disciple the young people. A Strong GenerationS Church is not built by pandering to youth culture but by challenging it. Guest speakers who preached long sessions of deep subjects in our church have expressed shock that our young people could follow and focus during their entire session. That didn't happen by accident. It is a fruit of wise discipleship. They are thermostats not thermometers.

Some church leaders have been too quick to conclude that the youth revival in HOGC is not possible in their culture. It is our loss if we from the West think like that. I choose to think differently. It is possible. We just have to decide whether we can receive from pastors who have borne fruit whether they are Western or Asian. There seems to be a subconscious mindset entrenched in some leaders that Westerners have more to offer to the church than Asians. But the Bible says that if we receive a prophet we will receive the reward of a prophet. Asian pastors are invited to the party but seldom given a seat at the table. That is why I say that it is not as extreme as #StopAsianHate but maybe some #Prejudice? My heart's strong desire is to make churches see the possibility of having youth revivals like the one I have been experiencing!

Pastor How and Pastor Lia have nothing to gain by travelling and preaching globally. They have their own business. They can afford to travel anywhere they want. In fact, they are introverts and prefer a low profile. If they ever preach overseas, it's only out of obedience to God.

Our church is having a revival. The atmosphere in our regular Sunday service is like the finale night of a conference. Every single weekend, we see people getting saved, people getting transformed. My pastors really don't need to preach anywhere else. But I know that they have so much to give to the whole *'white'* world. ☺

God wants to bring revival to all parts of the world, including the West. Young people must be saved and their hearts must be changed. Maybe it starts with us changing our hearts first!

A WESTERNER'S PERSPECTIVE ON AN ASIAN CHURCH

Regine Tan
on what goes on inside the Senior Pastors' office

Chief of Staff, Heart of God Church

My first job out of college was as an insights and analytics manager at Procter & Gamble, a Fortune 500 company. I quickly rose up the corporate ladder. At 23, I was handling a combined portfolio of US$500+ million across the Asia Pacific region. Truth be told, I only took on the stint at P&G to gain helpful skills for when I take over the reins of my family business. My family owns a multimillion-dollar business, has ventured into manufacturing and owns factories. Naturally, I grew up in a privileged family, with seven maids and three chauffeurs (think *Crazy Rich Asians*). I was all set to quit P&G and take on my rightful role as the heiress when I asked myself: *Is this all to life?* And that was when God called...

I heard Pastor How preach about *Giving God Our Best Years.* I hung onto every word he preached. The time to live for Jesus and His cause was *now*, in my *best years*. So I threw my grand homecoming plans out the window and decided to join HOGC for the ride of my life.

Today, I am the Chief of Staff at HOGC. I represent Pastor How and Pastor Lia's office to the staff and church. As their gatekeeper, I lead my team to plan and arrange their schedules and appointments.

I often get the question: *With your access to the senior pastors' lives offstage, how are they like away from the spotlight?*

Let me tell you three things.

1. They don't just build plans and strategies. They build people.

An analyst by training, I love collecting data and analysing numbers.

Below, I've taken the liberty to combine both Pastor How's and Pastor Lia's schedules together over a 52-week time frame to understand how they spend their time (categorised according to meeting type):

Table 1: Pastor How and Pastor Lia's 52-Week Work Schedule Categorised by Meeting Type

People: Conducting Discipleship Groups, Fireside Chats with Staff and Leaders, Leadership Trainings, One-on-one Discipleships, Loving and Caring for People	31%
Teachings: Preaching, Church Syllabus and Content Development	22%
Strategy: Church Macro Strategy and Planning	18%
Operations: Optimising and Progressing Church Operations	14%
Business	5–10%
Others	5–10%

While many write to Pastor How and Pastor Lia asking them for church-building strategies, the secret sauce lies in how they build people. Over a 52-week period, they spend most of their time on 'People'. You can clearly observe that in a typical weekend for Pastor How and Pastor Lia. Below, I extracted a sample schedule from Pastor How's calendar:

10:00 – 11:30 am	Discipleship Group - Pastor How met 8 university students
12:00 – 1:00 pm	Screens and Soundcheck, Briefing for Service
1:30 – 3:30 pm	Saturday Service Slot #1
4:30 – 6:30 pm	Saturday Service Slot #2
6:45 – 7:15 pm	Debrief Ministry Leaders for Service
8:00 – 10:00 pm	Dinner with Rising Young Adult Leaders - Pastor How encouraged 7 young adults

Almost religiously, Pastor How meets 10 to 15 people weekly to know them, speak into their lives or counsel them. Multiply 10 to 15 people x 40 weeks = that's a whopping 400 to 600 people. 🐢 If you multiply that by two, because Pastor Lia has a similar schedule meeting different sets of people, Pastor How and Pastor Lia personally interact with >1,000 in a church of 5,000.

Almost 1,000 unique relationships yearly. That's mad. Is that even humanly possible?

Even the anthropologist Dunbar postulates the 'magic 150' as the maximum number of meaningful relationships an individual can have. But somehow, with Pastors at the helm, a church of 5,000 feels so personal.

This does not happen by chance. Discipleship is deliberate and intentional.

The bigger a church is, the smaller it must feel.

Pastor How always says:

A Good Church is what you see on stage.

A Great Church is what you feel offstage and backstage.

They are more than just about plans and strategies. With them, it is always about *people.*

2. Building GenerationS is not their ministry. It is their life.

Nothing gets Pastor Lia more pumped up than *young people.* To date, she chairs the quarterly Deep Bench Meetings (akin to the corporate world's quarterly business reviews). A perennial sports fanatic, Pastor Lia ingeniously adapted the 'Deep Bench' concept into a church-building philosophy championing young people. In Deep Bench Meetings, she monitors 'how deep the bench is' across 60+ ministries and keeps tabs on our favourite metric: the average age of each ministry.

I can still clearly remember my first Deep Bench Meeting...

Topline numbers were good.

This particular ministry seemed 'healthy', with an average age of 20.

Pastor Lia asked to see the raw data and working sheets.

As she went through the report, something struck her:

"This group of 17-year-old boys – they're heading to the army soon, right?" (Yes, Singapore has mandatory army enlistment for all men. For two years.)

Pastor turned to us: "We need to fast track them. Time is running out. Let's help them become successful in serving God before they enlist."

Flipping the pages, Pastor Lia quipped: "So... Where are the 13 and 14-year-olds?"

The list of 13–14-year-olds was in the last few pages, because they were only at a crew level.

Pastor Lia then told the team: "Listen, we are too slow. Raise them to the next level. Give them a chance to lead!"

I live and breathe data, eat dashboards for breakfast. But I've never seen data read with the eyes of a carpenter. In one fell swoop, Pastor Lia's pointed questions unlocked the numbers. Immediately, we knew what was missing today and what the future should look like.

Pastor Lia tirelessly does this for all ministries. She is the voice of our 'Youth Conscience'.

She always asks: "Who's the youngest in the ministry?" "When can (Name) be promoted to the main team?"

To Pastor How and Pastor Lia, the cause of young people is not just a momentary focus or a strategy. *It is their life.*

Once, we organised a party of about 40 people for Pastor Lia's birthday. In true Pastor Lia fashion, the guest list was a rather eclectic mix. We had church veterans, the senior leaders, staff from Pastors' business and a bunch of 13–14-year-old leaders. Guess where Pastor Lia and Pastor How chose to sit?

Yes, they sat with the group of 13–14-year-olds – making that the VIP table.

I (literally) witnessed what our senior pastors have always taught: *Don't just invite youths to the party, give them a seat at the table.*

3. They are led by their vision but driven by their hearts.

I often get the question: 'What are Pastors' favourite meetings? Is it the strategy meetings or the vision casting meetings?' They like those meetings, but their happiest occasions are when Pastors have meetings to plan their... giving.

Yes, you did not read wrongly – Pastors have long meetings discussing in detail who to bless with monies and products from their business.

Through their business, they have already given away $500K+ worth of products to pastors and church staff all over the world. Beyond this, they have helped many of their own staff get their first car and even buy their first home through the business! Pastor How once told me, "My business will take care of my own needs and also 'those who were with me' – my team. Because they are more than just employees. They are family."

To Pastor Lia, the highlight of her 51st birthday celebration was passing a couple from the worship team a gift. Pastor Lia was just casually talking to this pair and found out that they were going to renovate their new home. Immediately, the next week, Pastor Lia met them. So right on her birthday, she passed this couple a cheque of $10K from the business and told them: "Go and build a home. Raise a generous, God-loving family." As the Chief of Staff, this is just one of the many acts of Pastors' generosity that I personally witness happening every month.

Let me give you another insider secret: Until today, Pastor How refuses to delegate the HR Department, preferring to personally handle staff salaries and benefits. Every plan is customised to the individual, down to their insurance. Each staff has a personal insurance plan that can follow them beyond their employment in church. That's the extent of

Pastors' care. What's in Pastor How and Pastor Lia's hearts is to provide for the team so we can serve God to our fullest potential!

They also look after young people who do not have either dad or mum. Until today, they still personally craft Father's Day and Mother's Day messages and handpick gifts for these youths.

Do that for a year: commendable. But do that consistently for 20+ years, that is commitment.

Having this access to my senior pastors' lives showed me that you can pursue vision while still being led by your heart.

So to answer that question people often ask, *this* is what my pastors are like. I have been so impacted by this access into their lives and that trumps any experience a Fortune 500 company can give.

ENDNOTES

CHAPTER 5: ONE GENERATION FROM EXTINCTION - CHRISTIANITY IN CRISIS

Aritonang, Jan and Steenbrink, Karel. *A History of Christianity in Indonesia.* Leiden, Boston: Brill, 2008.

Australian Bureau of Statistics. "Census Reveals Australia's Religious Diversity on World Religion Day." *Australian Bureau of Statistics,* January 18, 2018.

Bird, Warren. "Not a Boomer Phenomenon – Megachurches Draw Twice as Many Under 45." *Leadership Network,* June 24, 2014.

Korean Statistical Information Service, Statistics Office. *Census Bureau, Province/ Age/Gender Religious Population.* Daejeon, South Korea: Statistics Korea, 1985.

Korean Statistical Information Service, Statistics Office. *Census Bureau, Province/ Age/Gender Religious Population.* Daejeon, South Korea: Statistics Korea, 2015.

Lee, Morgan. "Where China's Crackdown Leaves the Hong Kong Church: Why Christians aren't all on the same page about the demonstrations and new ruling from Beijing." *Christianity Today,* June 17, 2020.

McCrindle Research. "A Demographic Snapshot of Christianity and Church Attenders in Australia." *McCrindle, National Church Life Survey, Australian Bureau of Statistics,* April 18, 2014.

Pew Research Center. "The Future of World Religions: Population Growth Projections, 2010–2050." *Pewresearch.org,* April 2, 2015.

Pew Research Center. "U.S. Teens Take After Their Parents Religiously, Attend Services Together and Enjoy Family Rituals." *Pewresearch.org,* September 10, 2020.

Plowman, Edward. "Demythologizing Indonesia's Revival." *Christianity Today,* March 2, 1973.

Pollack, Detlef and Rosta, Gergely. *Religion and Modernity: An International Comparison.* Oxford, United Kingdom: Oxford University Press, 2017.

United Nations, Department of Economic and Social Affairs, Population Division. *World Population Prospects 2019: Volume I: Comprehensive Tables.* New York, NY: UN Headquarters, 2019.

ENJOYED THE BOOK?

STAY IN THE KNOW

Sign up for our GenerationS newsletter
GenerationSmvmt.com

Find out more
@GenerationSmvmt

EXPERIENCE GENERATIONS FOR YOURSELF

HoGcX

HEART OF GOD CHURCH XPERIENCE

All-access intensive training course for
decision-makers, influencers and implementers

Find out more at **HoGcX.sg**

EXPLORE THE GENERATIONS SERIES

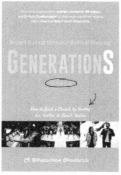

Check out
Volume 2 and more!

Volume 1   Volume 2

If you've read the paperback or eBook...

EXPERIENCE GENERATIONS VOL. 1
IN A FULL COLOUR
COMMEMORATIVE EDITION
HARDCOVER

Find out more on **GenerationSmvmt.com**

ABOUT HEART OF GOD CHURCH

HOGC Singapore is a youth church operated by youths, for youths, to reach youths. Even though it's been over 20 years since the church started, its average age is still a grand old... 22! It is home to thousands of young people. Find out more at **heartofgodchurch.org**

Images on cover:

HOGC Iconic Cross Stage
First conceptualised and built in 2007.

"On my most recent visit, one of my band was so wowed by the environment of the visual/video tech room – where he saw not just one operator at each station, but three... (This) was so impressive – there was one operator, one trainer and one trainee.

These were people in their mid to high teens, and some as young as 12 or 13... Considering the amount of responsibility a team carries in a large service, and how much specialised technical skill there is to learn... he was amazed. There was a beautiful trust being placed in these young people... and ultimately it's the Jesus model of discipleship."

MATT REDMAN
Two-time Grammy Award winner,
singer-songwriter and worship leader

ABOUT THE AUTHORS

Pastor How (Tan Seow How) and his wife Pastor Lia (Cecilia Chan) are co-founders, co-senior pastors of Heart of God Church (HOGC) Singapore and co-authors. A lot of 'co-this' and 'co-that' because they are like Siamese twins who even co-share the same office space. They share the same love for sports and steaks. The only thing they don't share is coffee as she needs a full cup every morning.

Lia is a former journalist, preacher, cancer survivor, worship team builder, trainer and CEO (Chief Entertainment Officer 😊). This serial discipler has been raising young leaders for more than 20 years. Her life verse is Isaiah 58:12 – "... You shall raise up the foundations of many GenerationS..."

How is the visionary, leadership, strategy and organisation guy. His passion and burden is to see Strong GenerationS Churches built, worthy of God's glory. He is also a businessman and funder but what matters most to him is being a godly father to GenerationS of young pastors and leaders!

They are Gen Xers who raised Millennial leaders to grow Gen Z leaders to reach Gen Alphas.

For more, check out **PastorHow.com** & **PastorLia.com**

Made in the USA
Las Vegas, NV
15 April 2023

70633321R00177